For two decades, Bishop Michael Putney has served the International Methodist-Roman Catholic Dialogue as its Co-Chair. In that capacity he has given exceptional leadership, which has helped to make this dialogue exemplary in terms of its working relationship and its output, most notably in terms of gifts which Methodists and Catholic can receive from each other. He is much loved and appreciated by Methodist and Catholic participants alike. He has also served as a member of the Vatican's Pontifical Council for Promoting Christian Unity, and his leadership and vision have shaped the Catholic Church's ecumenical mission in recent decades. He is an ecumenical giant whose witness has inspired many to imagine in new ways what a healthy reconciled Church could look like.

> Bishop Donald Bolen
> Catholic Bishop of Saskatoon
> Canada

Bishop Michael Putney has made a significant ecumenical contribution to the churches in Australia through his involvement in bilateral dialogues and participation in the National Council of Churches in Australia (NCCA). As President of the NCCA he actively worked to assist the churches to interact with the reports of bilateral dialogues so other churches may benefit from the rich insights. Bishop Michael has also been very involved in international dialogues and his wisdom is greatly valued by church leaders around the world. He has a conviction that the ecumenical space is the place where the churches can talk together and grow together to exhibit greater visible unity.

> Reverend Tara Curlewis
> General Secretary
> National Council of Churches in Australia

My Ecumenical Journey

Bishop Michael Putney

My Ecumenical Journey

Bishop Michael Putney

A Collection of Papers Selected and Edited by
Elizabeth Delaney SGS, Gerard Kelly and
Ormond Rush

ATF Theology
Adelaide

2014

National Library of Australia Cataloguing-in-Publication entry (pbk)

Author: Putney, Michael, author.

Title: My ecumenical journal / Michael Ernest Putney.

ISBN: 9781922239648 (paperback)
           9781922239679 (hardback)
           9781922239662 (ebook: pdf)
           9781922239655 (ebook: kindle, epub)

Notes: Includes index.

Subjects: Ecumenical movement.
           Christian union.

Dewey Number: 280.042

First printed 2014
Fourth reprint 2014

Front cover photograph: Ms Gillian Kingston (Methodist Church of Ireland), Bishop Michael Putney, Bishop Sunday Mbang of the Methodist Church of Nigeria, and President of the World Methodist Council, Pope Benedict XVI. The photo took place at a meeting on 9 December 2005 in the Vatican.

Cover design by Astrid Sengkey
Layout/Artwork by Anna Dimasi

Text Minion Pro Size 11

Published by:

An imprint of the ATF Ltd.
PO Box 504
Hindmarsh, SA 5007
ABN 90 116 359 963
www.atfpress.com

CONTENTS

I dedicate this book to all of my ecumenical friends who have so shaped my life over almost fifty years.

Foreword

by Cardinal Walter Kasper

His Eminence Cardinal Walter Kasper
President Emeritus
of the Pontifical Council for Promoting Christian Unity

It is with joy that I heartily endorse this collection of writings by Bishop Michael Putney.

He was appointed a member of the Pontifical Council for Promoting Christian Unity in 2004 when I was its President. In working with him, I came to appreciate his deep commitment to Christian unity. Bishop Putney was appointed Catholic Co-Chairman of the International Methodist-Roman Catholic Dialogue and he served in that role from 1996 to 2013.

His theological acumen is evident to all who work with him. He has a capacity to listen to others in dialogue and to clearly present the Catholic Church's understanding so that dialogue becomes a genuine exchange of gifts. This is a sure formula for the deepening of communion with our ecumenical partners. Bishop Putney knows and understands the meaning of spiritual ecumenism.

The chapters that follow deal with matters that are central to the Catholic Church's ecumenical engagement and will also speak to our ecumenical partners. The chapters demonstrate a depth of theological scholarship and a breadth of ecumenical experience, and this truly is a gift to be shared. I commend these articles for your reflection.

Walter Card. Kasper.

Foreword

by Reverend Dr Geoffrey Wainwright

My acquaintance with Bishop Michael Putney springs from our common participation in the Joint Commission for Dialogue between the World Methodist Council and the Roman Catholic Church. I served as chair on the Methodist side from 1986 to 2011; Bishop Putney held the equivalent position on the Catholic side from 1997 until illness hastened his withdrawal at the turn into 2013. In our doctrinal discussions and reflections Bishop Putney consistently demonstrated intellectual acumen (in earlier years his theological doctorate was gained *summa cum laude* from the Gregorian University in Rome); he embodied a constant pastoral concern for our Commission's anticipated results in the longer term; and he paid a careful practical attention to the working procedures of our group. In our preface to the Commission's 2011 'Durban Report' —*Encountering Christ the Saviour: Church and Sacraments*—we felt able to write: 'During the week-long meetings of the dialogue, the participants grew in friendship and mutual understanding. This friendship has in many cases developed over fifteen years. The mutual understanding is the result of serious, honest dialogue which, being authentically ecumenical, does not involve any compromise or ambiguity.' The doctrinal substance of our relationship found expression in the Joint Commission's thematic 'synthesis' of 'Forty years of Methodist and Roman Catholic dialogue' under the deliberate title *Together to Holiness* (Easter 2010).

Years before his engagement in the Catholic dialogue with the World Methodist Council, Dr Putney's theological and ecumenical insights had already been demonstrated at the global, and indeed the multilateral level, through his participation as an appointed Catholic in the workings of the Faith and Order Commission of the World Council of Churches. In particular, his doctoral work in pneumatology bore fruit in the strong contributions he made in the 1980s to the exposition of the person and work of the Holy Spirit according to the third article of the classic creeds when the WCC Commission on Faith and Order was studiously preparing the report that became 'Confessing the One Faith: An Ecumenical Explication of the Apostolic Faith as it is Confessed in the Nicene-Constantinopolitan Creed (381)' (Faith and Order Paper No.153, 1991). Bishop Putney's standing in the international ecclesiastical community is confirmed by the confidence placed in him by the Pontifical Council for Promoting Christian Unity (to which Roman body he was appointed by Pope John Paul II in 2004 and again by Pope Benedict XVI in 2010).

As an individual scholar and ecclesiastical leader, Bishop Putney has for decades been much in demand for lecture sessions during his visits to various parts of the world, and I have enjoyed the positive reception his presentations have typically received, thinking in particular of such occasions as our conversations at Duke University, North Carolina, in 2002 and 2006.

From colleagues in his home country we know of Michael Putney's various ecclesial activities, both in the framework of the National Council of Churches in Australia and, of course, within the more immediate range of the Catholic Church. In 2009, in company with Dr. Karen Westerfield Tucker—an American Methodist colleague within the International Dialogue Commission—I was able to pay a brief visit to Bishop Putney in his Queensland diocese of Townsville, where we saw for ourselves the high regard and deep respect in which he is held as pastor and teacher by those immediately under his episcopal care. More broadly, we encountered direct evidence of his engagement in the life of the city and its surroundings, and of his often voiced concern for people of all cultures in the region (we Dialogue Commission members had long known of his educational concerns and actions on behalf of the Aborigines and Torres Strait Islanders).

I consider myself fortunate to be Michael Putney's friend, and honoured by the confidence he has always shown me during our collaborative exercises.

> Geoffrey Wainwright
> Cushman Professor Emeritus of Christian Theology
> The Divinity School, Duke University

Editors' Introduction

In the first half of 2013, Elizabeth Delaney SGS, Gerard Kelly and Ormond Rush considered the idea of suggesting to Bishop Michael Putney that he agree to the publication of a collection of his papers and presentations on ecumenism. Each of the group knew Bishop Putney and his work over many years and in a number of contexts. Knowing his expertise and experience in ecumenism, each member of the group agreed that a collection such as this would serve the Church and the ecumenical movement itself very well. When he agreed to the project, the team read through a large collection of his published and unpublished papers and writings on the topic, and chose from among them a collection that would serve this purpose. The selected papers are contained in the volume we have here in this book.

Bishop Michael Putney has written and presented papers on a range of ecumenical topics over many years. In choosing from a wider collection of papers, the editors aimed to present papers that spanned the significant period of commitment to ecumenism in Australia as well as providing a sound background to topics that remain current.

The Seventh Assembly of the World Council of Churches held in Canberra in 1991 was significant for all Christians in Australia. It was significant for Catholics and especially so for Michael Putney as one of the Catholic Church's delegated observers. *The World Council of Churches, the Catholic Church and Ecumenism* presents an outline of some of the difficulties in this relationship.

In *Koinonia—An Ecumenical Breakthrough* Bishop Putney illustrates how this theme has underpinned ecumenical dialogue from the 1980s to the present day. Almost no ecumenical gathering occurs without some reflection on this crucial concept.

In Australia, the Catholic Church has engaged in dialogue with three churches: the Lutheran Church of Australia (from the 1970s); the Uniting Church (from 1977); and the Anglican Church. Of these, the first two dialogues commenced in the 1970s; the dialogue with the Anglican Church commenced only in 1993. While, the paper, *The Roman Catholic Church, Ecumenism and the Anglican Communion*, focuses on the international dialogue its inclusion honours both the dialogue and its members as well as the strong bonds that have developed.

A collection of papers from Bishop Michael Putney could not be complete without *The International Methodist—Roman Catholic Dialogue: Hopes for the Future*. As a member and co-chair of this dialogue for fourteen years, Michael Putney can speak of both dialogue—and of this dialogue in particular—with great understanding and respect. One of the most significant moments for ecumenism was the signing of the Joint Declaration on the Doctrine of Justification by the World Lutheran Federation and the Catholic Church in 1999. The affirmation of the Declaration by the World Methodist Council in 2006 gave him great cause for rejoicing. The inclusion of *Tenth Anniversary of the Formal Signing of the Joint Declaration on the Doctrine of Justification 29 October 2009* was essential!

Whenever Michael Putney speaks of dialogue, he recognizes the need for both the dialogue of love and the dialogue of truth as one. This means that dialogue must address the difficult questions. Consequently, *A Roman Catholic Understanding of Ecumenical Dialogue* presents a general approach to dialogue, while *The Papacy: is there a place for the papacy in a future united church?* offers an example of one of the topics that even Pope John Paul II has named as difficult. Likewise *Evangelisation and Ecumenism: is Common Witness Possible?* addresses another question raised by many involved in ecumenical endeavours.

In many ways, *A Contemporary Roman Catholic View of Martin Luther* recognizes the conversion or change of heart to which the Vatican Council's Decree on Ecumenism calls us. Bishop Putney presents the necessity and challenge of this call to conversion.

For many, the pontiffs, John XXIII, Paul VI, and John Paul II have been great leaders of ecumenism. Their words and actions have inspired many in their ecumenical endeavours. Bishop Putney's paper, *Ecumenism and Inter-religious Relations with Benedict XVI*, shows that this pope's commitment is no less.

Over the years, Michael Putney has engaged with Jewish people in Australia. Two papers, *An Australian Catholic Comment on We Remember: A Reflection on the Shoah*, and *Jewish—Catholic Meeting on Nostra Aetate* honour the friendships and respect that have grown in this relationship.

While most of the papers focus on the achievements and challenges of the ecumenical movement, *Baptism, Ecumenism and the RCIA* presents this as background and moves to a particular area of pastoral concern for the church.

The Approach of the Catholic Church to Ecumenism, while its title may sound like an introduction to ecumenism, presents a number of challenges for Catholics and other Christians alike. *Receptive Catholic Learning Through Methodist—Catholic Dialogue* shows the challenges inherent in dialogue and how the perspective of receptive ecumenism leads to greater understanding of both partners in the dialogue.

As those responsible for the selection of the articles which follow, we wish to acknowledge and thank the various journals and publishing houses where the articles were originally published for giving permission to re-publish. Without these permissions being readily given, we would not have been able to put this volume together. At the bottom of the first page of each article there are details of where that paper was originally given and/or where it was originally published.

Elizabeth Delaney SGS
Executive Secretary for Church Life
Australian Catholic Bishops Conference
Canberra

Gerard Kelly
President
Catholic Institute of Sydney
Sydney

Ormond Rush
Associate Professor and Reader
St Paul's Theological College/Australian Catholic University
Brisbane

One Man's Ecumenical Journey

My ecumenical journey began at Pius XII Seminary, Banyo, which I entered as a sixteen year old in 1963. This was the year after the opening of the Second Vatican Council. Consequently, my entire years of seminary formation until 1969 were shaped by that pivotal event. As a young man, I became part of the group of students whose imagination was fired by the news of what was being discussed and agreed to by the Bishops of the Council.

I was introduced to pre-conciliar developments in the areas of liturgy, ecumenism, biblical studies and the lay apostolate, and the more general theological movement known as *nouvelle théologie*, through reading about the Council rather than by any previous study, given my age. I read about all of this whenever I could find something available in a seminary which was not really prepared for this incredible event, and its attendant transformation of the Catholic Church.

My interest in ecumenism was initially just an interest in one of the new developments in the Church which I gave assent to with genuine enthusiasm. However, something pivotal occurred which meant that this particular stream of renewal became a deeper and more comprehensive part of my response to the Second Vatican Council.

In 1965 I participated in a seminary oratory competition and decided for some reason to speak about the life and message of Paul Couturier (+1953), a priest of the Archdiocese of Lyons, France, who was in some ways the father of the modern form of the *Week of Prayer for Christian Unity*. I expounded his call for 'spiritual ecumenism', and won the oratory competition. What happened more significantly for me was that he won me to ecumenism as a deep, spiritual commitment of my life. It was a real moment of conversion for me.

Perhaps as a result of this competition I was appointed by the staff of the seminary as the first Catholic representative on an inter-seminary committee involving Anglican, Methodist, Presbyterian, Congregational and Church of Christ students. We organised ecumenical gatherings in our respective seminaries and I experienced my first very exciting discussions with fellow Christians who were not Catholic. My ecumenical journey had begun.

I am immensely grateful to God that the beginning of my ecumenical journey was to lie in the spiritual and not simply in the practical part of my life. Ecumenism involves a great deal of practical activity and collaboration along with intense theological research and dialogue, but with its foundation in a spiritual conviction and a sense of a relationship to other Christians in the unity of the Holy Spirit. In the beginning I sometimes found collaboration and ecumenical practice a little difficult being more of an introvert than an extrovert, and more of a thinker than a planner, and hence I moved more easily into theological dialogue. I could always see the theological issues surrounding every step we wanted to take and I needed to resolve those before I could feel comfortable about the particular form of collaboration in question. Others were more enthusiastic about collaboration and gave theological reflection a second place. At the same time, I could never escape from this deep spiritual conversion which had occurred because of that oratory competition.

I was ordained a priest in 1969 and in 1971 was sent to Rome by the Bishops of Queensland to gain my Licentiate in Sacred Theology at the Gregorian University, and to continue my studies later in Louvain, Belgium, before returning to teach in Pius XII Seminary, Brisbane.

During my studies for the Licentiate in Theology at the Gregorian University, I took some courses dealing with ecumenical questions and came under the influence of one of the professors, Fr Jos Vercruysse SJ, with whom I took a course on contemporary ecumenical problems concerning baptism.

During this time I was also privileged, with the support of Fr Vercruysse SJ, to attend a Summer Seminar at the Institute for Ecumenical Research of the Lutheran World Federation in Strasbourg, which tackled the then very contemporary issue of the Holy Spirit and the Church, given the rise of the pentecostal/charismatic movement. Because of my participation, I both met some of the ecumenical giants of the day, especially Lutherans, and also was exposed for the first time to international multi-lateral dialogue. It was an exhilarating experience which shaped me irrevocably, though I did not realise it at the time. Many of the scholars I met then as a young priest continued to reappear in my ecumenical journey.

My studies in Rome at the Gregorian University and ecumenical experiences during that time in Rome, and then my ecumenical involvement in the Archdiocese of Brisbane, led to an interest in undertaking my doctoral work in the area of ecumenical studies. I had originally hoped to write on the ecclesiology of Pentecostal Churches, but was advised by Fr Francis Sullivan SJ that there was too little available in published form to write a doctoral dissertation at that time. Consequently, I went to Fr Vercruysse who was, in fact, a Luther scholar, and under his direction undertook doctoral studies in 1982. I eventually defended a thesis in 1985 entitled: *The Presence and Activity of the Holy Spirit in the Church, in the Documents of the Faith and Order Commission 1927 to 1983.*

As a consequence of my topic, I spent a lot of time in Geneva at the World Council of Churches working in the archives of the Faith and Order Commission, and became good friends with some key members of the Secretariate of the Commission such as Rev Michael Kinnamon who later became President of the National Council of Churches of the United States. Sometimes he would very kindly bring material to Rome for me to use in preparing my dissertation when he was coming there for ecumenical meetings. There were many others in Geneva who shaped my ecumenical understanding because of our personal exchanges, and their personal support and assistance at different times during my doctoral research, which led to enduring ecumenical friendships.

My years of study at the Gregorian University in Rome also involved another turning point in my ecumenical journey. I was nominated by the then Secretariat for Promoting Christian Unity in 1982 to attend as a Catholic graduate student a seminar at the Orthodox Centre of the Ecumenical Patriarchate, Chambésy, Switzerland entitled: *Luther and the German Reform in an Ecumenical Perspective.* I went to Geneva to study Luther and learnt a great deal about him, but I also learnt a great deal about the Orthodox Church through my time in Chambésy.

At the Chambésy Consultation I attended Greek Orthodox worship every day and then on Sundays slipped into Geneva for the Sunday Mass at Notre Dame, our own major church, in order that I might participate fully in the Eucharist and receive Holy Communion. One day, the Western Feast of the Ascension occurred and I spoke to the Catholic secretary of the Director, Metropolitan Damaskinos Papandreou, about the possibility of our having access to a little chapel or a room to celebrate our feast day with a Catholic Mass, to save the two of us slipping away from the seminar to go into Geneva for Mass. The message came back that the Metropolitan would cancel Orthodox worship for that day and I could celebrate a Catholic Mass in the Chapel of the Chambésy Orthodox Centre at an altar prepared outside the iconostasis, which I dutifully did. It was an extraordinary experience. I was able to invite a few more Catholics who were in Geneva at the time, though the congregation was largely Orthodox bishops and theologians from all over the world. On my return to Rome some marvelled that this had happened and wondered if it had ever happened before.

On my return to Australia I became a member of the Ecumenical Commission of the Archdiocese of Brisbane and so was involved in the ecumenical relationships which were part of the life of the Archdiocese in those years. We all had a very special example to follow in the friendship and collaboration of four wonderful men who led their respective churches: Archbishop Francis Rush (Catholic), Pastor Paul Renner (Lutheran), Archbishop John Grindrod (Anglican), Rev Rollie Busch (Uniting Church in Australia). Each of these men became friends and each taught me something about ecumenism through their leadership and friendship. In 1975 I had become one of the Roman Catholic representatives on the Faith and Order Commission of the Queensland Ecumenical Council which later became Queensland Churches Together. My friendship with some members from other Christian Churches continues to this day.

Also, on a very practical level I had to deal with ecumenical issues arising in Emmanuel Covenant Community in Brisbane because of the participation of other Christians in the intense spiritual and missionary life of that community to which I had been appointed Archdiocesan Liaison Priest in 1978.

In March 1982 I participated again as a student in Rome in an International Theological Congress on Pneumatology on the occasion

of the 1600th anniversary of the First Council of Constantinople and
the 1550th anniversary of the Council of Ephesus. It was held in the
Paul VI Audience Hall in Rome and involved such ecumenical giants
as Yves Congar OP, John Zizioulas, Emmanuel Lanne OSB, Max
Thurian, Jean-Marie Tillard OP and Jürgen Moltmann.

Later, at a lecture in Fribourg in 1985, I would hear Metropolitan
Damaskinos Papandreou say that when meeting Pope John Paul II
after the conference, the pope expressed the conviction that the major
issue separating our two communions had been settled through their
discussions. This was the issue of the *Filioque* clause added by the
West to the Nicene-Constantinopolitan Creed, and not accepted
theologically by the East. The Metropolitan said to Pope John Paul
that one more problem remained. When asked what it was he said
'You, Holy Father'. The pope apparently said he would set about
solving that problem as well, which he tried to do in his encyclical
letter, *Ut Unum Sint*, some years later.

My doctoral studies in Rome and the contacts I made because of my
ecumenical topic also led to my being appointed as a Roman Catholic
delegate to a Consultation of the Faith and Order Commission of the
World Council of Churches on the third article of the Nicene Creed
on the role of the Holy Spirit, in their study *Towards a Common
Expression in the Apostolic Faith Today*. It took place in Chantilly
near Paris in March 1985. I can remember Rev John Deschner, the
Chairman, saying after I had made an intervention at a plenary
session of the Consultation, that people should listen because I was
the only one who had read all the archives of the Faith and Order
Commission. Through my participation in that marvellous meeting
I developed a deeper understanding of multilateral dialogue and
the human as well as the theological dimensions of the interaction
between different Christian traditions in ecumenical dialogue.

At that consultation I also worked in a small team with an
American Greek Orthodox and a German Lutheran to draft the
section on the *Filioque* phrase in the Nicene Creed. This was the
basis for the development of a section in the study document of 1987,
Confessing One Faith, and the final report, *Confessing the One Faith:
An Ecumenical Explication of the Apostolic Faith as it is Confessed
in the Nicene-Constantinopolitan Creed (381),* published in 1991.
The final document did not resolve this division but it did lay the
foundation for that to happen.

On my return from my doctoral studies I became the Director of a Banyo Institute for the Study of Ecumenism, which was held every two years from 1987 to 1993. This obliged me to turn my intellectual and spiritual commitments again into something practical for ordinary men and women engaged in ecumenical work on a parish or diocesan level. Practical possibilities ranged from joint prayer, local dialogues, collaboration in work for the poor and in local councils, to ecumenical covenants between parishes in a local area. I believe this was the stimulus for a very important grounding of my theological understanding and commitment.

In 1991 I was a Delegated Observer to the World Council of Churches Assembly in Canberra and re-established contacts with many theologians and Church leaders whom I had known during my student years, particularly Fr Jean-Marie Tillard OP, who had a profound influence upon my ecumenical theology and my teaching of ecclesiology. I also learned how difficult it is to ensure that such a large representative body remains at the service of its member churches rather than becoming an identity with its own agenda alongside them; and how difficult it is to keep its agenda at the service of furthering unity between the churches when many delegates placed major socio-political issues higher on their agendas.

In 1993 I became Co-Secretary of the National Uniting Church-Roman Catholic Dialogue, which was a rich experience of not just ecumenical dialogue in a very thoughtful and practical way, but also of deep ecumenical friendship. I later became Catholic Co-Chairman in March 2010.

In 1994 I was invited to be a participant in a Regional Consultation on 'The Viability of Ministerial Formation' organised by the Sub-Unit for Ecumenical Theological Education of the World Council of Churches, in Sydney in November of that year. This led to my being a participant in the International Consultation: 'Ecumenical Theological Education—Its Viability Today' organised by the same Sub-Unit in Oslo in 1996.

I have a vivid memory that at the conference I spoke a little sharply when people were criticising the Catholic Church's ecumenical engagement in Latin America, having felt that the criticisms were somewhat unfair. I regretted my intervention but learnt from it that one must be ever-patient and ever-sensitive to what the real issues are in a dialogue and never react to an initial position being presented which often is not the full position of the person speaking, but rather, something about which they are passionate and speak a little intemperately.

Having become an Auxiliary Bishop in Brisbane in 1995, I was appointed a member of the Bishops' Commission for Ecumenical and Interfaith Relations in 2000, and Chair of its newly formed Commission for Ecumenism and Interreligious Relations in 2006. This again led to my working with others to apply all that I had learnt and all that touched my spirit deeply, in a practical way but on a national level.

In 1996 I was asked by the President of the Pontifical Council, Cardinal Edward Cassidy, if I would be willing to become Catholic Co-Chairman of the International Methodist-Roman Catholic Dialogue. I initially turned down his offer because I had never been a member of an international dialogue and I knew too little about Methodism. However, that night I discussed his offer with Mgr Tim Galligan who was a staff member of the Pontifical Council for Promoting Christian Unity and next morning said that I would take on this wonderful new role which instigated another profound step in my ecumenical journey. The staff of the Pontifical Council who served as secretaries of the Dialogue: Mgr Tim Galligan, Mgr Don Bolen and Mgr Mark Langham, are marvellous servants of the Church's ecumenical calling. I value their example and friendship enormously. Mgr Bolen is now the Bishop of Saskatoon and replaced me as Catholic Co-Chair of the Dialogue.

During three successive five-year phases I co-chaired the dialogue with my friend Rev Geoffrey Wainwright from Duke University, North Carolina. Through my relationship with him and so many other Methodist friends, I again discovered that the way forward is through ecumenical friendship based on our relationship to each other in Christ through the Holy Spirit, and through a dialogue that becomes increasingly sensitive because of this friendship.

We prayed together, talked together and produced wonderful documents, and the moments of ecumenical conversion, growth in understanding and bonding of spirits are too many to mention. I was delighted in my last *ad limina* meeting with Pope Benedict XVI to be able to tell him that Rev Geoffrey Wainwright, whom he knew as a theologian, was retiring from the dialogue and from his teaching position at Duke University. I asked the Holy Father if I could give Geoffrey his greetings. The pope reached his hand out to take my arm and said 'He is my good friend'. I wrote to Geoffrey to tell him what Pope Benedict had said, and then repeated it in a testimonial for his farewell from Duke University, so that the pope's words were read out at the dinner to honour this ecumenical giant and dear friend.

Because of my membership of the Dialogue I was invited to other Methodist meetings and was an Observer at an Executive Meeting of the World Methodist Council in Hong Kong in September 1999. This helped again to ground my understanding of Methodism in an experience of their normal processes of debate, struggle, dialogue and commitment that occur in any international body drawing together a huge array of member churches. The Council involved the very large United Methodist Church of the United States, which has members throughout the world, and many more local Methodist Churches including of course the founding church, the Methodist Church of Great Britain and Ireland. Moreover, the first has bishops and the second does not.

In 2004 I was appointed a member of the Pontifical Council for Promoting Christian Unity by Pope John Paul II and my membership was renewed by Pope Benedict XVI in 2010. My understanding of the ecumenical issues confronting us was grounded once more as I shared with the wonderful people of the Pontifical Council, their Consultors, the staff of the Council and its Prefect, Cardinal Walter Kasper and more recently, Cardinal Kurt Koch, the passion, the hopes and the concerns about the Church's participation in the ecumenical movement worldwide. The plenary meetings have always been a great experience for me and ones in which I felt able to play a full part making my own contribution to the plans of the Pontifical Council.

In June 2009 I was appointed Interim President of the National Council of Churches in Australia (NCCA) because the President had stepped down, and was then elected to that position in 2010 at the Seventh National Forum of the Council, which I was chairing as Acting-President. I had attended many Forums over the years as a member of the Catholic delegation. There were many highlights at these, with none greater than in Adelaide in 2004 when nineteen Churches signed the document 'Australian Churches Covenanting Together'. Another was at the Fourth Forum in Melbourne in 2001 when I spoke on the difficult question of joint mission in a paper entitled 'Evangelisation and Ecumenism: Is Common Witness Possible?' This is the dimension of our ecumenical commitment in which churches find it hardest to engage together.

Another highlight was presenting three Bible Studies on the Gospel of St John to the Fifth National Forum of the National Council of Churches in Adelaide in July 2004. This is not usually a Catholic contribution at ecumenical gatherings and the honour and challenge it offered led to a profound ecumenical experience for me. Interestingly, I attended every Forum of the National Council except its Inaugural Forum in Canberra in 1994 and its meeting in Melbourne in 2013.

Through the NCCA I was brought into a new working relationship with countless friends whom I had come to know over the years and had met with and worked with in other arenas. Together we tried to forge a way forward for the National Council which would ensure that it met the needs of the Australian Churches. My vision was always that people ought to want to come to Executive Meetings of the NCCA, because they would deal with the real agenda of the Australian Churches with the benefit of hearing the voices of other Christians. If the real agenda was not being talked about, then member Churches would not have sufficient enthusiasm for their participation in the National Council. We instigated plans to help this happen at the Forum in Canberra in 2010 and these were carried further at the Forum in Melbourne in 2013, which I was unable to attend.

Apart from this journey through meetings and conferences, there has been another journey which has been more one of teaching, writing and speaking. Pius XII Seminary where I taught became a member of the Brisbane College of Theology in 1983, along with the Anglican and Uniting Church Theologates. This meant that I was often teaching students from other churches and teaching with their professors. This ensured more than ever that all my teaching was attentive to the way other Christians would hear it. Apart from courses in the seminary, my life was also busy because of a great number of lectures given to clergy of different churches, ecumenical conferences and Catholic gatherings both in Australia and overseas.

I always had key messages to deliver in my teaching and writing on ecumenism as I sought to clarify what was involved. For example, I emphasised that ecumenical relationships must involve both love and truth. With only the former one can avoid the divisive issue. With only the latter one often cannot get past the obstacles they create. Ecumenism requires loving truth and truthful love. My ecumenical goal has always been the one mapped out by *Unitatis Redintegratio*, the Decree on Ecumenism, of the Second Vatican Council. For me it has to involve agreement in faith and not only a commitment to love. Ecumenical dialogue carried out in love, by God's grace, is essential if it is to come about.

I was also at pains to distinguish between non-denominational, inter-denominational and truly ecumenical gatherings, events, or projects. The first leaves church identities aside. The second acknowledges them but does not deal with them. While these can help foster fundamental relationships and friendships, of themselves they are not enough. Only the third deals fully with our identities, both what we share and what keeps us apart, and only in this way can significant ecumenical progress be made.

During this time I sometimes wrote specifically for publication but many of my addresses were not published, and some of my articles and addresses, published and unpublished, are gathered together in this publication, which is a very humbling experience for me.

The last ten years of my life have been spent as the Bishop of the Diocese of Townsville. Here I have experienced a wonderfully warm relationship between the pastors of Churches and congregations across the board from the Greek Orthodox to Wesleyan Methodists, from the Anglicans to independent Christian congregations. We collaborate on some major projects in the city of Townsville which are acts of Christian witness before the community, and many of us pray together at times. I also have regular meetings with the Anglican Bishop and the Presbytery Chair of the Uniting Church in Australia and a very warm friendship with both. We share with each other some of the difficulties we may be experiencing within our own communities and offer each other prayerful support.

One of the hallmarks of this period of my life has been a flowering of what previously was only a small part of my network of ecumenical relationships, and that is my friendships with Pentecostal and

Evangelical pastors. I pray with many of these of a Friday morning for an hour, and we have become deeply related to each other in Christ and in our desire to serve Him in the city of Townsville. Despite our different ecclesiologies and sometimes our different understanding of how we best receive the direction of the Holy Spirit for our communities, I have found that some of my closest ecumenical friendships are with these pastors.

While I have not had significant formal relationships with Pentecostal and Evangelical Churches, this informal and personal one is a deep and rich part of my ecumenical journey.

By way of conclusion, I could list an enormous number of men and women who have become my ecumenical friends and also fellow Catholic ecumenists, who together have taught me so much and inspired me so deeply. I cannot really do this as the list would be too long and I would hate to leave out any of the wonderful men and women I have come to know and love. So all I can do is simply say how grateful I am for everything I have received from them, and how each matters deeply to me and has become part of my sense of who I am because I am never without them in Christ.

Throughout all of this journeying I really just did what was asked of me or responded to what came along without reflecting on any overall pattern in my life. Only recently did I begin to wonder whether my ecumenical journey was a vocation and that God had been leading me and gifting me for this work. Certainly, I have had amazing encounters and opportunities, and been shaped year-by-year so that eventually I did not have to choose to be or do something ecumenical. I simply was always and am always ecumenical because there is no other me than one who is always in the deepest relationship with other Christians in my very soul because of Jesus and the Holy Spirit. At this stage of my life, I am just being myself. All I can do now is thank God for it all.

Most Reverend Michael E Putney
Bishop of Townsville

The World Council of Churches, the Catholic Church, and Ecumenism

At the Seventh Assembly of the World Council of Churches (WCC) in Canberra, February 1991, the Sixth Report of the Joint Working Group between the Roman Catholic Church and the WCC was presented to the assembly. The report celebrated twenty-five years of co-operation between the two bodies and five previous reports since the inauguration of the Joint Working Group (JWG) in 1965. In its report to the assembly the Reference Committee, as it was called, commented on the JWG Report and on the overall state of relationships between the WCC and the Catholic Church. It referred to an earlier decision 'not to pursue any further—at least for the time being—the question of membership'[1] by the Roman Catholic Church; and then called for the reconstitution of the JWG with the mandate of reviewing the relationships between the two bodies. In particular, it asked the new group to concentrate on obstacles which have prevented these relationships from developing more fully. Therefore a new and important phase of collaboration between the two bodies may well lie ahead of us. In order to understand the issues that will need to be dealt with, it is worth looking again at that earlier decision not to pursue the question of membership.

The possibility of Catholic Church membership of the WCC was raised in 1968 at its Fourth Assembly in Uppsala. Pope Paul VI publicly acknowledged the question in his visit to Geneva in 1969. Consequently the JWG took up the issue and a report was published in 1972. This report described the WCC as follows:

Paper presented at the 1991 Annual Conference of the Canon Law Society of Australia and New Zealand and published in *Canon Law Society of Australia and New Zealan:. Proceedings of the Twenty-Fifth Annual Conference* (1991): 202–8.

1. 'Report of Reference Committee', Document Number RC2, World Council of Churches Seventh Assembly, Canberra, Australia, 7–20 February 1991, 9.

The World Council of Churches is an attempt to bring together the now divided churches into a provisional fellowship in which they can meet one another. The World Council of Churches makes it possible for churches differing in tradition, form and size to search for fuller unity in the context of a fellowship which they already experience. In it the special character of each individual church is safeguarded and no church is required to compromise its convictions about doctrine or about the nature of the church. Through the Council, however, it becomes possible for the churches, within the limits imposed by their separation, even now to share their life, to bear joint witness to the Gospel and to strive together to serve the whole of mankind through the promotion of justice and peace.[2]

The claim that no church is required to compromise its convictions about the nature of the church is based upon what has become known as the Toronto Statement of 1950 which was forged especially to make it possible for the Orthodox Churches to be members of the WCC.

They could become members without having to accept other churches as churches in the full or true sense of the word.[3] The report's description of the Roman Catholic approach to the ecumenical movement was largely a summary of the Decree on Ecumenism.

In its account of the questions which Catholic Church membership of the WCC would raise, at least for some, it began with the ecclesiological issue. Even if the Toronto Statement made it clear that the Catholic Church would not have to renounce its ecclesiology, whereby it sees the Church of Jesus Christ subsisting in the Catholic Church, would this appear nonetheless to be compromised in fact? More concretely, would the authority of the pope be compromised or

---

2. John Cardinal Willebrands and Eugene Carson Blake, 'Patterns of Relationships between the Roman Catholic Church and the World Council of Churches', in *Ecumenical Review*, 24/3 (July 1972): 253.

3. *The Church, the Churches and the World Council of Churches: The Ecclesiological Significance of the World Council of Churches: A Statement Commended to the Churches for Study and Comment by the Central Committee of the Council, Meeting at Toronto, Ontario, July, 1950* (New York: WCC, 1953).

appear to be so? Would the distinctive witness of the Catholic Church be obscured by statements and programs of the WCC, despite the fact that member churches remain free to disassociate themselves from such activities? On the other hand, would other churches less numerically large and without the Catholic Church's inner cohesion have less authority and freedom if it were to join? For example, 'would statements emanating from the WCC have less authority . . . if the Roman Catholic Church disavowed certain of its statements?'[4] Finally, would the collaboration of two such large organisations smother the spiritual character of the ecumenical movement?

The report then proceeded to map out in considerable detail how it would be possible for the Catholic Church to join the WCC, and to deal with the above questions of concern. However the decision whether to apply for membership or not rested with the Church itself and, ultimately, it decided not to apply at that point. The reasons for this were named in the Fourth Report of the JWG to the Fifth Assembly of the WCC in Nairobi (1975).

> There is no doubt that the Roman Catholic Church could accept the basis of the World Council of Churches, but there are factors, some theologically based, which at present militate against membership as the visible expression of the relationship between the Roman Catholic Church and the World Council of Churches. To a much greater degree than other churches, the Roman Catholic Church sees its constitution as a universal fellowship with a universal mission and structure as an essential element of its identity. Membership could present real pastoral problems to many Roman Catholics because the decision to belong to a world-wide fellowship of churches could easily be misunderstood. Then there is the way in which authority is considered in the Roman Catholic Church and the processes through which it is exercised. There are also practical differences in the mode of operation, including the style and impact of public statements.[5]

4.   Willebrands and Blake, 'Patterns of Relationships', 265.
5.   *Breaking Barriers, Nairobi 1975: The Official Report of the Fifth Assembly of the*

Clearly the issues of ecclesiolog: the universal nature and mission of the Catholic Church, the role of the pope, and especially the question of public statement inhibited any move on its part for membership in the WCC. It was quite clear at the Canberra Assembly that there were no immediate plans to reconsider membership, despite the fairly open mandate of the new JWG.

Relations between the WCC and the Catholic Church have passed through a more difficult phase in recent years. Emilio Castro, the retiring Genera Secretary of the WCC, named some of the causes of this in an interview in 1991. He referred first of all to the issue of the troubled relationships between the Uniate Churches and the Orthodox Churches. Because the latter are members of the WCC, it has taken an interest in the matter,[6] which has not always been welcomed by the Pontifical Council for Promoting Christian Unity which would perceive this issue as one belonging to their bilateral relationship with the Orthodox Churches.[7] The other cause he listed is very interesting and deserves quoting:

> It is also obvious that the Roman Catholic Church has gone through an internal process of theological 'recentering'. In the wake of reaffirmation of the authority of the pope, the WCC's contacts with many sectors of the Catholic Church, while continuing, are inevitably seen in a different light. In that sense our dialogue risks becoming less free and more official.
>
> This has both promising and worrisome elements, and the participation of Roman Catholics in the activities of the WCC needs to be a permanent subject of conversation.[8]

World Council of Churches, Nairobi, 23 November–10 December 1975, edited by David M Paton (London: SPCK, 1976), 275.

6. Emilio Castro referred to this issue in his opening address to the Canberra Assembly, 'Report of the General Secretary', Document Number PL 2.1., World Council of Churches Seventh Assembly, Canberra, Australia, 7–20 February 1991, 13.

7. For an account of the theological and ecumenical issues involved, see Emmanuel Lanne, 'Eastern Catholics: Religious Freedom and Ecumenism', in *One in Christ*, 26 (1990): 308–27.

8. 'A Mirror of Diversity: A Conversation with Emilio Castro', in *One World,* 168 (Aug–Sep 1991): 16–17.

His concerns would be echoed by many other dialogue partners of the Catholic Church in 1991.

Emilio Castro also referred to the difficult doctrinal issues which separate the Catholic Church from the member churches of the WCC, especially the questions of ministry and the authority of the bishop of Rome. Finally he referred to the continuing difficulty of joint action or joint statements by the WCC and the Catholic Church on contemporary social questions. 'Joint action continues to evade us.'[9] This difficulty emerged with the joint initiative SODEPax[10] (Committee on Society, Development and Peace) at the end of the seventies and most recently with the inability of the two bodies to publish a common statement on racism and apartheid. Emilio Castro named some of the reasons for this difficulty:

> It is a question of the difference of the two bodies, one church, one council of churches. It is a question of the high visibility of Rome in the media. It is a question of Rome's being both a church and a state, and thus having diplomatic channels to operate in.[11]

These are certainly some of the factors which make such collaboration difficult. Central to them all is the papal role in the Catholic Church and in the world.

The sharpest illustration of this inability of the two bodies to act or speak together, and one also acknowledged by Emilio Castro, was the Convocation on Justice, Peace and the Integrity of Creation in Seoul, 1990. The convocation was the result of a process initiated in 1983 at the Vancouver Assembly which had called on the member churches to engage in a process of 'mutual commitment (covenant) to justice, peace and the integrity of creation'.[12] An act of covenanting did take place at the end of the Seoul Convocation. It included ten

---

9. 'A Mirror of Diversity', 17.
10. Konrad Raiser, 'Beyond Collaboration: Perspectives on the Work of the Joint Working Group between the Roman Catholic Church and the World Council of Churches 1972–1982', in *Ecumenical Review,* 35 (1983): 184.
11. 'A Mirror of Diversity', 17.
12. *Now Is the Time: The Final Document and Other Texts,* World Convocation on Justice, Peace and the Integrity of Creation, Seoul, 1990 (Geneva: WCC, 1990), 2.

affirmations about justice, peace and creation which touched upon many of the major issues of concern touching the lives of Christians and, indeed, all people in the world today.

The Seoul Convocation was not without its critics,[13] not least of all from the Catholic side. The Church had been invited to be a co-sponsor but had not done so because of 'unresolved difficulties'.[14] One officially named difficulty was the already cited one of the different nature of the two bodies.[15] There was also a Catholic concern about the meaning and nature of the 'conciliar process' which was to take place in Seoul, and about the decision to include in the convocation representatives of various movements for justice, peace and ecology. Finally, the Pontifical Council for Promoting Christian Unity had expressed increasing concern about what it perceived to be inadequate theological foundation for the positions taken by the WCC meeting on issues of justice, peace and now ecology.[16]

This latter concern would have been shared by many at the Canberra assembly where issues of justice, peace and the integrity of creation tended to dominate the agenda.[17] A broader frustration with the present state of the WCC was very forcibly expressed in a statement by the delegation from the Orthodox Church at the end of the Assembly. Their frustration would have been shared to varying degrees by many others, including Roman Catholics. The penultimate sentence of this statement asked the question, 'Has the time come for the Orthodox Churches and other member churches to review their relations with the World Council of Churches?'[18] Their causes for concern were named as follows: that the restoration of the visible

---

13. Janice Love, 'PIC and the Future of the Ecumenical Movement', in *Ecumenical Review*, 43 (1991): 107–19; Jerry D McCoy, 'A Promise Partially Fulfilled: The JPIC Convocation in Seoul', in *Mid-Stream*, 29 (1990): 407–17.

14. Joint Working Group between the Roman Catholic Church and the World Council of Churches, Sixth Report (Geneva: WCC, 1990), 10.

15. JWG, Sixth Report, 10.

16. 'Letter of Archbishop Edward I Cassidy to Dr Emilio Castro', in *Information Service*, 74 (1990): 57.

17. For a fuller account of this concern, see Michael E Putney, 'Ecumenical Moments', in *Ecumenical Review*, 43 (April 1991): 226–8.

18. 'Reflections of Orthodox Participants', Document Number A84, World Council of Churches Seventh Assembly, Canberra, Australia, 7–20 February 1991, 3.

unity of the Church remain the main aim of the WCC; that there has been an increasing departure from the basis of the WCC; that there has been a growing departure from biblically based Christian understandings of central doctrines; that the WCC is broadening in the direction of relations with other religions; that there was a tendency in the assembly to substitute a private spirit, the spirit of the world or other spirits for the Holy Spirit; that there was a lack of understanding shown for the Orthodox position on intercommunion; and that there was a changing process of decision-making in the WCC. These issues were seen to place in question the very nature and identity of the WCC.

While these criticisms are very strong, one needs to remember that ecumenical collaboration has always to be honest if authentic progress is to be made. Ecumenists are used to hard talking and eschew compromise as the end of genuine ecumenism. Moreover Roman Catholic concerns about the present state of the WCC need to be seen in the context of the immense amount of collaboration that takes place between the two bodies and which increases every year. For example, twelve Roman Catholic theologians are full members of the Faith and Order Commission of the WCC. Seven others are consultants to the Commission on World Mission and Evangelism which also has a full-time Roman Catholic staff member, Sister Monica Cooney SMSM from New Zealand. There is also a full-time Roman Catholic staff member of the Ecumenical Institute of the WCC at Bossey, Switzerland. The controversial Seoul Convocation had Roman Catholics on its preparatory staff and received funding assistance through the Pontifical Council for Promoting Christian Unity. There are yearly combined staff meetings between the WCC sub-unit on Dialogue with Living Faiths and the Pontifical Council for Interreligious Dialogue. Roman Catholic observer-delegates participate in most major WCC consultations, commission meetings, etc., including the Canberra Assembly. There is no significant area of WCC life which does not have some quite specific link to the Catholic Church through the Pontifical Council. Finally the charter for the new Joint Working Group should lead to a reassessment of these relationships and, it is hoped, an increase in collaboration in the future.[19]

Roman Catholic ecumenical activity is in no way limited to its relationship with the WCC. If anything, it is more at home with and certainly invests as much energy in its bilateral relationships with what have come to be known as Christian world communions. A listing of the various joint commissions established for dialogue with other communions indicates just how comprehensive and committed is the ecumenical involvement of the Catholic Church:

> Anglican Roman Catholic International Commission (1968–),
> Joint International Commission for Theological Dialogue between the Roman Catholic Church and the Orthodox Church (1979–),
> Roman Catholic–Lutheran Joint Commission (1967–),
> Reformed Roman Catholic International Dialogue (1970–),
> Joint Commission between the Roman Catholic Church and the World Methodist Council (1967–),
> International Joint Commission between the Catholic Church and the Coptic Orthodox Church (1974–),
> Joint Commission between the Roman Catholic Church and the Malankara Orthodox Syrian Church (1989–),
> Disciples of Christ–Roman Catholic International Commission (1977–),
> Baptist–Roman Catholic International Conversations (1984–),
> Pentecostal–Roman Catholic Conversations (1972–),
> Evangelical–Roman Catholic Dialogue (1977–)

These commissions vary from dialogues which have the stated goal of finding the way forward to the re-establishment of full communion, to longer term conversations aimed at clearing up misunderstandings, leading to fuller co-operation and mutual enrichment. The dialogues

---

19. For an analysis of the ecclesiological implications of the WCC and of Roman Catholic collaboration, with recommendations for the future, see Anton Houtepen, 'Towards Conciliar Fellowship: the WCC and the Roman Catholic Communion of Churches', in *Ecumenical Review*, 40 (1988): 473–87.

are the major illustration of a much larger Catholic Church involvement with the Christian world communions ranging from visits of heads of churches to collaboration on the local level.

This broad range of ecumenical activity in fact reaches its greatest intensity on the local level. In Australia the Catholic Church is a partner in dialogue with the Uniting Church and with the Lutheran Church. With the former, it described the possibilities which lay ahead in the statement 'Make Straight His Way Stages on the Road to Unity' (1985). With the latter, it has produced two extraordinary hopeful statements, 'Sacrament and Sacrifice' (1985) on the Eucharist, and 'Pastor and Priest' (1989) on the ministry. There were also very fruitful multilateral dialogues with the Australian Council of Churches (1967–72) which addressed issues from eucharist and ministry to authorities in moral behaviour. But these official dialogues are perhaps less significant than the vast array of ecumenical collaboration which takes place on a diocesan and parish level. This is so taken for granted these days that it often passes unnoticed, yet it is equal to anywhere else in the world. In a document published by the Secretariat for Promoting Christian Unity in 1975, Ecumenical Collaboration at the Regional, National and Local Levels, there is a long list of possibilities for ecumenical collaboration at a local level:

(a) shared prayer and worship,
(b) common bible work,
(c) joint pastoral care,
(d) shared premises,
(e) collaboration in education,
(f) joint use of communications media,
(g) co-operation in the health field,
(h) co-operation during national and international emergencies, relief of human need,
(j) resolution of social problems,
(k) promotion of justice and peace,
(1) bilateral dialogues,
(m) meetings of heads of communions,
(n) joint working groups,
(o) councils of churches and Christian councils.

In various ways all of these possibilities are being realised somewhere, at least, in Australia.

Of considerable interest in Queensland at the time of writing, 1991, is the entry of the Catholic Church in Queensland into a newly constituted ecumenical body called Queensland Churches Together. The Church in Queensland as such is joining the new body rather than dioceses. It will come into step with the Archdioceses of Melbourne, Adelaide, Hobart and Perth and the Dioceses of Parramatta and Ballarat which are already members of their regional councils of churches. Moreover there is considerable hope that the Catholic Church will become a member of a newly constituted Australian Council of Churches. This kind of collaboration is strongly encouraged by the Pontifical Council for Promoting Christian Unity which perceives it as easier for the Catholic Church to be involved in councils of churches on a regional basis rather than internationally (WCC).

No one knows what the future holds. That remains in the hands of God though one can surely argue that it will involve the WCC as well as the Christian world communions. It will involve dialogue and more dialogue. Above all, it will involve collaboration on the local level. As Pope John Paul II has said:

> the search for unity and ecumenical concern are a necessary dimension of the whole of the Church's life. Everything can and must contribute to it. I have already asked on more than one occasion that the re-establishment of unity among all Christians must be considered a pastoral priority. We are committed together with our brothers and sisters of the other churches and ecclesial communities in the ecumenical movement.[20]

---

20. Pope John Paul II, 'Address to the Roman Curia', in *Information Service*, 59 (1985): 2.

Koinonia—An Ecumenical Breakthrough

When one undertakes the task of analysing reports of ecumenical dialogues on the nature of the church, one is struck immediately by two significant facts. Firstly, it was really only in the second half of the past decade that the church itself became the explicit focus of international dialogues, with a few notable exceptions. The most important multilateral dialogue, the Faith and Order Commission (FOC), is only now beginning to take up the question. Of course this does not mean that there has not been significant ecclesiological reflection in many earlier dialogues and an implicit ecclesiology probably in most of them.

The second fact which becomes apparent is the emergence of *koinonia/communio/communion* as the over arching concept for speaking about the church, with a few exceptions. This is true not only in the bilateral dialogues but in the FOC as well. This also deserves study as a significant phenomenon in the modern ecumenical movement. *Koinonia* has been heralded by some as a sign of hope, a breakthrough concept which will enable more fruitful resolution of divisive ecclesiological issues. Certainly its fruitfulness is already apparent. It remains to be seen whether its more general acceptance will help to free up some of the remaining difficult blockages such as apostolic succession in the episcopacy, and papal primacy.

Commission on Faith and Order

At the Seventh Assembly of the WCC in Canberra February 1991, the

---

This paper was originally presented to Queensland Churches Together, Faith and Order Forum, on 13 May 1991. In 1994 it was revised for publication in Themes in Interchurch Dialogue: Koinonia, Scripture, Justification (Melbourne: Joint Board of Christian Education, 1994).

major contribution of the FOC occurred in the third section, 'Spirit of Unity: Reconcile Your People!' The most important work of this section was the redrafting of a statement prepared by the FOC, 'The Unity of the Church—Gift and Calling'. This document had been commissioned by the Central Committee to take another step forward in the WCC's very important attempt to describe the goal of the unity of the church being striven for in the ecumenical movement. The final statement produced by the third section, renamed 'The Unity of the Church as Koinonia: Gift and Calling', was the only document produced by any section which was open to amendment before voting in a plenary session of the assembly.

The New Delhi Assembly had produced the first really significant description of this goal in 1961. Its emphasis had been on 'all in each place' being brought together by the Holy Spirit into 'one fully committed fellowship', and at the same time being united with the whole Christian fellowship 'in all places and all ages'.[1]

The Nairobi Assembly of 1975 adopted the FOC language of conciliar fellowship to describe the united church as 'a conciliar fellowship of local churches which are themselves truly united'.[2] The key paragraph of the description produced in Canberra reads as follows:

> The unity of the church to which we are called is a *koinonia* given and expressed in: the common confession of the apostolic faith; a common sacramental life entered by the one baptism and celebrated together in one eucharistic fellowship; a common life in which members and ministries are mutually recognized and reconciled; and a common mission witnessing to all people to the gospel of God's grace and serving the whole of creation. The goal of the search for full communion is realised when all the churches are able to recognize in one another the One, Holy, Catholic and Apostolic Church in its fullness. This full communion will be expressed

---

1. *The New Delhi Report: The Third Assembly of the World Council of Churches 1961* (New York: Association Press, 1962), 116.
2. *Breaking Barriers, Nairobi 1975: The Official Report of the Fifth Assembly of the World Council of Churches, Nairobi 23 November–10 December 1975* edited by David M Paton (London: SPCK, 1976), 60.

on the local and the universal levels through conciliar forms of life and action. In such communion churches are bound in all aspects of their life together at all levels in confessing the one faith and engaging in worship and witness, deliberation and action.[3]

The ecclesiology of *koinonia* or communion emerged as a fruitful way forward for ecumenical reflection on the church. In this the FOC statement was faithful to the original recommendations of the preparatory documents for the Assembly which likewise focused on the church as 'koinonia in the Spirit'.[4] In his report, Heinz Joachim Held, then the Moderator of the Central Committee, had also prepared the Assembly for this development by describing *koinoni* as 'the central concept or rather the decisive reality of living on which everything is meant to converge',[5] including everything undertaken by the WCC. This new statement integrated the conciliar forms of life and action described at Nairobi into the deeper reality of ecclesiological *koinonia*. The preceding paragraph in the statement pointed to the level of communion which already exists between the churches and challenged them to draw the appropriate consequences for their life. In a subsequent paragraph it celebrated diversity as integral to communion but affirmed that diversity has its limits, without spelling out in any details what these were.[6] The statement also called the churches to recommit themselves to working for justice, peace and the integrity of creation and to link more closely the search for sacramental communion with this broader project. The report of the third section went on to recommend that a study be undertaken within the WCC of the ecumenical perspective of ecclesiology.[7]

---

3. *Signs of the Spirit: Official Report, Seventh Assembly, Canberra, Australia, 7–20 February 1991*, edited by Michael Kinnamon (Geneva: WCC, 1991), 173.
4. *Resources for Sections: The Theme, Subthemes and Issues: World Council of Churches Seventh Assembly 1991* (Geneva: WCC, 1990), 56–7.
5. Kinnamon, *Signs of the Spirit*, 139.
6. In a contribution to the collection of preparatory articles for the assembly, Jean MR Tillard OP dealt with the theological notion of 'reconciled diversity' from a Roman Catholic perspective, and more fully with the limits of diversity in an ecclesiology of communion in 'Spirit, Reconciliation, Church', in *Ecumenical Review*, 42 (1990): 237–49.
7. Kinnamon, *Signs of the Spirit*, 99.

Already at the Dunblane, Scotland, meeting of its Standing
Commission in August 1990, the FOC had outlined the programme
of a study to be entitled 'Ecumenical Perspectives on Ecclesiology or
'The Church in Ecumenical Perspective'. The first reason advanced for
undertaking this study was that 'the understanding of the nature and
mission of the church has moved to the forefront of all ecumenical
dialogues and encounters in recent years'.[8] Moreover many of the
still controversial issues between churches and the difficulties
discovered in ecumenical collaboration have their basis in different
understandings of the church. The purpose of this new study will not be
to develop a detailed work of ecclesiology or some kind of ecumenical
ecclesiology. Rather 'its aim is to bring together basic ecclesiological
perspectives which have emerged in ecumenical dialogues
. . . and which could lead to a shared vision of the nature, unity and
mission of the church'.[9] The study would consider how the separated
churches are related to the one Church of Christ and how different
ecclesiologies could be transformed so that remaining differences
were complementary rather than mutually exclusive. Furthermore,
the Standing Commission recommended studying how the model of
the eucharistic communion in local churches being the basis for a
conciliar communion between the churches might be applied to the
relationship between the presently separated churches.

This focus on *koinonia* (communion/participation/fellowship)
emerged as well in the first FOC analysis, in 1990, of the responses
from the churches to the 1982 Lima document, 'Baptism, Eucharist
and Ministry'. In its reflection on the ecclesiological perspectives
contained in these responses the FOC discovered that many of the
churches themselves described the church in terms of *koinonia*.
So once again it recommended that this notion be taken up by
the commission as a way forward towards a convergent vision of
ecclesiology, without suggesting this was the only possible approach.

It also tried to show how the different emphases in the ecclesiology

---

8. *Minutes of the Meeting of the Standing Commission Held at the Scottish Churches
   House Dunblane, Scotland, 16–24 August 1990*, Faith and Order Paper Number
   152 (Geneva: WCC, 1990), 69.
9. *Minutes of the Meeting of the Standing Commission Held at the Scottish Churches
   House Dunblane, Scotland, 16–24 August 1990*, 70.

of the various churches could contribute in a complementary way to an ecclesiology of *koinonia*. Such emphases were: the church as gift of the word of God, the church as mystery or sacrament of God's love for the world, the church as the pilgrim people of God, the church as servant and prophetic sign of God's coming kingdom.[10]

Again in the 1990 study document produced by the FOC, *Church and World: The Unity of the Church and the Renewal of the Human Community*, we find the same emphasis on *koinonia*. This study document is a first major step taken by the FOC to try to overcome the increasing polarisation, manifest again in Canberra in 1991, between the two great strands of the ecumenical movement, the search for visible unity and work for the transformation of the world. It attempts to show the indissoluble relationship between the nature of the church and the mission of the church in the world. All the images it uses to describe the church and its mission, such as 'mystery' and 'prophetic sign' it once again saw as embraced by the notion of *koinonia*.[11] Clearly then, in this arena of multilateral dialogue one can undoubtedly speak of the emergence of ecclesiology as the present focus of ecumenical concern and of *koinonia* as the theological notion emerging at the centre of the dialogue. FOC dialogue will take another step forward in August 1993 when the Fifth World Conference on Faith and Order convenes in Santiago de Compostela, Spain, to draw together the work of the previous thirty years with the theme 'Towards *Koinonia* in Faith, Life and Witness.'[12]

---

10. *Baptism, Eucharist and Ministry 1982–1990: Report on the Process and Responses*, Faith and Order Paper Number 149 (Geneva: WCC, 1990), 148–51. For a more detailed analysis of these differing emphases and the churches in which they were to be found, see Anton Houtepen, 'Towards an Ecumenical Vision of the Church', in *One in Christ*, 25 (1989): 217–37.

11. *Church and World: The Unity of the Church and the Renewal of the Human Community*, Faith and Order Paper Number 151 (Geneva: WCC, 1990), 34. More recently again a consultation took place between representatives of the FOC and those concerned with the Justice, Peace and Integrity of Creation (JPIC) project in an attempt to overcome the tension between the two streams of WCC work. It was entitled 'Koinonia and Justice, Peace and Integrity of Creation'. The report is published as *Costly Unity* (Geneva: WCC, 1993).

12. For an introduction to this conference, see 'The Fifth World Conference on Faith and Order', in *Ecumenical Review*, 45/1 (January 1993): 1–121.

Joint Working Group

The Sixth Report of the Joint Working Group (JWG) between the Roman Catholic Church and the World Council of Churches (WCC) contains as an appendix a new study document which the JWG had commissioned. It is entitled 'The Church: Local and Universal'. In its introduction it acknowledges that the document was prepared with the conviction 'that the ecclesiology of communion can be a way of expressing and especially of building on the real although imperfect communion already existing between churches despite their continuing divisions'.[13] The study document deals in turn with the ecclesiology of communion, local and universal communion in ecumenical perspective, the ecclesial elements of communion, and the structuring of communion. It also draws attention to the Christian WorldCommunions and their recognition of the importance of this ecclesiology, quoting from the seventh assembly of the Lutheran World Federation (1984): 'We give witness and affirm the communion in which Lutheran Churches of the whole world are bound together'.[14] It is worth noting that Christian world communions were formerly referred to as World confessional families. The change in name is in itself very significant.

Orthodox Dialogues

One finds a similar emphasis upon *koinoia* in the ecclesiology outlined in the first statement produced by the Joint Commission between the Roman Catholic Church and the Orthodox Church, *The Mystery of the Church and of the Eucharist in the Light of the Mystery of the Holy Trinity*, which was published in 1982. There one finds the church described as 'the sacrament of the Trinitarian *koinonia*, the "dwelling of God with men" (cf Rev 21:4)'.[15] The trinitarian

---

13. *Joint Working Group between the Roman Catholic Church and the World Council of Churches. With Two Study Documents Commissioned and Received by the Joint Group: The Church: Local and Universal The Notion of 'Hierarchy of Truths': an Ecumenical Interpretation, Geneva–Rome 1990* (Geneva: WCC, 1990), 24.

14. *Joint Working Group between the Roman Catholic Church and the World Council of Churches. With Two Study Documents*, 27.

15. 'Joint Commission for Theological Dialogue between the Roman Catholic Church and the Orthodox Church. Second Plenary Meeting Munich, June 30 to July 6 1982. The Mystery of the Church and of the Eucharist in the Light of the Mystery of the Holy Trinity', in *Information Service*, 49 (1982): 108.

koinoia is communicated to the church through the eucharist, and the eucharistic celebration in turn reveals how the *koinonia* takes shape in the local church itself. It is an eschatological, kerygmatic, ministerial and pneumatological *koinonia*. A similar ecclesiology can be found in the Moscow Statement (1976) produced by the Commission for Anglican Orthodox Joint Doctrinal Discussions: 'The Church celebrating the Eucharist becomes fully itself; that is *koinonia*, fellowship—communion.'[16]

In the second statement of the Joint Commission between the Roman Catholic Church and the Orthodox Church, *Faith, Sacraments and the Unity of the Church* (June 1987), one can find the same constant recourse to an ecclesiology of *koinonia*. It speaks of the human person's integration into the Body of Christ through his or her *koinonia* with the visible church and bases its whole account of the possibility of communion between churches on the necessity of communion in faith which enables communion in the sacraments.[17] Similarly, in the third statement produced in 1988 on the sacrament of order, the role of the ordained ministry is described very much in terms of ecclesial communion.[18] It is not surprising that one should find an ecclesiology of communion taken for granted in dialogues with the Orthodox Church. Such an ecclesiology has been theirs from the beginning[19] and, in some ways, they have encouraged its acceptance by the West.

Anglican–Roman Catholic International commission

The increasing significance of an ecclesiology of communion for the various dialogues sponsored by the WCC and the Orthodox is also borne out by a study of other recent bilateral dialogues. This is

16. *Growth in Agreement: Reports and Agreed Statements of Ecumenical Conversations on a World Level*, edited by Harding Meyer and Lukas Vischer (New York: Paulist Press, 1984), 45.
17. 'Joint International Commission for the Theological Dialogue between the Roman Catholic Church and the Orthodox Church. Bari, June, 1987. Faith, Sacraments and the Unity of the Church', in *Information Service*, 64 (1987): 82–7.
18. 'The Sacrament of Order in the Sacramental Structure of the Church with Particular Reference to the Importance of Apostolic Succession for the Sanctification and Unity of the People of God', in *Information Service*, 68 (1988): 173–8.
19. See John D Zizioulas, *Being as Communion: Studies in Personhood and the Church* (New York: St. Vladimir's, 1985).

nowhere more apparent than in the Work of the Anglican–Roman Catholic International Commission (ARCIC). The preface to the Final Report of ARCIC I named *koinonia* as its 'governing principle'.[20]

In its introduction, it showed how *koinonia* was the unifying theme of its three agreed statements. 'In them we present the eucharist as the effectual sign of *koinonia*, *episcope* as serving the *koinonia*, and primacy as a visible link and focus of *koinonia*.'[21] The *koinonia* requires visible expression because the church is meant to be the sacrament of God's saving work. Therefore it is not surprising that ARCIC II produced as its second agreed statement one entitled *Church as Communion*. If one is to study the ecclesiology of communion *(koinonia)* and its ecumenical ramifications, this statement is probably the best place to start.

The statement endeavours to give an account of the real though imperfect communion which already exists between Anglicans and Roman Catholics. It is also founded on the conviction that the ecclesiology of communion will enable the two churches to understand more clearly the differences between them and to resolve them more easily.[22] The first section of the document is devoted to establishing the scriptural foundation for an ecclesiology of communion. Secondly, it explores how the church as communion is sacrament of God's merciful grace intended for the whole of humanity. This was already a theme in its first agreed statement, *Salvation and the Church*. Thirdly, it takes up the relationship between communion and the apostolicity, catholicity and holiness of the church. Then it looks at the elements necessary for unity and ecclesial communion before describing both the existing communion between the two churches and the remaining divisive issues.

In a very brief overview of the scriptural account of God's dealings with humanity, the statement illustrates how right from the beginning of creation God has endeavoured to draw human beings into communion with Godself and with each other as stewards of

---

20. Anglican–Roman Catholic International Commission, *The Final Report. Windsor, September 1981* (London: SPCK, 1982), 3.
21. Anglican–Roman Catholic International Commission, *The Final Report*, 6.
22. *Church as Communion: An Agreed Statement by the Second Anglican Roman Catholic International Commission. ARCIC II.* (London: Anglican Consultative Council, 1991), 8–9.

creation. All the biblical images used to describe the Christian community it sees as attempts to express different dimensions of the reality to which they all refer:, 'communion, a shared life in Christ . . . which no one image exhaustively describes. This communion is participation in the life of God through Christ in the Holy Spirit, making Christians one with each other.'[23]

Already in the New Testament various dimensions of *koinonia* become apparent. At its centre is communion with the Father, through Christ, in the Spirit. It is entered through faith and baptism and both nourished and expressed in the eucharist. It is necessarily lived out in a visible human community of mutual service and sharing of spiritual and material gifts between both individuals and communities. Its integrity and building up requires appropriate structure, order and discipline. It will reach its fulfilment when the whole creation is brought into communion with God in Christ.

The second section of this agreed statement relates the church as *koinonia* to God's purpose of bringing all people into communion with God through a transformed creation. Christ, through his life, death and resurrection became the sign, instrument and first fruits of this divine purpose of transforming the whole creation. By the power of the Holy Spirit, the riches of God's grace are made present for all time through the church. So the statement is able to say:

> It (the church) is rightly described as a visible sign which both points to and embodies our communion with God and with one another; as an instrument through which God effects this communion; and as a foretaste of the fullness of communion to be consummated when Christ is all in all. It is a 'mystery' or 'sacrament'.[24]

As an instrument of the Holy Spirit, the church is an 'effective sign',[25] both the embodiment and bearer of salvation in Christ. This is despite the sinfulness of its members; and does not suggest that God's saving work is limited to those who explicitly confess Jesus Christ. Therefore the communion of the church is a pledge and foretaste of

---

23. *Church as Communion*, 13.
24. *Church as Communion*, 16.
25. *Church as Communion*, 17.

the universal communion of love which is still to come. The agreed statement highlights the celebration of eucharist as the paramount manifestation of this 'sacramentality' of the church:

> Here, celebrating the memorial of the Lord and partaking of his body and blood, the Church points to the origin of its communion in Christ, himself in communion with the Father; it experiences that communion in a visible fellowship, it anticipates the fullness of the communion in the Kingdom; it is sent out to realize, manifest and extend that communion in the world.[26]

In its first agreed statement, 'Salvation and the Church,' ARCIC II focused less on the church as communion than on the stewardship by the church as the free gift of God:

> For the Church is servant and not master of what it has received. Indeed, its power to affect the hearer comes not from our unaided efforts but entirely from the Holy Spirit, who is the source of the Church's life and who enables it to be truly the steward of God's design.[27]

It also emphasised more fully the need of the church for constant purification and renewal.

When describing the apostolicity of the church in its ecclesiology of communion, the agreed statement describes apostolic tradition as that which links the present both to the past and to the future and so enables the communion to span both time and space.[28] Apostolic tradition is the Spirit-preserved living memory of Christ which is realised and freshly expressed in every age and culture. All Christians have responsibility for the faithful maintenance of the one apostolic faith in its diverse expressions. Those with oversight in the community have the particular responsibility of keeping the

---

26. *Church as Communion,* 19.
27. *Salvation and the Church: An Agreed Statement by the Second Anglican–Roman Catholic International Commission. ARCIC II* (London: Anglican Consultative Council, 1987), 24.
28. *Church as Communion,* 22.

community within the bounds of the apostolic faith. They discern the insights of the community and sometimes give authoritative expression to them. The community in turn assimilates the content of this teaching into its life if it recongnises in it the apostolic faith. This mutual interaction takes place under the guidance of the Holy Spirit in whom all members share. Succession in episcopal ministry serves to assure each community that its faith is the apostolic faith. Moreover the communion among episcopal ministers themselves enables the local church to find its own particular place in the communion of all the churches and its perceptions and concerns to be shared with other churches.

Catholicity in this ecclesiology expresses the power of the one gospel to bring together all the diversity of the human family for mutual enrichment in one communion. 'As the result of communion with God in Christ, diversity does not lead to division; on the contrary, it serves to bring glory to God for the munificence of his gifts.'[29] The communion of local churches is integral to catholicity because it enables the diverse gifts of one to be shared with the others. Unity is maintained in this catholic diversity as follows: 'by the common confession of the one apostolic faith, a shared sacramental life, a common ministry of oversight, and joint ways of reaching decisions and giving authoritative teaching.'[30]

When exploring unity more fully the agreed statement returns to these constitutive elements and expands on them. Fundamentally communion means sharing in the life of the triune God, but this spiritual communion requires expression in a visible ecclesial communion which both embodies and promotes the spiritual communion. When the essential constitutive elements of communion are present and mutually recognised, local churches are able to be together in communion, and their ministers likewise in communion with each other. The primary constitutive element to which all others are subordinate is the common confession of Jesus as Lord. Next the statement speaks of the confession of the one apostolic faith, revealed in the scriptures and set forth in the creeds. Baptism is the foundation of the communion and the celebration of the eucharist its pre-eminent expression and focus. It involves a shared commitment

29. *Church as Communion*, 24.
30. *Church as Communion*, 26.

to the mission of the church, a life of mutual concern, the acceptance
of the same basic moral values and the same vision of humanity, and
the common confession of the one hope in the final consummation
of the kingdom of God.

Concerning the ministry of oversight referred to previously, the
agreed statement summarises some of the conclusions of the *Final
Report* of ARCIC I, locating the fullness of oversight in the episcopate.
It goes on to say:

> This ministry of oversight has both collegial and
> primatial dimensions. It is grounded in the life of the
> community and is open to the community's participation
> in the discovery of God's will. It is exercised so that unity
> and communion are expressed, preserved and fostered
> at every level—locally, regionally and universally. In
> the context of the communion of all the churches, the
> episcopal ministry in the universal primate finds its role
> as the visible focus of unity.[31]

In one little paragraph, the agreed statement situates its treatment
of these constitutive elements in a very nuanced perspective. It too
deserves to be quoted in full:

> All these inter-related elements and facets belong to the
> visible communion of the universal Church. Although
> their possession cannot guarantee the constant fidelity of
> Christians, neither can the Church dispense with them.
> They need to be present in order for one local church to
> recognize another canonically. This does not mean that
> a community in which they are present expresses them
> fully in its life.[32]

In the light of this statement of shared ecclesiological vision the
document was then able to go on to discuss the degree of communion
already existing between Anglicans and Roman Catholics, to name
the major issues still unresolved, and to express the hope that this

---

31. *Church as Communion*, 41.
32. *Church as Communion*, 30.

agreed ecclesiology of communion would prove to be the appropriate context for resolving them. There can be no doubt that in this bilateral dialogue at least such an ecclesiology has already proved to be an immensely fruitful way forward.

Methodist Roman Catholic Dialogue

Another international bilateral dialogue on the church in which *koinonia* plays a central role is that between Methodists and Roman Catholics. In the Nairobi Report of the Joint Commission between the Roman Catholic Church and the World Methodist Council (1982–86) entitled, *Towards a Statement on the Church*, one finds not only that the church is described in the first paragraph as 'a visible *koinonia* of Christ's disciples',[33] but later on one reads: 'We have found that *kononia,* both as a concept and an experience, is more important than any particular model of Church union that we are yet able to propose.'[34] Jean M Tillard OP, who plays such a vigorous role in the FOC, ARCIC and the Orthodox–Roman Catholic dialogue and whose own writing on the subject[35] has been so influential ecumenically, has suggested that the opening paragraph of this report is among the most beautiful definitions of the church one can find and deserves to be adopted by the FOC.[36] The paragraph reads as follows:

> Because God so loved the world, he sent his Son and the Holy Spirit to draw us into communion with himself. This sharing in God's life, which resulted from the mission of the Son and the Holy Spirit, found expression in a visible *koinonia* of Christ's disciples, the Church.[37]

The Methodist–Roman Catholic statement also speaks of the church as 'sign, sacrament and harbinger of the Kingdom of God'[38] in a way

---

33. *Towards a Statement on the Church: Report of the Joint Commission between Roman Catholic Church and World Methodist Council 1982–1986, Fourth Series* (Lake Junaluska: World Methodist Council, 1986), 4.
34. *Towards a Statement on the Church,* 8.
35. Jean MR Tillard OP, *Church of Churches: The Ecclesiology of Communion* (Collegeville: Glazier, 1992).
36. Jean MR Tillard OP, 'Commentary on *Towards a Statement on the Church*', in *Information Service,* 62 (1986): 216.
37. *Towards a Statement on the Church,* 4.
38. *Towards a Statement on the Church,* 5.

reminiscent of ARCIC II. In commenting on the way the statement deals with the sacramentality of the church, Tillard pointed to a protestant diffidence about affirming a clear, effective link between the church and the actualisation of salvation in Jesus Christ, that is the church as *effective* sign or sacrament, a diffidence which is lacking in the treatment of the sacraments of baptism and eucharist themselves,[39] and which is overcome in the statement of ARCIC II.

The Methodist–Roman Catholic statement deals next with various models for organic unity in the *koinonia* of the one Body of Christ, affirming both the need to protect legitimate variety but also the necessity of limits to this variety. Such limits arise both from the need for cohesion and co-operation but also from the basic structures of the church which exclude anything which would disrupt communion in faith, order and sacramental life. Here unresolved issues begin to emerge. These can be grouped under three headings: the normativeness or otherwise of the pattern of ministry developed from the New Testament in the second and third centuries, apostolic succession, and papal primacy. Since then the Methodist–Roman Catholic dialogue has published a new report entitled 'The Apostolic Tradition' which situates the ordained ministry in a much richer context than is often the case.[40] Jean Tillard raised two rather perceptive questions for this continuing dialogue: Why is there almost a silence on the relationship between local church and universal church in this dialogue, given that the church is a communion not just of disciples with various traditions and structures but a communion of local churches?[41] Can one any longer continue to characterise Methodists as essentially a devotional movement or a spiritual tradition when one is concerned about identifying the ecclesial nature of one's dialogue partner?[42]

Lutheran–Roman Catholic Dialogue

The ecclesiology of communion/*koinonia* plays an interesting part in the statements produced by the Roman Catholic–Lutheran

---

39. Tillard, 'Commentary', 217.
40. 'The Apostolic Tradition: Report of the Joint Commission between the Roman Catholic Church and the World Methodist Council', in *Information Service*, 78 (1991): 212–25.
41. Tillard, 'Commentary', 219.
42. Tillard, 'Commentary', 218.

Joint Commission. In its 1980 statement *Ways to Community* the word is used only rarely. For example, the question is asked, 'What steps toward unity are implied by the nature of ecclesial fellowship (*communio*) as a gift of God's grace which precedes all our efforts?'[43] However 'community' or 'fellowship' seem to be the preferred words.

While it is true that the full riches of the notion of communion/ *koinonia* are not exploited in this document, nonetheless many of the ecclesiological elements that such a notion encompasses are present, and the document is compatible with such an ecclesiology.

This is apparent when reading the 1985 statement, *Facing Unity*. Right at the beginning under the heading of 'The Church as Fellowship' one reads 'The Church is therefore a communion (*communio*) subsisting in a network of local churches.'[44] *Communion/ communio* is used to describe the relationship between the variety of local churches, an element of ecclesiology not really addressed in the earlier statement. It is also the language used when describing the role of sacraments in the church:

> The sacraments are part of God's trinitarian act of salvation: the work that God performed in Christ once for all for the salvation of the world is mediated by the Holy Spirit who works through word and sacrament so that *communio sanctorum* is formed, i.e. church as participation in the gifts of salvation and as communion of the faithful.[45]

The document acknowledges that a view of the church as communion was determinative for the early church, is still so for the Orthodox churches, and has become central to Roman Catholic ecclesiology. Moreover it also acknowledges that such a view is in accord with Lutheran ecclesiology; and the worldwide Lutheran community is cited as an example of a *communio* of local churches.[46] As in the

---

43. 'Lutheran–Catholic Joint Commission: Charting a Future Course for Ecumenism', in *Origins*, 11 (31 September 1981): 252.
44. 'Roman Catholic/Lutheran Joint Commission. Facing Unity. Models, Forms and Phases of Catholic–Lutheran Church Fellowship', in *Information Service*, 59 (1985), 45.
45. 'Facing Unity', 58.
46. 'Facing Unity', 45–6. For an analysis of the history and significance of the Lutheran

two previous dialogues an ecclesiology of communion leads easily to reflection on the sacramentality of the church itself. While acknowledging a reticence of Lutherans towards this concept, the statement suggests that the intention behind the use of the word 'sacrament' for the church should be acceptable to them. It defines this as follows:

> as the body of Christ and *koinonia* of the Holy Spirit, the church is the sign and instrument of God's grace, an instrument that of itself can do nothing. The church lives by the word as it lives by the sacraments and at the same time stands in their service.[47]

Overall the document is concerned with describing the various models of church unity, the actual relationship between the two communions, and concrete steps which need to be taken to restore full communion. As such it is a ground breaking document and an ecumenical first. At the same time, while the statement does not explore exhaustively the ecclesiology of *koinonia* and naturally dwells on specific questions which at present divide Lutherans and Roman Catholics, it does deal in turn with the elements intrinsic to such an understanding of the church. The more intentional inclusion of this ecclesiological approach seems again to have proved fruitful for another bilateral dialogue.[48]

Lutheran–Methodist Dialogue

This dialogue was more comparative than the previous ones. The final report, *The Church: Community of Grace*, devotes a major section to the two themes of the authority of the scriptures and salvation by grace through faith, before its explicit treatment of the church. This

---

World Federation adopting this language to describe itself, see Kjell Nordstokke, 'The Ecclesiological Self-Understanding of the Lutheran World Federation: From *Free Association* to *Communion of Churches*', in *Ecumenical Review*, 44 (October 1992): 479–90.

47. 'Facing Unity', 58.

48. For a Lutheran assessment of this document from the perspective of an ecclesiology of *koinonia*, see Ola Tjorhorn, 'The Goal of Unity: Searching for a Common Ecumenical Vision', in *One in Christ*, 26 (1990): 80–93.

latter is fairly brief though a larger section is devoted to the mission of the church. In between there is a treatment of baptism and eucharist as means of grace. In its treatment of eucharist one reads, 'There is a new awareness of the corporate character of the act of worship, expressing and making real the communion (*koinonia*) with Jesus Christ and one another.'[49] The church itself is variously called 'the community of grace', 'the communion of saints', 'the community of Jesus Christ called into being by the Holy Spirit'.[50] It is the corporate nature of Christian life which is emphasised in this fairly brief ecclesiological exposition.

Lutheran–Uniting Church Dialogue

This dialogue appears to be the only Australian bilateral dialogue which has dealt explicitly with ecclesiology. It takes a fairly comparative approach and places particular emphasis on the visibility and invisibility of the church. Agreement was reached on the understanding that the one holy church will, in the strict sense, only become visible when Jesus Christ comes again. Denominations as visible organisations are properly called 'churches' but they are only so called in a looser sense because they are a mixture of faithful and unfaithful members.[51] The unity in Christ that the justified have by faith is not visible. Nor can it ever be lost. Work to restore the unity of Christians is not the restoration of the unity of the Body of Christ which can never be destroyed, and could never be achieved by human formulations. However such ecumenical endeavour is necessary to achieve agreement in the pure word and the sacraments which are the visible marks of the church and the mission of Christ, because visible disunity is a scandal and an obstacle to faith.[52]

Baptist–Roman Catholic Dialogue

Official conversations have been taking place between representatives

---

49. *Final Report of the Joint Commission between the Lutheran World Federation and the World Methodist Council 1979–1984. The Church: Community of Grace* (Geneva: LWF, 1984), 19.
50. *The Church: Community of Grace*, 12–13.
51. 'Uniting Church–Lutheran Church Dialogue: Agreed Statement on the Church (December, 1986)' (unpublished document), 1–2.
52. 'Agreed Statement on the Church', 7.

of the Baptist World Alliance and the Roman Catholic Church since 1984. In 1988 the first report of these conversations was published under the title *Summons to Witness to Christ in Today's World*. When dealing with the church this report resorts entirely to an ecclesiology of *koinonia*. As it says, 'Koinonia of the Spirit (Phil 2:1, cf 2 Cor 13:14) is a helpful description of our common understanding of the church'.[53] The briefer description of *koinonia* in the report is consistent with the fuller description in the report of ARCIC II, though it does devote greater space to a description of the role of the Holy Spirit in the *koinonia*.

Within the context of this ecclesiology the report describes the differing ecclesiological emphases of the partners to the conversation. Baptists refer primarily to the local congregation gathered by the Spirit in obedience and service to God's word when they speak of the church. It is divine in its origin, mission and scope but human in its historical existence and structure. For Roman Catholics the church as a community is a visible structure established and sustained by Christ. The Body of Christ and the visible structured society are not two realities but one reality composed of a divine and a human element. Consequently the concrete realisation of the *koinonia* of the Holy Spirit is perceived of somewhat differently by Baptists and Catholics. In other words, the Spirit is conceived of as working through different structures. For Baptists the Spirit is seen to work through the various interdependent associations, conventions and alliances; but structures are avoided which would threaten the freedom of individuals and the autonomy of local congregations which are the primary locus of the Spirit's work. For Roman Catholics the *koinonia* which the Spirit achieves in the local congregation is simultaneously a *koinonia* of various local congregations in the one universal church. Therefore the Spirit is perceived as working in the various spiritual and institutional bonds between congregations presided over by bishops and by the bishop of Rome.[54] While these are quite major differences between the partners to the conversations,

---

53. 'Summons to Witness to Christ in Today's World: A Report on the Baptist–Roman Catholic International Conversations', in *Information Service*, 72 (1980): 8.
54. 'Summons to Witness to Christ in Today's World', 12.

it is from within the common ecclesiological foundation of a *koinonia* of the Spirit that they are seeking further mutual understanding.

Pentecostal–Roman Catholic Dialogue

The third phase of a dialogue between the Pontifical Council for Promoting Christian Unity and some classical Pentecostal churches and leaders produced a report in 1989 entitled *Perspectives on Koinonia*. It acknowledges that the topic was chosen not only because the subject of the communion of saints had emerged in the previous phase of their dialogue but because the theme of communion/*koinonia* was arousing such ecumenical interest in other dialogues and was already proving to be fruitful.[55] Given the identity of the dialogue partners, the title of the report is well chosen. It illustrates two differing perspectives on various dimensions of the ecclesial *koinonia*. As such it is a fascinating ecumenical document. It ranges over a broad canvas, dealing in turn with scripture and tradition, baptism and faith, the church itself, the church and salvation, the communion of saints, ministry, and holiness. While many areas of agreement are named, this is far from being an agreed statement. At the same time each party often acknowledges the challenge that the other party offers to their own understanding or practice. Sometimes the hope is expressed that differing perspectives will be discovered that are complementary and mutually enriching. For example, Pentecostals remind Roman Catholics of the personal dimension of the *koinonia* with God 'which comes from the Holy Spirit who converts persons of sin and brings them to faith in Jesus Christ.'[56] Roman Catholics remind Pentecostals of the communitarian dimension of the New Testament understanding of *koinonia*. These are complementary dimensions of ecclesial *koinonia*. Once again an ecclesiology of *koinonia* seems to have proved fruitful in a dialogue; and on this occasion between very different partners.

Reformed–Roman Catholic Dialogue

This dialogue has produced two reports with significant ecclesiological content. The first, *The Presence of Christ in Church*

---

55. 'Pentecostal–Catholic Dialogue. Perspectives on Koinonia', in *Information Service*, 75 (1990): 179–90.
56. 'Perspectives on Koinonia', 182.

and World (1977), deserves being borne in mind when one reads the latest and more innovative *Towards a Common Understanding of the Church* (1990). The latter statement is innovative because it is the first dialogue to explicitly deal with the event of the Reformation and its interpretation in the separated communions. It strives for what it calls 'a reconciliation of memories'. When dealing with the church directly the statement starts from the premise that there are two different conceptions of the church operative in the dialogue partners.

In the Reformed tradition the church is conceived of as *creatura verbi*, the creation of the Word of God.

> The Church depends upon this word the Word incarnate, the Word written, the Word preached—in at least three ways:
> – the Church is founded upon the Word of God;
> – the Church is kept in being as the Church by the Word of God;
> – the Church continually depends upon the Word of God for its inspiration, strength and renewal.[57]

At the time of the Reformation any appeal to continuity, custom or institution was rejected in favour of the living voice of the living God found in the Bible, as the essential and decisive factor by which the church must live as *creatura verbi*. But the church as the community of grace, community of faith, is not merely the community in which the word is preached. It also becomes itself a medium of confession and its faith a 'sign' or 'token' to the world.[58]

The Catholic conception of the Church is then described in terms of the church as sacrament, rather than communion/*koinonia*; though, as other dialogues would indicate, these are normally intimately connected. The statement is at pains to point out that the application of sacramental language to the church must respect the absolute lordship of Christ over the church. Christ is the unique foundational sacrament in the sense that he is the visible manifestation in the world

---

57. 'Towards a Common Understanding of the Church: Reformed/Roman Catholic International Dialogue: Second Phase (1984–1990)', in *Information Service*, 74 (1990): 107.
58. 'Towards a Common Understanding of the Church', 108.

of 'the active and original power of the whole economy of salvation'.[59] The church is a sacrament only by the gift of Christ who gifts it to be his sign and instrument.

> The Church then is only a sacrament founded by Christ and entirely dependent on him. Its being and its sacramental acts are the fruit of a free gift received from Christ, a gift in relation to which he remains radically transcendent, but which, however, he commits to the salvation of humankind.[60]

In relation to the unique mediation of Christ, the Church is 'the servant, but never either its source or its mistress'.[61] The Church is an instrument of Christ's unique mediation and a sign of the efficacious presence of that mediation. It lives out of the word which brought it to birth and which it proclaims, and hence is the sacrament of the Word of God.

> If the Church is seen in relation to its source, it may be described as the sacrament of God, of Christ, and of the Spirit—as sacrament of grace. If it is seen in relation to its mission and calling, it may be called the sacrament of the kingdom, or the sacrament of salvation.[62]

The report of the dialogue acknowledges that while both partners agree about the radical dependence of the Church on the gift of God, they do not understand the activity of the Church in the salvation of humanity in the same way. The Reformed are said to often allege that Catholics appropriate to the church the role that is proper only to Christ. Catholics are said to often allege that the Reformed hold the church apart from the work of salvation and hence leave aside the assurance that Christ is present and active in his church. These are caricatures of each position but yet are seen as illustrating two tendencies in ecclesiology. The report expresses the hope that these

---

59. 'Towards a Common Understanding of the Church', 108.
60. 'Towards a Common Understanding of the Church', 108.
61. 'Towards a Common Understanding of the Church', 109.
62. 'Towards a Common Understanding of the Church', 109.

different aspects could be seen as complementary and the poles of a creative tension between the churches.

The question of the continuity of the Church focuses this creative tension rather sharply. The Reformed give priority to continuity in the confession of faith and in the teaching of gospel doctrines. This constitutes the apostolicity of the church and therein ministers can be said to be in apostolic succession. Roman Catholics consider that the apostolicity found in faith and preaching, and in the administration of the sacraments, is linked to certain visible signs through which the Spirit works, especially the apostolic succession of bishops. Similarly the Reformed see the scriptures as sufficient witness to the gospel message, a message 'that constantly creates the understanding of itself afresh',[63] while acknowledging that tradition is an expression of faithful communion through the centuries. Roman Catholics accept the scriptures as *norma normans* for all doctrine but they perceive the tradition as the living interpretation of the scriptures transmitted in an uninterrupted way through the ages. It has real authority, as do magisterial decisions about its meaning, though these are founded again on submission to the message of the scriptures.

Other examples are dealt with in the report, including sinfulness in the Church, the Reformation itself, the church visible and invisible, ministerial order. The differing ecclesiological tendencies are manifested in the account of each of these topics. In the first report of this dialogue, *The Presence of Christ in Church and World* (1977), their differing tendencies were described as follows:

> This difference in attitude may rest on a difference in pneumatology: Catholic thought is primarily sustained by confidence in the *continuing* presence of the Holy Spirit, whereas the Reformed Church experiences the presence of the Spirit as a *constantly renewed* gift of the ascended Lord.[64]

Clearly the Reformed–Roman Catholic dialogue has found a way of describing the differences between the ecclesiologies of the

---

63. 'Towards a Common Understanding of the Church', 110.
64. 'The Presence of Christ in Church and World. Dialogue between the World Alliance of Reformed Churches and the Secretariat for Promoting Christian Unity: 1970–72', in *Information Service*, 35 (1972): 23.

two communions but always on the foundation of what they have in common and with the hope of finding the differences to be complementary rather divisive. In his assessment of this dialogue and the level of communion between Reformed and Roman Catholics, Jos Vercruysse SJ drew attention to the section of this report containing a common confession of faith and pointed out that though the bonds of communion may be imperfect, they have already gone beyond those created simply by baptism.[65] Reformed–Roman Catholic Dialogue is based on the communion already shared and strives for a deepening of that communion.

However, Jean Tillard, when speaking about the so-called 'basic difference'[66] between the Roman Catholic Church and the Churches of the Reformation, situated this difference in ecclesiology. More specifically he situated it in different perspectives on the relationship of the Word of God to the church and hence the role of the church in salvation, precisely the perspectives named in this dialogue, in which he played no part. He went so far as to say:

> Our fundamental visions of the Church on earth are so different that they perhaps cannot be reconciled as they stand, without a radical debate leading to an ecclesiological change or 'conversion' . . . is it necessary for one of our ecclesiological traditions or perhaps for each of them to modify in some concrete way its basic ecclesiologicl position?'[67]

Jos Vercruysse, on the other hand, argued that the report 'rightly states that the two conceptions can be envisaged as complementary', and further 'why not even a challenge and a necessary correction of possible imbalance?[68]

Certainly this dialogue highlights both the centrality of the ecclesiological issue in contemporary ecumenical dialogue and the

---

65. Jos E Vercruysse SJ, 'A Comment and Reflection on "Towards a Common Understanding of the Church"', in *Information Service*, 74 (1990): 125.

66. For an overview of the discussion on this debated ecumenical question, see Harding Meyer, 'Fundamental Difference—Fundamental Consensus', in *Mid-Stream*, 25 (1986): 247–59.

67. JMR Tillard OP, 'We Are Different', in *Mid-Stream*, 25 (1986): 286.

68. Vercruysse, 'A Comment', 123.

difficulties that sometimes have to be faced once one does begin to tackle this topic. It is interesting that the report recommends reflection on the WCC Nairobi (1975) description of the unity we seek in terms of a conciliar fellowship,[69] as a possible way forward for the dialogue. One wonders whether the WCC Canberra description of this goal in terms of *koinonia,* will be taken up and whether such an ecclesiology would offer a liberating way forward or a further blockage to the dialogue.

Reformed–Anglican Dialogue

In 1984 the Anglican–Reformed Commission produced a report entitled *God's Reign and Our Unity* representing the fruit of work over four years. This report has a unique approach to Christian unity because it situates it in the wider missionary and eschatological context of the kingdom of God. It acknowledges that the members of the commission from the Third World assisted it to come to the realisation that the unity of the whole human race was the goal of the gospel and so the kingdom of God was the correct focus for ecclesiology. These members also led it to recognise the necessity of taking orthopraxia into account and not just orthodoxy. Many of the issues of orthodoxy deemed to be divisive in traditional ecumenical dialogues were considered by these members to be largely irrelevant to the mission of the Church today.[70] Given this starting point the report argues that only a more missionary and eschatological vision of the church gives any urgency to the quest for unity and enables it to be properly understood.[71]

The description of the Church which emerged within the commission is very expressive of this missionary and eschatological perspective:

> The Church is sent into the world as a sign, instrument and first-fruits of a reality which comes from beyond history—the Kingdom, or reign of God. The unity of the church is not simply an end in itself because the church

69. 'Towards a Common Understanding', 117.
70. *God's Reign and Our Unity: The Report of the Anglican–Reformed International Commission 1981–1984. Woking, England, January 1984* (London: SPCK, 1984), 14.
71. *God's Reign and Our Unity*, 9.

does not exist for itself but for the glory of God and as a sign, instrument and first-fruits of his purpose to reconcile all things in heaven and earth through Christ. Nor is the Church merely a means to an end, for the Church already enjoys a foretaste of that end, and is only a sign and instrument in so far as it is a foretaste. Life in Christ is the end for which all things were made, not a means to an end beyond it.[72]

This appears to be a much stronger ecclesiological agreement than was able to be reached in the Reformed–Roman Catholic Dialogue where the role of the church itself in salvation was named as an as yet unresolved issue.

When attempting to describe the form of unity to be sought by the two communions, as they are called in the report, it turns to the descriptions of the goal put forward by the New Delhi, Uppsala, Nairobi and Vancouver Assemblies of the WCC.[73] Once again it will be interesting to see whether this dialogue is affected in any way by the Canberra description in terms of *koinonia*/communion. Such an ecclesiology is already foreshadowed towards the end of the report when it names seven things which need to be borne in mind by those who read this report. The first of these is:

Participation in Christ and in the life of the Triune God. In our different communions we are all participating, in the Spirit, in what Christ has done and is doing, and in his communion with the Father and his mission to the world and his will for peace and justice.[74]

Conclusion

The ecclesiology of *koinonia*/*communion* has proved to be a reconciling ecclesiology, and an ecclesiology very clarifying of unresolved differences, in most major bilateral dialogues on the church in this past decade. It is also emerging as the preferred language of the WCC

---

72. *God's Reign and Our Unity*, 19.
73. *God's Reign and Our Unity*, 68–9.
74. *God's Reign and Our Unity*, 79.

and its FOC. It is clearly congenial to the Orthodox, Anglicans,[75] and Roman Catholics.[76] It is increasingly the language of Lutherans; and has been deemed appropriate by Baptists and some Pentecostals, as the recent bilateral dialogues well illustrate. But it has not really surfaced in dialogue with the Reformed Churches. Therefore, it is extremely important for the ecumenical movement and any future convergence on ecclesiological issues that the voice of the Reformed Churches be heard on this fundamental question. Certainly there are significantly different approaches to the church in 'reformed' and 'catholic' traditions. It would be a pity if the more 'catholic' churches moved ahead in their dialogues around the central concept of ecclesial *koinonia* without hearing the concerns of the 'reformed' churches. Maybe in discussing *koinonia* together they will be able to deal with what leads to one being 'reformed' and the other 'catholic' and ultimately, by the grace of God, discover a new way forward to becoming the one communion of God in Jesus Christ through the Holy Spirit.

75. See *The Truth Shall Make You Free: The Lambeth Conference 1988: The Reports, Resolutions and Pastoral Letters from the Bishops* (London: Anglican Consultative Council, 1988), 144–8.

76. The Extraordinary Synod of Bishops (1985) said 'The ecclesiology of communion is the central and fundamental idea of the Council's [Vatican II] documents'. *Documents of the Extraordinary Synod of Bishops November 28–December 8 1985* (Homebush: St Paul, 1985), 35. The 1992 document of the Congregation for the Doctrine of the Faith, 'Some Aspects of the Church as Communion', reaffirms the centrality of this ecclesiology but at the same time raises new questions for those involved in ecumenical dialogue because of its treatment of the relationship between the local and universal church. For the document itself and some ecumenical responses, see 'The Church as Communion', in *Catholic International*, 3/16 (1–30 September 1992): 761–76.

The Roman Catholic Church, Ecumenism, and the Anglican Communion

In his letter to the gathering in Mechelen, Belgium, to celebrate the seventy-fifth anniversary of the Malines Conversations, Pope John Paul II wrote:

> Despite the difficulties—some of them sadly of recent origin—which Anglicans and Catholics have yet to resolve, I am heartened by the providential growth in effective co-operation which has taken place in recent years. It is my fervent prayer that the International Commission will continue its mission of pursuing and expressing 'the whole truth into which the Holy Spirit guides Christ's disciples' *(Ut Unum Sint, 36)* in ways which reflect the profound spiritual bonds linking the Catholic Church and the Anglican Communion . . .
>
> . . . It is my hope that this Seventy-fifth Anniversary of the Malines Conversations will give fresh impetus to the dialogue between Catholics and Anglicans. I join all those taking part in the anniversary celebration in fervent prayer that the Lord will indeed grant us that unity for which he himself prayed.[1]

Archbishop Carey of Canterbury, who was himself in Mechelen, expressed similar sentiments. He spoke of his gratitude for those who

This previously unpublished paper was presented in October 1996 at the annual Catholic clergy day in Brisbane.

1. 'John Paul II Seeks "Fresh Impetus" in Anglican Roman Catholic Dialogue', in *Church Scene*, 5/43 (6 September 1996): 2.

took part in the original consultations and went on to say: 'We know there is still a long way to go until we realise their dream of visible unity between our two Communions, and yet I am struck that . . . their sense of vision and hope has not been lost.'[2]

However when one reads the writings of some of those who would have gathered in Mechelen, as members or former members of ARCIC, one is confronted with the seriousness of the 'difficulties' the pope referred to. In his address for the second Richard Stewart Lecture in Cawley, West Sussex, on 4 December 1995, Jean Tillard OP, a member of both ARCIC I and II, and one whose very valuable contribution to the drafting of texts has often been acknowledged, said this about the present relations between the Anglican and Roman Catholic Communions:

> In this tragic situation our two Churches share a common responsibility. The delayed response of the *Curia Romana* created the sad impression, first that the Roman Catholic Church was not very interested in making real the unity of the two Churches, and, second, that the officials of the Congregation for the Doctrine of the Faith were no longer in tune with the mandate Paul VI gave to the Catholic members of the commission. But on the other side, the way the Anglican Communion was dealing with the burning issue of the ordination of women to the presbyterate and even episcopacy, without taking into account the letters written by those of the Roman curia who were deeply desirous of unity and working for it, made Catholic people believe that for the Anglicans the question of unity was secondary, unimportant. The consequence of such a situation is that it is now impossible to expect the coming together of the two Churches under one and the same ordained ministry in order to form what ARCIC-I called 'an organic unity', no matter what concrete shape this organic unity may have been supposed to adopt. Since we cannot affirm that the Catholic Church will accept the validity of Eucharist and ordination celebrated by

2. 'The Church in the World', in *The Tablet* (7 September 1996): 72.

a female minister, and since we cannot affirm that the Anglican communion *as such* will reverse the synodical decision to ordain women, one may evidently fear that there is a dead-end, a wall, a final stop we shall never cross, never bypass.

Consequently, for a few years Anglicans have now been looking for full communion with the Lutherans, even if they know that some of the statements or concordats they propose may create more difficulties in relations with the Catholic Church. This also explains why the Catholic Church is now making so many efforts to remove the obstacles separating itself from the Orthodox Churches, initiating so many gestures of fellowship with the main Orthodox leaders. If there is an organic unity to be expected by either the Roman Catholic Church or by the Orthodox Churches, it is now clear that it will happen only between these two communions of local Churches. The consequence of this exclusive possibility is the risk of dividing Christianity into two huge blocks of Churches, the so-called Protestant family and the so-called traditional family.[3]

I have quoted Jean Tillard at length because he is one of the finest ecumenical theologians in the Catholic Church and, secondly, he has committed a great deal of his life to achieving the restoration of unity between our two communions. His assessment of the situation is very bleak, though he proceeds to explore what he calls the possibilities of '*in-between communion*'. He argues for this as an alternative to settling simply for some form of collaboration with a partner with whom union, one believes, is impossible—an alternative he rejects. His description of the possibilities is creative and even adventurous. Some suggestions certainly exceed what is considered possible at the moment. Moreover, he hopes that through this kind of relationship some of the present obstacles to full communion may disappear. In other words, his analysis is stark and confronting but his prognosis remains hopeful.

---

3. JMR Tillard OP, 'Roman Catholics and Anglicans: Is There a Future for Ecumenism?' in *One in Christ*, 32 (1996): 107–8.

I believe it is very important to speak the truth to each other in ecumenical relationships and not to avoid the hard, even tension-filled, issues. So I am very grateful to the dedicated Jean Tillard for his bluntness, and equally grateful for his hopefulness. This issue of the ordination of women needs to be set out clearly before both partners in our relationship as truly a new obstacle. Tillard, you will notice, speaks of our common responsibility for the present impasse. Catholics contributed their alienating performance of delaying for ten years a response to ARCIC I, thereby making it hard for anyone to believe we were serious. Anglicans went ahead to ordain women without a consensus on the question among all the major Christian Churches of East and West.

Some may describe the causes differently. Many Anglicans may prefer to speak in terms of an Anglican willingness to respond positively to the changed cultural interpretation of the role of women and the recognition of the injustice they have suffered in the past, and a Catholic obstinacy as manifest in the 1994 papal letter, *Ordinatio Sacerdotalis*, and Cardinal Ratzinger's commentary on it.[4] Others may believe the issue will pass quickly, as soon as the Catholic Church realises what they perceive to be the untenability of its position. However one sees the situation, it is important not to trivialise it. There is a real and very serious difference between our churches on this question and we need to define our relationship with this difference very clearly before our eyes. While Tillard's description may be a little bleak, there is no point in acting as if this new obstacle were not confronting us on our road ahead. In a recent very interesting interview, Cardinal Edward Cassidy of the Pontifical Council for Promoting Christian Unity had this to say: 'the ordination of women to the priesthood is obviously a fundamental problem for the dialogue with those Communions which consider ordained priesthood an essential ministry in their understanding of the Church.'[5] At the same time, he went on to say that every dialogue has such fundamental questions to deal with and that this was the very reason for dialogue. What must happen to resolve the question will only be discovered through dialogue. 'We have to go on with the dialogue', was what he said.[6]

---

4. 'Reply to the *Dubium* concerning the Teaching Contained in the Apostolic Letter *Ordinatio Sacerdotalis*', in *Origins*, 25/4 (30 November 1995): 401–5.
5. Gerard O'Connell, 'Dialogue Must Go On', in *The Tablet* (20 April 1996): 507.
6. O'Connell, 'Dialogue Must Go On', 507.

As if Jean Tillard's impressions were not enough, another Roman Catholic member of ARCIC I and foremost English ecumenist, Edward Yarnold SJ, suggested in 1994 that the Porvoo Statement between the Church of England and Nordic Lutheran Churches may have created another obstacle between our two communions on the path to full communion. The Porvoo Statement is interpreted by Anglican Bishop David Tustin, Chairman of the Council for Christian Unity, in its most irenic way, as follows:

> What the text does say, building on these strong statements on apostolicity and succession, is that a Church which, like the Church of England, has preserved the sign of historic episcopal succession is free to acknowledge an authentic episcopal ministry in a Church which has preserved continuity in the episcopal office by an occasional presbyteral ordination at the time of the Reformation. At the same time, a Church, like the Church of Norway, which has preserved continuity through an episcopal succession, but with an occasional break in the laying on of hands at the Reformation, is free without denying its own past to enter a relationship of mutual participation in episcopal ordinations with a Church which has retained the episcopal succession with no such a break.[7]

Edward Yarnold uses different language to describe the principles of Porvoo, language rejected by Bishop Tustin, and he comes to a rather tough conclusion:

> Among Catholics the 'extraordinary route to episcopal office' remains a tentative suggestion; the tradition that certainty is required in matters concerning the sacraments is likely to prevent the Church from recognizing orders without episcopal succession, even on the accepted principle of *ecclesia supplet* (the implicit action of the Church makes up defects in the administration of sacraments). The Porvoo signatories, on the other hand, are much more confident, wishing to

---

7. David Tustin, 'Porvoo Principles', in *The Tablet* (23 July 1994): 924.

commit their Churches to the interchange of ministries even before the sign of episcopal succession has been re-established. They consider themselves justified in taking such an unprecedented step, feeling 'free' to acknowledge 'authentic episcopal ministry' even if there is no unbroken line of bishops, on what can only be the balance of theological probabilities . . .

The declaration has thus important implications for Roman Catholic–Anglican relations. If Roman Catholics could accept the Porvoo principle, many of the objections to Anglican orders would be nullified. If on the other hand, as seems more probable, they are bound to reject it, a new and important disagreement on the doctrine of ministry will have emerged.[8]

George Tavard AA, also a member of ARCIC I, a continuing member of the Methodist–Roman Catholic Dialogue, and like Jean Tillard one of the best ecumenists among contemporary Catholics, acknowledges the difficulties the statement raises for Catholic doctrine. He said interestingly enough:

In order to accept this conclusion from a Catholic point of view, one has to be persuaded that the order of episcopacy is transmitted by intention and ritual, whether the ordainers themselves are or are not in the episcopate. This implies restoring a more radical doctrine of *opus operatum* than the Catholic sacramental theology that Protestant theology has commonly rejected.[9]

Nonetheless he believes the Porvoo Statement will have beneficial effects because it will lead to developments in the theology of reception and of communion. One could add that the statement's understanding of the apostolic succession of bishops in relation to that of the whole Church,[10] while not new, is significant for the

---

8. Edward Yarnold SJ, 'In Line with the Apostles', in *The Tablet* (9 July 1994): 879.
9. George Tavard AA, 'A Catholic Reflection on the Porvoo Statement', in *Mid-Stream*, 33/3 (July 1994): 356.
10. Compare: Christopher Hill, 'Anglican Orders: An Ecumenical Context', *in*

practical conclusions to which it has led. From that point of view, it seems clear that despite ARCIC I the discussion of the question of apostolic succession between our two communions is still incomplete. Certainly the Catholic Church needs to explore even more vigorously the fruit of renewed and richer understandings of apostolic succession which have emerged in ecumenical dialogue and in contemporary theological discussion, to see whether they can extend to the theology of the Porvoo Statement.

It is not Catholic members of ARCIC I alone who have expressed some heavy-hearted views. Henry Chadwick said in an address in New York entitled 'The Ecumenism of the Possible', and concerning the new Ecumenical Directory, which overall many found to be a step forward:

> The recently published Vatican 'Directory for the application of the principles and norms of Ecumenism' (25 March 1993) reads as if its authors felt bound by the positive Decree of the Second Vatican Council *(Unitatis Redintegratio)*, but in practice regarded ecumenical dialogue as virtually certain to end in treachery and a betrayal of authentic principles. When the Congregation for the Doctrine of the Faith published its critical evaluation of the ARCIC statement 'Salvation and the Church', the statement was recognised to be fully compatible with the Catholic faith, but with a crucial qualification, namely that if the Anglicans could equally accept it, it must be ambiguous.[11]

Ecumenical dialogues are obviously not producing a team of optimists to lead us easily into the future. But they are producing men and women who can speak honestly about the obstacles confronting our two communions, and yet who do so with hope, not optimism, hope

---

Anglican Theological Review, 78/1 (Winter 1996): 90–1; Alec Graham, 'It's More Than Just a Chain of Bishops', *in Church Times* (26 August 1994): 10; Ola Tjørhom, 'The Porvoo Statement: A Possible Ecumenical Breakthrough?', *in Ecumenical Review,* 46/1 (January 1996): 100–1; Henrik Roelvink, 'The Apostolic Succession in the Porvoo Statement', in *One in Christ,* 30/4 (1994): 344–54.

11. Henry Chadwick, 'Anglican Ecclesiology and its Challenges', in *One in Christ,* 31/1 (1995): 38.

in God and the grace of Jesus Christ and the power of the Holy Spirit. No-one wants us to stop. Now is the testing time. Now is the time for faith, the time for hope, and the time for a love that is truthful and realistic. As Cardinal Cassidy said: 'We have to go on with the dialogue'.

One other question always arises and causes pain in discussions between Anglicans and Catholics. That is the question of mutual recognition of ministries. Obviously all the issues already noted have both complicated and yet enriched any discussion of this topic; 1896 is the centenary year of *Apostolicae Curae* in which Pope Leo XIII declared: 'We pronounce and declare that ordinations carried out according to the Anglican rite have been and are absolutely null and utterly void'. This has meant a renewed focus not only on this document and its historical context, but also on the whole question of validity of ordination and how it is discerned. A number of things need to be noted initially. Firstly, even though the Vatican does not intend to publish any statements itself about *Apostolicae Curae*, it is publishing the complete archival holdings on the matter, making them thereby available for more general historical scrutiny. Moreover, one needs to recognise that a new context has been established for the study of this question by the Canterbury (1973) and Salisbury (1979) Statements on 'Ministry' of the Final Report of ARCIC I. Both our communions have acknowledged the acceptability of this section of the Final Report.[12]

Another new factor is the recent decision of Catholics in England to ordain or re-ordain *sub conditione* Bishop Graham Leonard, though an emphasis placed not only on Old Catholic co-consecrators but also on the personal intention of the candidate raises some new concerns for ecumenical theologians.[13]

The only major conference to celebrate the centenary of this troubling document was held at General Theological Seminary,

---

12. For the Catholic Church response, see 'Clarifications on Certain Aspects of the Agreed Statements on Eucharist and Ministry of the First Anglican–Roman Catholic International Commission', *in Information Service, 87* (1994/IV): 237.

13. Christopher Hill, 'Anglican Orders: An Ecumenical Context', in *Anglican Theological Review*, 78/1 (Winter 1996): 93–4; Edward Yarnold SJ, 'A New Context: ARCIC and Afterwards', in *Anglican Theological Review*, 78/1 (Winter 1996): 72–3; Christopher Hill, 'The Utrecht Connection', in *The Tablet*, 245 (7 May 1994): 577–8; 'Anglican Bishop Becomes Roman Catholic Priest', in *Origins*, 23/46 (5 May 1946): 793–5.

New York, in the Spring of 1996. In his introduction to the collection of papers, R William Franklin, Professor of History and Mission at the General Theological Seminary, argued that the newly opened archives studied so carefully by Giuseppi Rambaldi SJ of the Gregorian University reveal an uncertainty concerning the historical foundations of *Apostolicae Curae* on the part of half the papal commission, and saw this as justifying a reconsideration of Leo XIII's judgement.[14] In this he was echoing the interpretation of the Anglican–Roman Catholic Consultation USA of which he is a member.[15] In his conclusion Franklin saw the question as ultimately one concerning the *magisterium* of the Catholic Church.[16] In his paper George Tavard analysed the theology of tradition of Pope Leo XIII and concluded:

> Pope Leo, however, felt no substantive need to obtain a consensus from his commission. By himself he could proclaim the truth. But if he extricated the commission on Anglican orders from a historical labyrinth, it was at the cost of falling into the snares of a defective theology of tradition, to say nothing of the additional cost of indefinitely delaying the reconciliation of the Churches.[17]

Edward Yarnold, on the other hand, analysed the supposed 'new context' for a look at the possibility of mutual recognition of ministry. His conclusion was not at all as hopeful as are most commentators these days:

---

14. R William Franklin, 'Introduction: The Opening of the Vatican Archives and the ARCIC Process', in *Anglican Theological Review*, 78/1 (Winter 1996): 18.
15. 'ARC/USA Statement: Anglican Orders: A Report on the Evolving Context of their Evaluation in the Roman Catholic Church, 8 May, 1990', in *One in Christ*, 26/3 (1990): 256–79; R William Franklin and George H Tavard, 'Commentary on ARC/USA Statement on Anglican Orders', in *Journal of Ecumenical Studies*, 27/2 (Spring 1990): 261–4.
16. Franklin, 'Introduction: The Opening of the Vatican Archives and the ARCIC Process', 29.
17. George H Tavard, '*Apostolicae Curae* and the Snares of Tradition', in *Anglican Theological Review*, 78/1 (Winter 1996): 47.

It must however in conclusion be stated that not all changes have increased the likelihood of Roman recognition. The ordination of women (at the time of writing there were said to be ten women bishops in the Anglican Communion), the movement for lay presidency at the Eucharist, the weakening of Anglican insistence on the indissolubility of marriage, the spread of theological liberalism, and a lack of firmness in some aspects of moral teaching combine to make it less easy for the justifiably demanding Roman authorities to acknowledge in Anglicanism the context which would make the native character of the ordination rite acceptable. On the other side, the Vatican criteria for recognition have become clearer, perhaps also stricter. I regret to have to conclude that the 'new context' in which Anglican orders should be judged is not in every respect more favourable than the setting a hundred, or even nine years ago.[18]

It seems clear to me that *Apostolicae Curae* deserves to be looked at again in the light of these and other studies,[19] though there may be no consensus from such a second look. Furthermore, as with the Porvoo Statement, the whole question of validity and mutual recognition of ministry for churches which hold to episcopal apostolic succession needs to be clarified ecumenically between our communions.

In order to appreciate changes in the relationship between the Anglican and Catholic Churches, it is also important to see them against the backdrop of larger developments in the Catholic Church's own approach to ecumenism. But before doing this it may be worth reminding ourselves of the sadness surrounding the Roman Catholic

---

18. Yarnold, 'A New Context', 74.

19. Examples include: George H Tavard, *A Review of Anglican Orders: The Problem and the Solution* (Collegeville: Liturgical Press, 1990); JMR Tillard OP, 'Recognition of Ministries: What Is the Real Question?', in *One in Christ*, 21/1 (1985): 31–9; Thomas Ryan, 'Reflections on a New Context for Discussing Anglican Orders', in *One in Christ*, 22/3 (1986): 228–33; George H Tavard, 'The Recognition of Ministry: What is the Priority?', in *One in Christ, 23/1* (1987): 21–35.

response to the Final Report of ARCIC I, which stated after a very positive overview that 'the Catholic Church judges, however, that it is not yet possible to state that substantial agreement has been reached on all the questions studied by the commission'.[20] Most commentators perceived the problem as one of methodology, and feared that the whole methodology of ARCIC was at stake.[21] Moreover Francis Sullivan SJ, formerly of the Gregorian University, has written a very perceptive comparison of the methodological issues in the Response to ARCIC I and the methodology employed in the Roman Catholic dialogue with Oriental Orthodox Churches.[22]

Of perhaps greater significance are Cardinal Cassidy's own words in the interview cited previously when he reaffirmed the Vatican's confidence in the ARCIC method: 'The method ARCIC has tried to follow from the beginning is very important, going behind formulas which originated in controversy not to relativise them but to discover if there can be common ground underlying them'.[23] Such an affirmation followed his letter to the co-chairmen of ARCIC II who had forwarded to Rome their clarifications of questions raised by Rome in its official response. Cardinal Cassidy was able to say in that letter:

> The Pontifical Council for Promoting Christian Unity is therefore most grateful to the members of ARCIC II, and to those from ARCIC I who prepared these clarifications. The agreement reached on Eucharist and Ministry by ARCIC I is thus greatly strengthened and no further study would seem to be required at this stage.[24]

20. 'Vatican responds to ARCIC I Final Report', *in Origins*, 21/28 (19 December 1991): 441.
21. Kevin McDonald, 'Clarifying Objectives and Methodology', in *Catholic International*, 3/3 (1–14 February 1992): 130–2; Edward Yarnold SJ, 'Response to the Response: I', in *The Tablet* (7 December 1991): 1524–5; Christopher Hill, 'Response to the Response: II', in *The Tablet* (7 December 1991): 1525–7; Henry Chadwick, 'Blocked Approaches', in *The Tablet* (1 February 1992): 136–7.
22. Francis Sullivan SJ, 'Lessons We Have Learned from Participation of Rome in Ecumenism', in *Milltown Studies*, 34 (1994): 13–30.
23. Gerald O'Connell, 'Dialogue Must Go On', in *The Tablet* (20 April 1996): 506.
24. 'Clarification on Certain Aspects of the Agreed Statements on Eucharist and Ministry of the First Anglican–Roman Catholic International Commission', in *Information Service*, 87 (1994/IV): 237.

In order to understand developments in Catholic approaches to ecumenism even this past five years one would need to look at the *Directory for the Application of Principles and Norms on Ecumenism* of 1993, which has been welcomed but not uncritically by different commentators from other churches.[25] One most critical review is that of George Tavard AA, who had worked on the predecessor to this *Directory*.[26]

But much more important than this is Pope John Paul II's twelfth encyclical, *Ut Unum Sint*. There are many things one can say about this very significant document,[27] but I wish to focus only on one aspect. In paragraph 95 one reads the following words:

> As Bishop of Rome I am fully aware, as I have reaffirmed in the present encyclical letter, that Christ ardently desires the full and visible communion of all those communities in which, by virtue of God's faithfulness, his Spirit dwells. I am convinced that I have a particular responsibility in this regard, above all in acknowledging the ecumenical aspirations of the majority of the Christian communities and in heeding the request made of me to find a way of exercising the primacy which, while in no way renouncing what is essential to its mission, is nonetheless open to a new situation.

The pope goes on to refer to an exchange he had with the Patriarch of Constantinople, Dimitrios I, in 1988, when he confessed that the papacy which should have been a service to the unity of the church sometimes 'manifested itself in a very different light' and that he prayed for the Holy Spirit to enlighten all pastors and theologians of the two communions so that they could seek together ways in which his ministry might accomplish 'a service of love recognised by all'.

---

25. For example, in *Ecumenical Review,* 47/4 (1995): Reinhard Frieling, 'Some Remarks on the New Ecumenical Directory', 411–8; Diane C Kessler, 'The New Catholic Ecumenical Directory: A Protestant Reading', 419–25; and Damaskinos of Switzerland, 'The New Ecumenical Directory: An Orthodox View', 426–9.
26. George H Tavard, 'The 1993 Directory for Ecumenism', in *Ecumenical Trends* (October 1995): 3–10.
27. See Jean-Marie R Tillard OP, 'From *Unitatis Redintegratio* to *Ut Unum Sint*', in *Catholic International,* 7/2 (February 1996): 76–80.

Finally he calls again for church leaders and theologians of all churches 'to engage with me in a patient and fraternal dialogue on this subject, a dialogue in which, leaving useless controversies behind, we could listen to one another' (96). In these two short paragraphs this encyclical has gone to the very heart of the division between the other great Christian world communions and the Catholic Church, that is, the role of the bishop of Rome. This was made clear in ARCIC I and, in one way or another, in all the major dialogues involving the Catholic Church.

The way forward to deal with this question can only be the way of ecumenism. The Roman Catholic Church can never explain its understanding clearly enough or reform its practice of papacy decisively enough on its own. The fundamental truth of the ecumenical movement is that the truth which will set us free (to unite) can only be found together. What is most heartening about this recognition that the exercise of the papal ministry will need to change, is that the interpretation and recommendation comes from Pope John Paul II himself.

Perhaps the best context for understanding the positive tone of his encyclical is a papal document of November 1994 entitled, *Tertio Millennio Adveniente,* in English 'As The Third Millennium Draws Near'. There is an urgency in this document about what needs to be done if the year 2000 is to be celebrated as a Year of Jubilee. Within the wide-ranging renewal Pope John Paul II wants to see are 'ecumenical initiatives so that we can celebrate the Great Jubilee, if not completely united, at least much closer to overcoming the divisions of the second millennium' (34). Given that there are only four years left before to the Year of Jubilee, I think this new encyclical is an attempt to provoke those ecumenical initiatives he considers essential to its celebration.

I was also struck by paragraph 37 of *Tertio Millennio Adveniente* where the pope made the claim that at the end of the second millennium the church had once again become a church of martyrs as in the beginning of the first millennium. He pointed out that 'the witness to Christ borne even to the shedding of blood has become a common inheritance of Catholics, Orthodox, Anglicans and Protestants . . . *This witness must not be forgotten'*. Many in this century have been, he says, nameless 'unknown soldiers' and urges us all to find their names and safeguard their memories. He says very interestingly: 'This gesture cannot fail to have an ecumenical character and expression. Perhaps the most convincing form of ecumenism is the ecumenism of the saints and of the martyrs. The *communio sanctorum* speaks louder than the things which divide us' (37). Archbishop Sergio Sebastiani, General Secretary of the Central Committee in Rome preparing for the Year of Great Jubilee, explained that behind this invitation to us all to venerate the martyrs of all the churches is the conviction that 'the death of even a single Christian, for faith in Christ, is an act of full commitment to the salvation and unity of all'.[28] Of course, different churches will respond differently to the notion of venerating such martyrs and Catholics must continually make it clear that it is only God they honour, God who has, by the grace of Christ, achieved such heroism in his human creatures. Already, as if in anticipation, Fr Theo Aerts MSC has produced a volume entitled *The Martyrs of Papua New Guinea: 333 Missionary Lives Lost during World War II*,[29] which chronicles the death and, in some cases, the lives of 333 missionaries and locals who died during the Second World War. His examples are drawn from seven different churches and provide an extraordinary record of Christian witness unto death.

All in all there is a great deal happening in the Catholic Church's approach to ecumenism and in the relationship between our two communions. While recent developments may seem to have created more obstacles than ever before, we need to remember that we are committed to this relationship forever because our common baptism and faith in Jesus Christ demand it. Indeed Jesus Christ demands it. We dialogue because there are obstacles, not because there are none. And in all things let us take to heart the words of Cardinal Cassidy in a 1992 interview, precisely concerning our relationship:

> When we enter into ecumenical dialogue we take our faith as it is today. We bring our identity. But we also try to remain open to the Holy Spirit who is working for the unity of Christians. It is not for us to tell the Holy Spirit what's to be done. He should be telling us and we should be taking heed.[30]

---

28. 'Dennis McManus Interviews Archbishop Sergio Sebastiani on the Church's Celebration of the Jubilee year 2000', in *Catholic World*, 239 (Jan–Feb 1996): 14.
29. *The Martyrs of Papua New Guinea: 333 Missionary Lives Lost during World War II*, edited by Theo Aerts (Port Moresby: University of Papua New Guinea Press, 1994).
30. Gerard O'Connell, 'Cardinal Cassidy's Future for Dialogue with Anglicans', in *The Tablet* (28 November 1992): 1521.

A Contemporary Roman Catholic View
of Martin Luther

When I was a newly ordained priest working in my first parish I went one day to the parish primary school to spend their 'religion class' with the grade seven pupils. It so happened that the religious sister teaching that class was taking them through the ten commandments. Not being very good with children in big numbers and knowing little about the art of catechesis, I resorted to the tried and true method canonised by Socrates, and began to ask questions.

Enquiring in turn as to specific sin ruled out by each commandment, I arrived at the fifth, *'Thou shalt not kill'*. To my surprise, one young fellow from the bush told me that eating too much was surely a sin rightly condemned by this commandment. I decided to investigate further and asked him why this was so.

To my even greater surprise, he then developed a logical argument that left me speechless. He said: 'Take Henry VIII. He used to eat a lot and he always wanted more and more food. Then he wanted women and lots of different women. So he started a new church to get them'. His attribution of the cause of the English Reformation to Henry VIII's eating too much made his religious teacher blush with embarrassment.

There are two aspects of this anecdote relevant to my topic today. Firstly, to accuse the reformers—not that Henry VIII exactly fits that category—of gross moral failure as a way of explaining their actions was typical of the popular Catholic understanding of the Reformation just twenty-five years before this four hundred and fiftieth anniversary

This paper was previously published in *Perspectives on Martin Luther: Papers from the Luther Symposium held at Luther Seminary Adelaide, South Australia, 22–23 March 1996, Commemorating the 450th Anniversary of the Reformer's Death,* edited by MW Worthing (North Adelaide: Openbook Publishers), 35–47.

of the death of Martin Luther. Secondly, if I had asked that same pupil
to tell me about Martin Luther or the Continental Reformation, he
would probably have been completely ignorant.

This ignorance may not have been widespread in South Australia,
but it almost certainly was in Queensland. In an address I gave to the
first Lutheran–Catholic Clergy Day to discuss *Pastor and Priest* in
1993, I said concerning relations between our two communions in
my own state of Queensland, that they had moved to a new, deeper
level in recent years, at least on the official level, but I wondered how
widely this has been appreciated on the parish level. Too often contact
on that level, I suggested, has been at best sporadic and sometimes
marked by a certain unease or suspicion of the other. No doubt there
are reasons for this which can be found in the membership of both
communions. On the Catholic side one factor is probably a popular
misconception that because they attribute to Luther the beginning
of the Reformation then Lutherans must be the representatives of
Protestantism *par excellence*, and so very different to Catholics in
every way.[1]

The relationship between the Lutheran Church and the Catholic
Church in Queensland has moved to a new level with the entry of
both our communions for the first time into an ecumenical body in
our state, the newly formed *Queensland Churches Together*. Perhaps
the now regular contact between our communions will ensure not
only that there is education in our Catholic schools about Martin
Luther but also that it does not fall into the trap of 'demonising' the
other, which was an easy way of dealing with differences even twenty-
five years ago in Queensland, and perhaps elsewhere. This will only
be true if the resources to which the religious educators turn offer
a fairer picture of Martin Luther. My address is really an attempt to
indicate what they might find.

In the week beginning 12 February 1996, and so the week prior
to Luther's death four hundred and fifty years ago, I was in Rome
for a meeting of bishops to plan a Year of Great Jubilee to mark the
two thousandth anniversary of Christ's birth (2000). I could not help
but be struck by the irony that I was researching a paper on Luther

---

1. Michael Putney, 'Pastor and Priest: A Roman Catholic Reflection', in *Apples of
    Gold: Essays in Honour of HPV (Paul) Renner, on the Occasion of his Retirement*,
    edited by Inari Thiel (Brisbane: Sophia Collective, 1992), 92–3.

whose death we would soon commemorate while I was, at the same time, preparing for a Holy Year. I was reminded of the two Holy Years which Luther would have known, 1500 and 1525.

The former was presided over by Alexander VI and was notable not only for instituting the rite of opening Holy Doors in the four major basilicas of Rome but also for the suspension of all local indulgences in favour of those to be attained as a result of pilgrimage to Rome, and finally the indulgences for the souls in purgatory attained by giving alms to St Peter's Basilica, among other spiritual requirements. An official commentary on Pope John Paul II's letter calling the Year of Great Jubilee (2000), *Tertio Millennio Adveniente,* which I was given at the planning meeting I attended in Rome, had this to say about the 1500 jubilee:

> The jubilee brought many pilgrims to Rome, so many that Sigmund de Conti wrote, *Orbis in Urbe.* In the registers of the confraternity of the Hospital of the Holy Spirit one finds recorded the names of many Hungarians and Germans. And among the *romei,* Nicholas Copernicus, who arrived around Easter time, and taught a mathematics course for scientists. The flood of the Tiber from November 1st to November 4th disturbed the city: the jubilee was extended until Epiphany, then extended to a few cities of Italy, and to other regions all the way until Pentecost of 1501, with the same practices and after the payment of a sum of money.
>
> The Alexandrian Jubilee constituted the apex of the external organisation of the jubilee—the aspect of the popular religious phenomenon was less important— and the question of indulgences placed it as a premise of the Lutheran protest.[2]

The jubilee of 1525 was a much more complex event and deserves to be treated by someone more competent, an historian, in the context of Luther's relationship with Rome at the time.

---

2. Alessandro Galuzzi, 'The Jubilee Years in the History of the Church', in *Preparing for the Year 2000,* edited by Sergio Sebastiani (New Hope: Urbi et Orbi Communications, 1996), 82–93.

Given this irony of my being involved in a quest to answer the question of how a Catholic would view Luther today and my being in Rome to prepare for a Holy Year with all the problematical historical and theological issues which that raises, I decided to ask the question of the city of Rome itself: 'How do you view Luther?' How are you acknowledging that he died four hundred and fifty years ago?

As part of my quest for an answer, I walked to St Peter's and observed the great basilica which, as one Roman Catholic friend and Luther scholar said, 'caused the Reformation'. His judgement is provocative and was intended to be so. Still it was salutary to look at something so truly beautiful and to realise that the fund-raising for it at one period did unthinkable damage to the church.

From there, I walked to Santa Maria del Popolo, the church attached to the convent where Luther surely stayed when he came to Rome in 1510–11. I was eager to find out what was there when Luther visited, and the prior of the Augustinian community happily obliged. One can still see the ancient main altar, now preserved in the sacristy, two small altars in the first chapel in the south aisle and the tomb of Christopher Della Rovere, all attributed to Andrea Bregno or his pupils. More significantly, the prior passed on to me the proceedings of an international conference organised by the Augustinianum in Rome on the occasion of the fifth centenary of Luther's birth in 1983. I could not help but think how the Catholic appreciation of Luther had changed in recent decades to permit Pope John Paul II to urge participants at the conference to seek only the truth in their historical research and to appreciate the purification that the truth can bring.[3]

From Santa Maria del Popolo I walked to San Agostino, which Luther may have visited as well, because the superior general of his order lived there when he was in Rome. Finally, I went to the Gesù, a Jesuit Church of the Catholic Reform. It is interesting because in the altar-piece depicting the vanquishing of heresy there are books by Luther and Calvin lying alongside the vanquished heresy. However, one can no longer see this without careful study because the Jesuits have removed the colour which drew attention to the authors, a gesture of ecumenical sensitivity.

---

3. 'Discorso di SS. Giovanni Paolo II', in *Martin Lutero: Atti del convegno internazionale nel quinto centenario della nascita* (1483–1983) (Rome: L'Agostiniana di Roma, 1984), 18.

Rome had still more to offer after this day of pilgrimage. In the bookstores, I saw displayed the latest copy of *Jesus,* a popular Catholic monthly published by St Pauls Publications. On the front cover was pictured Pastor Martin Beer, Lutheran pastor of the Berlin cathedral. The heading on the front cover was 'Forty Years Ago the Reformer Died' and, I think we would say in English, 'There was once a man called Luther' *(Cera una volta Lutero).* Twenty-three pages of the one hundred and twenty-eight were devoted to Luther or Lutheranism, including an interview with Wolfhart Pannenberg where he speaks of Protestants needing to be ready to accept a role for the bishop of Rome in terms similar to the Orthodox, as a bishop *primus inter pares.*[4] This ministry would require a major change within the Catholic Church as well, he pointed out.

The article on historical research was entitled 'Neither Angel, Nor Demon but Witness to Christ'. Another article on the 'Dialogue Towards Unity' informed the reader that in Hong Kong, in 1997, at the Ninth Assembly of the Lutheran World Federation, debate will take place over the observations from Lutheran communities around the world on the 1994 report of the third phase of the Lutheran–Catholic International Dialogue. It is entitled 'Church and Justification: Understanding the Church in the Light of the Doctrine of Justification'.

At the meeting of bishops I actually attended there were observers from other churches and from the World Council of Churches (WCC). The Lutheran World Federation representative was Professor Dr Juhani Forsberg, I think from Finland. There was a remarkable emphasis throughout the meeting on the need to celebrate the two thousandth anniversary of Christ's birth in an ecumenical manner. This priority was consistent with the overall programme for the next few years leading up to the year 2000. It emphasises forgiveness, seeking it and giving it, in all areas of life. The focus for reflection is Jesus Christ himself and the Holy Trinity. I was reminded sharply of previous Holy Years when I heard the word 'indulgences' used in the meeting—not in any official presentations or documentations, and only by one bishop from Latin America.

---

4. Wolfhart Pannenberg, 'Quando si dimentica lo scandalo della croce', in *Jesus,* 18 (February 1996): 71.

On my last day in Rome I was watching a religious news programme on television. It was 18 February and a major news item was the four hundred and fiftieth anniversary of Luther's death, that very day. The director of my doctoral dissertation, Fr Jos Vercruysse SJ, was being interviewed. He situated Luther's teaching in his religious consciousness, Luther's spirituality, and spoke very positively of the results of the International Lutheran–Catholic Dialogue. Conversation while in Rome with Fr Vercruysse SJ and Fr Jared Wicks SJ, Dean of Theology at the Gregorian University, both of whom are leading ecumenists and Luther scholars, confirmed the conviction borne out of my research that there had been a shift of enormous proportion in recent decades in the Catholic perception of Martin Luther.

The question I had asked of Rome itself, 'How do you view Luther?', could not be answered only be the observations of a pilgrim observer. One needed also to ask what is the view of the bishop of Rome. The opinions of Leo X, Adrian VI and Pius IV are known well enough to students of the Reformation, and easily understood given their historical situations. Then in 1623, Urban VIII, in his bull canonising Ignatius of Loyola, *Rationi congruit*, called Luther a dreadful monster, a sacrilegious blasphemer who had tried to corrupt and revolutionise religion.[5]

Again, just over a hundred years ago, Leo XIII had this to say about all the reformers, in his 1881 encyclical, *Diuturnum*, on the origin of civil power:

> In truth, sudden uprisings and the boldest rebellions immediately followed in Germany the so-called Reformation, the authors and leaders of which, by their new doctrines, attacked at the very foundation religious and civil authority; and this with so fearful an outburst of civil war and with such slaughter that there was scarcely any place free from tumult and blood-shed. From this heresy there arose in the last century a false philosophy—a new right as it is called, and a

---

5. Boris Ulianich, 'Esiste una storiografia cattolica relative a Lutero?', in *Martin Lutero*, 127.

popular authority, together with an unbridled license which many regard as the only true liberty. Hence we have reached the limit of horrors, to wit, communism, socialism, nihilism, hideous deformities of the civil society of men and almost its ruin.[6]

Early in the twentieth century, Pope St Pius X commented on the Reformation in his encyclical of 1910 on St Charles Borromeo:

> In those days passions ran riot and knowledge of the truth was almost completely twisted and confused. A continual battle was being waged against errors. Human society, going from bad to worse, was rushing headlong into the abyss. Then those proud and rebellious men came on the scene who are 'enemies of the cross of Christ ... Their god is the belly ... they mind the things of earth.' These men were not concerned with correcting morals, but only with denying dogmas. Thus they increased the chaos. They dropped the reins of law, and unbridled licentiousness ran wild. They despised the authoritative guidance of the church and pandered to the whims of the dissolute princes and people. They tried to destroy the Church's doctrine, constitution and discipline. They were similar to those sinners who were warned long ago: 'Woe to you that call evil good, and good evil'. They called this rebellious riot and perversion of faith and morals a reformation, and themselves reformers. In reality, they were corrupters. In undermining the strength of Europe through wars and dissensions, they paved the way for those modern rebellions and apostasy.[7]

Given these robust examples of papal perceptions of Martin Luther and other reformers, it is all the more surprising to hear Pope John

---

6. Pope Leo XIII, Encyclical Letter, *Diuturnum*, 'On the Origin of Civil Power', in *The Papal Encyclicals, Volume 2, 1878-1903*, compiled by Claudia Carlen IHM (Wilmington: McGrath Publishing Company, 1981), 56.

7. Pius X, Encyclical Letter, *Editae Saepe*, 'On St Charles Borromeo', in *The Papal Encyclicals, Volume 3, 1903-1939*, compiled by Claudia Carlen IHM (Wilmington: McGrath Publishing Company, 1981), 117.

Paul II speak in these words on the occasion of the five hundredth anniversary of Martin Luther's birth:

> In fact, the scientific researches of Evangelical and Catholic scholars, researches whose results have already reached notable points of convergence, have led to the delineation of a more complete and more differentiated picture of Luther's personality and of the complex texture of the social, political and ecclesial historical realities of the first half of the sixteenth century. Consequently there is clearly outlined the deep religious feeling of Luther, who was driven with burning passion by the question of eternal salvation. Likewise, it has become clear that the breach of Church unity cannot be traced back either to a lack of understanding on the part of the authorities of the Catholic Church, or solely to Luther's lack of understanding of true Catholicism, even if both factors played their role.[8]

Two factors have made this shift possible: the developments in Roman Catholic historiography of Martin Luther and the contemporary dialogue between the Lutheran and Catholic Churches, both international and national, including the very fruitful one here in Adelaide. The developments in historiography have been mapped many times. Though I am not an historian, I would like to indicate who the pivotal agents of change would appear to have been.

The first major shapers of a Catholic view of Luther this century were Heinrich Denifle OP and Hartman Grisar SJ. The former attributed the Reformation to Luther's immorality, the unbridled lust of a fallen and theologically illiterate monk. This powerful and self-satisfying portrayal of 'the enemy' filtered down even to my childhood perceptions of the divisions in the church being caused because some men must have been very bad. For Grisar, Luther was not so much bad as perhaps 'mad'. His mental instability caused him to deny dogma and divide the church. Despite the gross distortion of the former and the very serious bias of the latter, their work is not surprising. James M Kittleson has argued:

---

8. 'Pope John Paul II's Letter on Fifth Centenary of Birth of Martin Luther', in *Information Service*, 52/3 (1983): 83.

> Until recently, Catholic scholars have begun their work by asking, 'Where did Luther go wrong?' while their Protestant counterparts have wondered, 'Where (or when) did he go right?' The ensuing praise and condemnation have, for the most part, centred on his theological thinking and tended to explain it by reference either to his great moral stature or to his utter lack of any such thing.[9]

It was not long before Catholic historians disputed the work of these scholars, men such as Sebastian Merkle and Hubert Jedin. Richard Shauffer described this change as a movement from 'destructive criticism to a respectful encounter'.[10] No doubt the change had much to do with the integrity of the scholars but one must not forget that already the modern ecumenical movement was underway. Shortly after his ordination and commitment of his life to the ecumenical movement, this century's greatest Catholic ecumenical theologian, the late Yves Congar OP, travelled through Germany to visit the most important centres of Luther's life and work. He would later say: 'I know that nothing really worthwhile with regard to Protestantism will be achieved so long as we take no steps truly to understand Luther, instead of simply condemning him, and to do him historical justice'.[11]

However, it is Joseph Lortz, originally from Luxembourg, to whom all scholars attribute the most influential shift in perception in Roman Catholic scholarship. His *Die Reformation in Deutschland*, of 1939–40, painted a picture of late medieval Europe with theology in decline because of Occamism, and with the rise of humanism, which laid the groundwork for the Reformation; rather than Luther's morals or personality. For Lortz a Reformation had become historically necessary, and Catholics had their share of guilt for the division which ensued. Luther himself, for Lortz, was a genius and a deeply religious man, though guilty of subjectivism. This was an incredible shift in perception and, despite occasional revivals of Denifle's and

---

9. 'Luther the Theologian', in *Reformation Europe: A Guide to Research II*, edited by William S Maltley (St Louis: Center for Reformation Research, 1992), 21.
10. *Luther as Seen by Catholics*, Ecumenical Studies in History Number 7 (London: Lutterworth Press, 1967), 7.
11. Quoted in *Luther as Seen by Catholics*, 8.

Grisar's views, Catholic historians would begin from that point on
with a fundamentally positive view of Martin Luther. More recently,
one could mention Lortz's students, Erwin Iserloh and Peter Manns,
and Iserloh's student, Jared Wicks SJ. Another major contributor is
Otto Hermann Pesch who compared Luther's existential theology
with Aquinas' sapiential theology and recognised the legitimacy of
both approaches.

Cardinal Jan Willebrands was able already in 1970, in the light
of this research, to make the first official positive statement about
Martin Luther in an address to the Lutheran World Federation. There
he was able to paint a picture of Luther as, in a sense, 'our common
teacher'.[12] He said among other things:

> Who . . . would still deny that Martin Luther was a deeply
> religious person who with honesty and dedication
> sought for the message of the gospel? Who would deny
> that in spite of the fact that he fought against the Roman
> Catholic Church and the Apostolic See—and for the
> sake of truth one must not remain silent about this—he
> retained a considerable part of the old Catholic faith?
> Indeed, is it not true that the Second Vatican Council
> has even implemented requests that were first expressed
> by Martin Luther, among others, and as a result of which
> many aspects of Christian faith and life now find better
> expression than they did before? To be able to say this
> in spite of all the differences is a reason for great joy and
> much hope.[13]

My own theological education in the 1960s was influenced by Josef
Lortz because Dr Thomas Boland, my lecturer in church history, had
been introduced to the work of Lortz during his studies in Rome,
even if the reading available to me in English was the moderate but
still classical view of Luther put forward by Philip Hughes in his
The Reformation: A Popular History. That I did not wrestle with the
question of Luther then was not only a consequence of my age but

---

12. Quoted from Otto Pesch by George Yule in *Luther: Theologian for Catholics and
    Protestants* (Edinburgh: T&T Clark, 1985), 41.
13. Quoted in 'Martin Luther—Witness to Jesus Christ', in *Information Service*, 52/3
    (1983): 87.

also of *the* age, when ecumenism was only just beginning for most Catholics; and of the place: Catholics in Queensland in the 1960s did not have much awareness of Luther or Lutherans because of their smallness in number, when compared with Anglicans, Presbyterians and Methodists.

If developments in Catholic historiography changed the Catholic perception of Martin Luther and made possible the irenical statement of Pope John Paul II in 1983 and the irenical response to my question of Rome only a month ago, the other major factor has been ecumenical dialogue between the two communions. Official international dialogue began at the end of the Second Vatican Council. Discussion in 1965 and 1966 led to the establishment of a dialogue to engage in 'serious discussions on theological issues' which 'both separate and unite the two communions'. Its goal was named as 'visible unity' which indicates both the seriousness of the dialogue and the perception that the two communions had much in common. Where dialogue partners have less in common, the goal is named less definitively.

The first report was produced in 1972, *The Gospel and the Church* (Malta Report). It did not attempt to deal with the sixteenth-century controversies as such, but, 'to examine confessional differences in the light of contemporary biblical theology, church history and the perspectives opened up by Vatican II'. The second report, in 1978, was *The Eucharist.* The third in 1980 was entitled *Ways to Community* and dealt with concrete steps necessary for the resolution of obstacles to full communion. The fourth report of 1981, *The Ministry in the Church,* dealt with the third issue recognised at the end of the first five years as needing thorough research. These second, third and fourth reports were the work of sub-committees working during the seventies.

In 1980, the International Dialogue put out an agreed statement on the Augsburg Confession, *All Under One Christ,* and in 1983 a Joint Statement on the 500th anniversary of the birth of Martin Luther, *Martin Luther—Witness to Jesus Christ.* Much of that Joint Statement is indicative of the major shift in Catholic historiography of Luther that I have just mapped. For example, paragraph 22 sums up one aspect of this shift:

> There has developed in our century—first of all in German-speaking areas—an intensive Catholic re-

evaluation of Luther the man and of his Reformation concerns. It is widely recognised that he was justified in attempting to reform the theology and the abuses in the church of his time and that his fundamental belief—justification given to us by Christ without any merit of our own—does not in any way contradict genuine Catholic tradition, such as is found, for example, in St Augustine and Thomas Aquinas.[14]

On the occasion of that same 500th anniversary, Cardinal Willebrands said in an address in the Church of St Thomas, Leipzig:

The basic power of evil, the impotence of man and the all-pervading might of God were the central questions of life that Martin Luther, professor of theology, man of prayer, preacher and pastor, posed himself. He pursued them with such passion and coherence that, in this respect, one is in a certain sense justified in describing him as the standard bearer of the majesty, the honour and the judgeship of God and, at the same time, as the spokesman of man, who—mortal and turned inwards onto himself—can rely on nothing other than God's mercy. A merciful, saving God and man weighed down by guilt! Many of our contemporaries, even in so-called Christian countries, have lost sight of the reality to which these words refer. They speak about the absence of God, about emancipation and self-realisation. But they are no longer aware of their basic condition, they no longer see the world and themselves as subject to God's anger and mercy. And therefore I ask whether the time is not more than ripe for us to join hands in trying to see to what extent, face to face with this world of ours, we can today bear witness to the good news of our redemption, the message that the Church is intended to serve. Ought we not, driven on by the memory of history and guilt, jointly to mould and shape our present?[15]

---

14. 'Martin Luther—Witness to Jesus Christ', in *Information Service*, 52/3 (1983): 87.
15. Cardinal Johannes Willebrands, 'Address of Cardinal Willebrands on the

The fifth report of the International Dialogue was published in 1984, *Facing Unity: Models, Forms and Phases of Catholic–Lutheran Church Fellowship.* Finally, in September 1993, the latest report was produced, *Church and Justification: Understanding the Church in the Light of the Doctrine of Justification.* Of greater significance still is a document entitled *Joint Declaration on the Doctrine of Justification* which is being analysed by Lutherans and Catholics at the time of writing (1996). Circulated by the Lutheran World Federation and the Pontifical Council for Promoting Christian Unity it has been compiled from already existing dialogue documents which include the reports of the International Dialogue and of the Lutheran–Roman Catholic Dialogue in the USA, and the German study, *The Condemnations of the Reformation Era: Do They Still Divide?* This latter is, I think, one of the most important and exciting ecumenical works ever produced.

The *Joint Declaration* claims that, while differences remain, they are not, or should not be, church dividing. The request to both Churches is that they test this claim and if they believe it is sustainable, then to affirm it in some way so that both communions can together declare that the condemnations of each other concerning justification no longer hold. This is particularly relevant given that 1997 will be the 450th anniversary of the *Decree on Justification* of the Council of Trent, the same year as a meeting of the Lutheran World Federation.

Historians studying Martin Luther do so in a new context established by this dialogue. Only through dialogue is it possible for the truth of the gospel to be heard in different contexts in all its life-giving authenticity. For many centuries we have each been exploring the Christian mystery in isolation. Within our secure boundaries our exploration has revealed to us the riches of that mystery. It has been life-giving for us because the Holy Spirit has ensured that Jesus Christ would live in our unique confessional culture despite our disunity.

At the same time this exploration in isolation has also been an exploration over against the other, for example Protestants versus Catholics, Evangelicals versus Liberals, Reformed versus Lutheran, Lutherans versus Catholics. This has meant that each of us has emphasised in our tradition whatever distinguishes us from the other, and has interpreted the other as a damaged or limited

Occasion of the 500th Anniversary of the Birth of Martin Luther', in *Information Service*, 52/3 (1983): 93–4.

form of ourselves, which has really been to imprison each other. The boundaries of our isolation have been the walls of our mutual imprisoning.

Our exploration of the Christian mystery, while nonetheless by the grace of the Holy Spirit an entry into the mystery of Christ, has at the same time been so only with difficulty because of the inhibiting force of our prison walls. Our confessional culture has filtered and nuanced and even steered the gospel into certain specific channels while still being a bearer of Christ to us.

Since we are being led by the Holy Spirit into the ecumenical movement the walls of our mutual imprisonment are rapidly falling. This gives us a freedom which brings incredible bonuses. Now we are free to be ourselves, to reclaim the breadth and depth of our traditions, including those elements which were emphasised by 'the other' and which we held onto only tentatively or under another guise.

Not only are we free to reclaim the wholeness of our traditions, but we are led to deeper insights into them by hearing the questions, the challenges, the difficulties and the positive interpretations of the other. Truth can best be found through such dialogue; and the truth so found emerges more and more as the same truth, the same gospel, the same Christ.

Ultimately the goal of such dialogue is for each of us to recognise the one apostolic tradition, the one gospel in the faith confessed by the other, and so to recognise the one church of Christ in its fullness in the other. When such recognition has taken place, then reconciliation is possible.

Conclusion

I believe it is no longer necessary for Catholics and Lutherans to presume that their views of Martin Luther and the causes of the Reformation need be opposed. The climate of dialogue, and the integrity of historians, has ensured that Catholic views of Luther have changed dramatically. The dreadful monster and sacrilegious blasphemer of Urban VIII, the proud and rebellious men pandering to the whims of princes of Pius X, have given way to the man of deep religious feeling with burning passion for the question of salvation of John Paul II, and the man of prayer, standard bearer of the majesty of God of Cardinal Willebrands.

The next topic we must be brave enough to tackle is not so much an historical one, but a theological one, that is, the interpretation of the event of church division itself, which occurred with Luther's movement of reform. Now that we are free to be more dispassionate about the actual historical causes, we need to ask the deeper question of how we differ in our theological interpretation of the event of the Reformation itself. In the report of the Reformed–Roman Catholic (not the Lutheran–Roman Catholic) International Dialogue (1990), *Towards a Common Understanding of the Church*, there is a lengthy account headed 'The Church We Confess and Our Divisions in History'. The key paragraph revealing differing interpretations of the event of the Reformation is the following:

> Accordingly, our respective interpretations of the division in the sixteenth century are not the same. The Reformed consider that the Reformation was a rupture with the Catholic 'establishment' of the period. This establishment had become greatly corrupted and incapable of responding to an appeal for reform in the sense of a return to the purity of the Gospel and holiness of the early Church. Nevertheless, this does not mean that the resulting division was a substantial rupture in the continuity of the Church. For Catholics, however, this break struck at the continuity of the tradition derived from the apostles and lived through many centuries. Insofar as the Reformed had broken with the ministerial structure handed down by tradition, they had deeply wounded the apostolicity of their churches. The severity of this judgment is moderated today because ecumenical contacts have made Catholics more aware of the features of authentic Christian identity preserved in those churches.[16]

The most recent report of the Lutheran–Catholic International Dialogue, *Church and Justification: Understanding the Church in the Light of the Doctrine of Justification*, lays out in extraordinary detail

---

16. 'Reformed–Roman Catholic International Dialogue: Towards a Common Understanding of the Church', in *Information Service*, 74/3 (1980): 111.

the various theological perspectives which would lead to differing theological interpretations of what happened in the Reformation, but does not actually deal with the event itself. I think we are mature enough now to address it. As we struggle to respond to Christ's imperative for all of us, to allow him to unite us again so that the world may believe, we have to be able to deal with our past painful separation not only through careful, purifying historical scholarship which frees us from simply blaming each other, but also by sharing with each other our spiritual perceptions about what happened. How could Lutherans break with Rome? How could Catholics put union with Rome above faithfulness to the gospel? We feel deeply here because it concerns the contours our fidelity to Christ has taken. The International Dialogue has laid it out for us. Now it is time to talk about it, and I am not afraid. If the Holy Spirit has led us this far, we can surely believe that God's will that we be one is stronger than all our pride and foolishness. 'Father, may we truly be one.'

The International Methodist–Roman Catholic Dialogue: Hopes for the Future

In 1749 the Irish city of Cork had its peace tragically disturbed by riots led by Nicholas Butler, himself a Protestant, against the small Methodist community which gathered in that city. One serious suggestion for an explanation of the cause of the riots is that the Methodists were suspected of being fundamentally a Jesuit movement.[1] At the same time, the Catholics of Cork appeared either to have stood by and allowed Nicholas Butler's mob to do its damage; or to have joined in, despite their own lack of civil rights in Ireland at the time. Whatever the full story, these riots and others elsewhere prompted John Wesley to write *A Letter to a Roman Catholic* which, in a sense, is the first, if isolated, attempt at ecumenical dialogue between Methodists and Catholics.

It was only the publishing initiative of the great Albert C Outler, who was then an observer at the Second Vatican Council, and Michael Hurley SJ, who participated with Outler in the Joint Commission between the World Methodist Council and the Catholic Church for its first ten years, which brought this letter to everyone's attention again.[2] Its opening paragraphs deserve to be heard because they are probably more typical of the sentiments of both parties to the present dialogue, at least when it first began in 1967, than they were of Methodists or Roman Catholics in 1749. Wesley wrote:

This paper was presented as *The Rollie Busch Memorial Lecture* in 1996, and was subsequently published in *Trinity Occasional Papers*, XVI/2 (December 1997): 41–57.

1. David Butler, *Methodists and Papists: John Wesley and the Catholic Church in the Eighteenth Century* (London: Darton, Longman & Todd, 1995), 43.
2. Geoffrey Wainwright, *Methodists in Dialogue* (Nashville: Ringswood Books, 1995), 37.

My dear friend,

1. You have heard ten thousand stories of us, who are commonly called Protestants, of which, if you believe only one in a thousand, you must think very hardly of us. But this is quite contrary to our Lord's rule, 'Judge not that ye be not judged;' and has many ill consequences, particularly this—it inclines us to think as hardly of you. Hence we are on both sides less willing to help one another, and more ready to hurt each other. Hence, brotherly love is utterly destroyed; and each side looking on the other as monsters, gives way to anger, hatred, malice, to every unkind affection, which have frequently broke out in such inhuman barbarities as are scarce named among the heathens.

2. Now, can nothing be done, even allowing us on both sides to retain our own opinions, for the softening our hearts towards each other, the giving a check to this flood of unkindness, and restoring at least some small degree of love among our neighbours and countrymen? Do you not wish for this? Are you not fully convinced that malice, hatred, revenge, bitterness, whether in us or in you, in our hearts or yours, are an abomination to the Lord? Be our opinions right or be they wrong, these tempers are undeniably wrong. They are the broad road that leads to destruction, to the nethermost hell.

3. I do not suppose that all bitterness is on your side. I know there is too much on our side also. So much, that I fear many Protestants (so called) will be angry at me too for writing to you in this manner, and will say, 'It is showing you too much favour; you deserve no such treatment at our hands.'

4. But I think you do. I think you deserve the tenderest regard I can show, were it only because the same God has raised you and me from the dust of the earth, and has made us both capable of loving and enjoying him to eternity; were it only because the Son of God has bought you and me with his own blood. How much more, if you are a person fearing God (as without question many

of you are) and studying to have a conscience void of offence towards God and towards man?[3]

Though Wesley's kindly sentiments were probably typical of many Methodists as the dialogue began in 1967, his concerns were also probably quite accurate later as well. In the late sixties, some people on both sides would have seen the other as living a very diminished form of Christianity. Some Methodists in 1967 would have perceived Catholics as not truly Christian because of their unbiblical teaching and superstitious practices that were Wesley's own concerns.[4] Catholics would have seen Methodists as outside the true church and needing to return within. However, Wesley's more irenic sentiments found a home in enough Methodist and Catholic hearts for a dialogue to begin.

When one looks again at Wesley's letter, one finds a very sound theological foundation for dialogue. Firstly, he allowed both sides to retain their own opinions but, at the same time, he asked them to soften their hearts, and to replace unkindness with 'at least some small degree of love'. The foundation for this love lay in the recognition that both Methodists and Catholics were created by God to share his life in heaven, and that Jesus Christ died for both. More interestingly still, he was prepared to acknowledge that he saw real signs of a Christian life in some Catholics. In other words, one can be led to love and to dialogue, and away from rejection and unkindness, by discerning signs of Christ and the Holy Spirit in the other. The three principles here enshrined remain valid. Be true to one's own beliefs. Recognise the signs of God's presence in the other. Love them, and so dialogue with them.

Wesley's attempt to speak to Catholics through this letter of 1749 not only serves to help them respond positively today to the Methodist tradition but it also reveals a very significant difference between the two traditions and an apparent obstacle to their reconciliation. In his letter Wesley endeavoured to give a brief explanation of Protestant, not specifically Methodist, belief through some simple fundamental creedal statements. He concluded with the following thoughts:

---

3. 'Letter to a Roman Catholic', in David Butler, *Methodists and Papists*, 211–12.
4. Butler, *Methodists and Papists*, 159–64.

11. Now, is there anything wrong in this? Is there any one point which you do not believe as well as we? But you think we ought to believe more. We will not now enter into the dispute. Only let me ask, if a man sincerely believes thus much, and practises accordingly, can any one possibly persuade you to think that such a man shall perish everlastingly?[5]

Later in the letter he adds:

16 . . . We ought, without this endless jangling about opinions, to provoke one another to love and to good works. Let the points wherein we differ stand aside: here are enough wherein we agree, enough to be the ground of every Christian temper and of every Christian action.[6]

Paragraphs 114–16 of the 1996 agreed statement produced by the Methodist–Roman Catholic Joint Commission, *The Word of Life: A Statement on Revelation and Faith,* refer on one hand to John Wesley's clear distinction between 'essentials' and matters of 'opinion' and, on the other, to the Catholic emphasis that 'the whole teaching of the Church constitutes an organic unity'.[7] This, at first glance, would imply that when these two communions seek to find agreement about a confession of faith, Catholics will have a much longer list of doctrines about which they seek agreement than Methodists. This is a very serious issue and will be explored a little more later.

Another very relevant aspect of Wesley's approach to affirming doctrinal unity was his claim to be giving an account of Protestant, not specifically Methodist, beliefs. This illustrates that in a dialogue between the Methodist and Catholic Communions, it may not be necessary to deal with all the divisive issues of the Reformation. If these are being dealt with in Roman Catholic–Reformed, Roman Catholic–Lutheran and Roman Catholic–Anglican Dialogues, the Methodist–Roman Catholic Joint Commission might be able to leave some Protestant–Catholic issues to the other dialogues and to

---

5. 'Letter to a Roman Catholic', 213.
6. 'Letter to a Roman Catholic', 215.
7. Methodist–Roman Catholic Joint Commission, *The Word of Life: A Statement on Revelation and Faith* (Lake Junaluska: World Methodist Council, 1996), 39–40.

concentrate on those matters which arise uniquely when Methodists and Catholics encounter each other. What these might be can be discovered in part by a study of the statements already produced by the Joint Commission.

The distinction of Wesley between 'essential' beliefs and 'opinions' is related to his impatience with theological disputes which distract one from what really matters, 'to provoke one another to love and to do good works'. For example, after giving an account of his Protestant confession of faith, he moves immediately to ask the question: 'But does he practise accordingly?' He goes on to say 'If he does not, we grant all his faith will not save him'[8] before proceeding to illustrate what good Protestant practice would be. This crucial link between Christian belief and Christian practice and hence the centrality of the latter for Wesley, explains his readiness to dialogue with some Catholics for he recognised that some at least were people 'fearing God . . . and studying to have a conscience void of offence towards God and towards man'. It also points both communions to an area where they can find a great deal in common about which to dialogue and in which to collaborate.

In February 1997 I was in Durham, North Carolina, meeting with Reverend Geoffrey Wainwright, of Duke University, Reverend Joe Hale, General Secretary of the World Methodist Council, and Father Tim Galligan, of the Pontifical Council for Promoting Christian Unity. We were the respective chairmen and secretaries of the dialogue between the World Methodist Council and the Catholic Church. Our meeting took place at Duke University. One moment of that very happy and successful meeting caught me quite by surprise. The Duke University campus is presided over by a beautiful university chapel first used in 1932 and dedicated in 1935. Its style is English Gothic in inspiration and it fulfils the wish of the university's founder, James Buchanan Duke: 'I want the central building to be a church, a great towering church which will dominate all of the surrounding buildings'.[9]

I entered this great, towering, and beautiful church late one afternoon for Evensong. As I walked through the portal, I saw ranged around me a host of important figures. John Wesley was in the centre.

---

8. 'Letter to a Roman Catholic', 213.
9. Quoted in Guidebook, *Duke University Chapel*.

Above him were Thomas Coke (1747–1814), English Methodist missionary and bishop of the Methodist Episcopal Church; Francis Asbury (1745–1816), pioneer Methodist preacher and bishop; and George Whitefield (1714–1770), English Methodist evangelist and missionary. On his left were Thomas Jefferson, President; Robert E Lee, Southern General; and Sidney Lanier, Southern poet. On his right were John Wycliffe (1324–1386), 'English translator of the bible and martyr'; and Martin Luther. However, to my utter astonishment, I also saw Girolamo Savonarola (1452–1498), described in the guidebook as 'fiery Dominican Preacher and reformer'.

I had left my seminary historical studies with an impression of Savonarola consistent with Nicholas Cheetham's description of the Dominican's later years:

> It seemed that, intoxicated by his own eloquence, he had lost control of himself and was behaving like a crazy fanatic. Excommunicated by the Pope, disavowed by the Florentines whose city had been laid under an interdict, he was eventually removed from power, tried, defrocked and publicly executed.[10]

Savonarola was the prior of San Marco in Florence. He was a scholar, very gifted preacher, extremely zealous reformer, and appeared to be a mystic gifted with visions and prophecy. When Charles VIII of France invaded Florence, the Medici rulers fled and Savonarola assumed the city government. A change in political fortunes for the city, his extreme disciplinary measures, and conflict with Pope Alexander VI led to his condemnation.

Some have seen in Savonarola an influence on other European reformers. He was praised by Luther and some even suggest he influenced Luther's doctrine of justification.[11] One historian ironically comments that Savonarola 'had hurled at the Borgia pope missiles far more deadly than Luther's gentlemanly theses aimed at the Medici'.[12] He has been acclaimed by some, therefore, as in the

---

10. Nicholas Cheetham, *Keeper of the Keys: The Pope in History* (London: Macdonald & Co., 1982), 197.
11. Cheetham, *Keeper of the Keys*, 196.
12. ER Chamberlin, *The Bad Popes* (New York: Dorset Press, 1969, reprinted 1986),

great line of the reformers; and condemned by others for the same reason. His Catholic orthodoxy has been debated for centuries. The classic Catholic historian of the popes, Ludwig Pastor, flatly denied that he was a precursor of the Reformation and defended his Catholic orthodoxy, while still calling him 'fanatical', with 'tendencies' which were, in his characteristic phrase, 'practically uncatholic'.[13]

Despite these harsh and unattractive images of Savonarola which have come down to us today there was, right from the time of his death, a continuing movement of veneration for him. Pastor claims that for a whole century Dominican superiors had to combat his veneration by other Dominicans and actually had to forbid his name being mentioned or any painting of him being on display.[14] However, in the 1983 General Chapter of the Order of Preachers (Dominicans) the introduction of his cause for beatification was recommended, and in May 1996 the Cardinal Archbishop of Florence set up a commission to investigate the matter.

This 'fiery Dominican preacher and reformer', who is honoured alongside Wesley and Luther on the walls of a Methodist chapel, and who may eventually be honoured as a saint in the Catholic Church, raises some interesting questions for any discussion of Methodist–Catholic relations. Firstly, do the Methodist acknowledgement and the Roman Catholic acknowledgement of Savonarola's contribution depend on two different, even opposed, interpretations of the significance of his life? I do not believe this is necessarily true. While Methodists may approve of Savonarola partly because he attacked the pope, and Catholics partly because he apparently remained an orthodox Catholic, would not both want to acknowledge above all that he preached the gospel tirelessly and without fear and that he tried to reform the church from top to bottom? Is there not in this strange figure of the fiery friar a sign of what certainly mattered most to John Wesley and ought to matter most to both communions, namely our faithfulness to Jesus Christ and our commitment to proclaiming him and his message to the whole world? Is this not a bond between us that provides the only worthwhile foundation for ecumenical

---

243.
13. Ludwig Pastor, *History of the Popes from the Close of the Middle Ages*, Volume 6 (London: Kegan Paul, Tench, Trubner & Co, 1923), 51.
14. Pastor, *History of the Popes from the Close of the Middle Ages*, Volume 6 , 52-3.

dialogue? A dialogue which seeks to further the possibilities of full communion between two Christian world communions can only be fruitful if both parties are engaged in the dialogue for the sake of the foundational commitment they share, to Jesus Christ and his mission. The only truly appropriate motivation is one's own love of Jesus Christ and one's desire to serve him. Any other motivation would not be a work of God's grace and would neither sustain one through the tough times nor protect one from seeking all too easy solutions. Was not John Wesley motivated by this deeper concern for Christ and his cause in his *A Letter to a Roman Catholic* already cited?

A second question which Savonarola raises is whether Methodists at Duke University might be offended if Catholics were ever to begin calling the hero of their portal 'Blessed' or 'Saint' Girolamo Savonarola? I am reminded here of a paper my friend, Reverend Dr Han Spykerboer, delivered at a Faith and Order Forum of *Queensland Churches Together* in May 1995. This was the year of the beatification of Mary MacKillop by Pope John Paul II in Sydney. The topic for the forum was 'The Saints: What Do They Mean for Us?', and Han was asked to speak from a Uniting Church in Australia perspective. I can still remember his conclusion:

> The Uniting Church does not recognise individual Saints and is not likely ever to do that. But IF the Uniting Church were going to have a real personal Saint, then it would be a Saint who would meet the various contrasting elements present within the Uniting Church; it would be a Saint with a strong evangelical fervour, a Saint who in prophetic and non-conformist ways would bring this Saint in conflict with the church and its leaders, it would be a Saint with vision and courage, it would be a Saint like Mary MacKillop.[15]

What then of a Saint Girolamo Savonarola? Would some Methodists or Uniting Church members find this at least an intelligible choice of someone to canonise, more perhaps than I would? Even so, the fact remains that Wesley charged Catholics with idolatry because of their

---

15. Han Spykerboer, *The Saints: What do They Mean for Us? A Uniting Church Perspective* (private circulation).

cult of images, their 'worship' of Mary and their offering of prayers to saints;[16] and Methodists have continued to be inclined to do the same. At the very first meeting of the International Dialogue in 1967, Catholic doctrines about Mary were named as 'hard core issues of radical disagreement'.[17]

This question has been largely avoided in contemporary dialogues involving Catholics, despite the figure of Mary being, as Geoffrey Wainwright says, that which 'most obviously distinguishes Roman Catholicism from Protestantism'.[18] The one major exception is the Lutheran–Roman Catholic Dialogue in the United States which produced *The One Mediator, the Saints and Mary* in 1990.[19] Another important and very relevant contribution is that of the British Methodist–Roman Catholic Committee. Their report is entitled *Mary, Mother of the Lord: Sign of Grace, Faith and Holiness: Towards a Shared Understanding.*[20] Given Wesley's concerns, it is to be hoped that the International Dialogue might one day be able and ready to address this issue.

Another question which this image of Savonarola raises specifically for the Catholic Church is whether it might be time for it to acknowledge publicly the holiness of John Wesley and his positive contribution to Christ's cause. Already, Pope John Paul II has spoken of 'the deep religious feeling' of Martin Luther, and Cardinal Willebrands has called Luther a 'man of prayer, preacher and pastor', and 'a deeply religious person who with honesty and dedication sought for the message of the gospel'.[21] I believe that a similar official

---

16. David Butler, *Methodists and Papists*, 111–14.
17. 'Denver Report, 1971' in *Growth in Agreement. Reports and Agreed Statements of Ecumenical Conversations on a World Level*, edited by Harding Meyer and Lukas Vischer (Geneva: WCC, 1984), 321.
18. Geoffrey Wainwright, *The Ecumenical Moment: Crisis and Opportunity for the Church* (Grand Rapids: Eerdmans, 1983), 169.
19. *The One Mediator, the Saints, and Mary: Lutherans and Catholics in Dialogue VIII*, edited by H George Anderson, T Francis Stafford, Joseph A Burgess (Minneapolis: Augsburg, 1992).
20. *Mary, Mother of the Lord: Sign of Grace, Faith and Holiness: Towards a Shared Understanding* (Peterborough: Methodist Publishing House, 1995).
21. Quotations found in Michael Putney, 'A Contemporary Roman Catholic View of Martin Luther', in *Perspectives on Luther. Papers from the Luther Symposium held at Luther Seminary, Adelaide, South Australia, 22-23 March, 1996. Commemorating the 450th anniversary of the Reformer's Death*, edited by MW

development of language about Wesley would be an important contribution to relations between our two communions, and one easily made. However, in an article on 'Wesley and the Communion of Saints', Geoffrey Wainwright has very perceptively linked the recognition of John Wesley, even as an official saint by the Catholic Church, to its recognition of the origins of the Methodist movement as a work of the Holy Spirit.[22]

This takes us to the question which Savonarola and Wesley raise for both communions: How do we each interpret theologically the beginning of Methodism, and can our interpretations be reconciled? A fundamental question at the heart of all Western ecumenical dialogues with the Catholic Church is how the Reformation is interpreted. Consequently, at the heart of the Methodist–Roman Catholic Dialogue is the question of how the later division of Methodism from the Church of England is to be interpreted.

It must be remembered that the Methodist and Catholic Communions never officially separated from each other. Geoffrey Wainwright suggests this ought make the relationship easier as sometimes the relationship between a grandmother and her children is easier than that between a child and its parent, as would be the relationship between Anglicans and Rome or Methodists and Canterbury.[23] The most helpful and challenging contribution to our finding together an answer to these questions is found in the Singapore Report of the Joint Commission. There one reads that Wesley's action in appointing Francis Asbury and Thomas Coke as 'superintendents' in America without Church of England episcopal ordination was 'part of a fresh and extraordinary outpouring of the gift of the Spirit who never ceases to enliven and unify the Church'.[24] Whether Catholics give this event such a positive recognition is the question at the heart of the dialogue.

In a paper I gave in 1996 in Adelaide to mark the 450th anniversary of Martin Luther's death, I said to a largely Lutheran audience:

Worthing (Adelaide: Faculty of Luther Campus, 1997).
22. Wainwright, *Methodists in Dialogue*, 248.
23. Wainwright, *Methodists in Dialogue*, 39–40.
24. 'Roman Catholic–Methodist Dialogue', in *Catholic International* 3/3 (1–14 February 1992): 119.

The most recent report of the Lutheran–Catholic International Dialogue . . . lays out in extraordinary detail the various theological perspectives which would lead to differing theological interpretations of what happened in the Reformation, but does not actually deal with the event itself. I think we are mature enough now to address it. As we struggle to respond to Christ's imperative for all of us, to allow him to unite us again so that the world may believe, we have to be able to deal with our past painful separation not only through careful, purifying historical scholarship which frees us from simply blaming each other, but also by sharing with each other our spiritual perceptions about what happened. How could Lutherans break with Rome? How could Catholics put union with Rome above faithfulness to the gospel? We feel deeply here because it concerns the contours our fidelity to Christ has taken. The International Dialogue has laid it out for us. Now it is time to talk about it . . .[25]

I would wish to raise the same questions about the Methodist–Roman Catholic Dialogue. While the break between Luther and the Church of Rome was the fundamental one which led to different major forms of Western Christianity, each of which, until this century, defined the other as a defective form of itself, the same basic questions arise between the Catholic Church and all Protestant churches. How does one justify not doing as the other did? How do Protestants justify breaking from the continuing church or how do Catholics justify not reforming so that a break was unnecessary? Any dialogue which can find a common and acceptable answer to these questions has travelled a great distance towards reconciliation.

If this is the issue at the heart of the Methodist–Roman Catholic Dialogue and Wesley has already mapped out a methodology for such a dialogue, what has it been able to achieve up to this point? A Joint Commission was established after the Second Vatican Council, and the World Methodist Conference of 1966. There had been Methodist observers at each of the four sessions of the Second Vatican Council,

---

25. Michael Putney, 'A Contemporary Roman Catholic View of Martin Luther', 47.

sixteen in all. The Joint Commission had its first meeting in Ariccia, near Rome, in 1967, and submitted its first report to the World Methodist Council meeting in Denver, 1971. This first phase was entitled 'conversations' between the two communions and covered a host of topics from the practical to the doctrinal. This was true also of the second phase which concluded with the World Methodist Conference in Dublin, 1976. No Australians were involved in either of these phases of the dialogue. In each phase the participants were very concerned about communicating the experience and fruits of their conversations to ordinary Methodists and Roman Catholics and producing reports which would assist relations between the two communions in a practical way.

From these we can discover something about how these two communions engaging in dialogue for the first time saw each other. How did they see themselves related to each other ecclesiologically? The Denver Report recognised certain similarities between the two communions. Firstly, both place the growth in holiness of their members at the centre of their priorities. Parallels to Methodism were seen in the renewal movements which often became religious orders in Catholicism. Both are strongly missionary as well. Finally, Catholics find much of the theology of Charles Wesley's hymns very congenial,[26] though this raises the question of the relationship between contemporary Methodism and the Wesleys. How strict is the continuity, how close the affinity? In 1993, a description of the present relationship between the two communions was offered by the English Methodist–Roman Catholic Committee in a document entitled *Can the Roman Catholic and Methodist Churches Be Reconciled?*:

> What unity exists at present?
> A great deal, and this perhaps is not always sufficiently emphasised in our dialogue. This unity includes a common faith in the Holy Trinity; a common baptism into Christ; our sharing of the Holy Scriptures; our belief enshrined in the Apostles' and Nicene Creeds; our common appropriation of the western spiritual tradition; the living tradition of worship; the common concern for

---

26. 'Denver Report, 1971', 308–9.

holiness; the concern for social righteousness. Much more could be noted but these represent important areas of convergence, best expressed as a real but imperfect communion between our two churches.[27]

The third phase of the dialogue produced its report for the World Methodist Conference in Honolulu, 1981. This report was more focused than the very wide-ranging reports of Denver and Dublin. It concentrated on the Holy Spirit, and then on Christian moral decisions and Christian marriage. The first section began with the illuminating sentence: 'Methodists and Catholics repeatedly discover a notable rapport when they speak of spirituality, the life of the Spirit'.[28] Six paragraphs were devoted to 'the Holy Spirit at work in justification and regeneration' with no apparent difficulties for either party, referring as easily to the Council of Trent as to John Wesley. The convergence or consensus described in the section on 'Christian Experience' is particularly impressive, with Catholics affirming Wesley's teaching on spiritual experience and Methodists affirming some teachings of the Second Vatican Council. They said together: 'we have found new meanings in the evident similarities between Wesley and the mainstream of Catholic spirituality'.[29] In a rather lyrical paragraph they described the very rich experience they were referring to as 'Christian experience':

> Together, then, we affirm that the Christian experience toward which we aspire as one includes mystery and clarity, feeling and reason, individual conscience and acknowledged authority, charisms and sacraments, spiritual exercises and service, individual and communal 'discernments of spirits', local community and worldwide mission, fidelity to the past and openness to the present and future. We are agreed that Christian experience requires for its development the disciplines of prayer and devotion, the truth accessible in Holy Scriptures, the

27. 'English Methodist–RC Committee: "Can the Roman Catholic and Methodist Churches be Reconciled?"', in *One in Christ*, 29 (1993): 168.
28. 'Honolulu Report, 1981', in *Growth in Agreement*, 368.
29. 'Honolulu Report, 1981', 374.

nourishment of the sacraments, the encouragement that comes from God's abundant gifts of grace and wisdom, for witness and service in the world.[30]

The final paragraph of the report gives an account of a very rich ecumenical spirituality, which provides a profound basis for the continuing dialogue between the World Methodist Council and the Catholic Church:

> What we have shared and said together about the Holy Spirit enhances our confidence about the future of our relations. We are all alike under the judgement of God, but all alike confident of the presence and power of his Spirit, which is Love. That Spirit brought us into dialogue; has produced fruits of that dialogue; while we continue joyfully to accept this authority and prompting we cannot presume to set limits to what he may yet work in us. While we continue to work at our problems we are challenged to neglect no opportunity of witnessing in common to what God does for us and offers to all persons. Such witness we can be sure will already carry its own authority.[31]

At the end of this phase of the dialogue they decided to 'concentrate more intensive study on such problems or differences as have recurred and seemed most obstinate in the past three quinquennia'.[32] To that end they chose to begin with 'The Nature of the Church'. There were two Australian participants in this phase of the dialogue, Reverend Eric Osborne and Reverend Norman Young.

In the report of this next phase, which was presented at Nairobi in 1986, there is an interesting paragraph early on which contributes something to the quest for an answer to the fundamental question of how each partner interprets the origin of Methodism:

---

30. 'Honolulu Report, 1981', 375.
31. 'Honolulu Report, 1981', 386.
32. 'Honolulu Report, 1981', 385.

> The Church is judged, transformed and empowered for mission by the Word of God as appropriated through the Spirit. The reforming power of the Word is evident in such instances as some of the medieval reforms (monastic, papal, mendicant), the Reformation and the Catholic renewal of the 16th and 17th centuries, the evangelical revival of the 18th century, the ecumenical movement of the 20th, and many other movements of renewal.[33]

The origins of Methodism are positively acknowledged by both parties as an instance of 'the reforming power of the Word'.

When exploring different models of 'organic unity in the koinonia of the one Body of Christ', the most intriguing was the analogy drawn between Wesley's movement and religious orders founded by reformers such as Benedict of Norcia and Francis of Assisi, a comparison already found in the first report of Denver 1971. Though these latter were fully integrated in the unity of the Church, they had a real, though relative autonomy.[34]

Concerning the ministry of leadership in the church, the report affirmed that from the New Testament and the history of the church it was clear that there has always been a need for a God-given ministry. In addition, Catholics and some Methodists would see a similar work of the Holy Spirit in the establishment of the scriptural canon, the classical creeds and the threefold ministry (bishop, presbyter, deacon). However, there was no agreement on how far this development of the threefold ministry was unchangeable and 'how far loyalty to the Holy Spirit requires us to recognise other forms of oversight and leadership that have developed, often at times of crisis or new opportunity in Christian history'.[35] Despite this unresolved issue, not unrelated to the question about the theological significance of the origins of Methodism, this section of the report concluded rather pragmatically: 'Practically, however, the majority of Methodists already accept the

---

33. *Towards a Statement on the Church: Report of the Joint Commission between the Roman Catholic Church and the World Methodist Council, 1982–1988. Fourth Series* (Lake Junaluksa: World Methodist Councils 1986), 5.
34. *Towards a Statement on the Church*, 9.
35. *Towards a Statement on the Church*, 10.

office of bishop, and some Methodist Churches that do not have expressed their willingness to accept this for the sake of unity'.[36] It noted that in British Methodism, which lacks bishops because of the historical circumstances of its origins, *episcope* was exercised through the conference and was shared among those chairing districts and superintendent ministers. If such Methodist Churches were to adopt bishops while not considering them essential, it would be to promote unity. They would accept them as a focus of unity and a sign of the historic continuity of the church. The report devoted nearly half its text to a study of papacy.

At the conclusion of this report, it was proposed to take up a study of the apostolic tradition, which is what they did. This is not surprising given the focus in the previous report on ministry, papacy, and, above all, on 'authoritative teaching'. The fifth report was completed in time for submission to the World Methodist Council meeting in Singapore, April 1991. By then, Australians among the members were Archbishop John Bathersby, then Bishop of Cairns, who joined in 1987, and Reverend Norman Young, who had been a member since 1977. It is worth noting that the Methodist–Roman Catholic Dialogue was by then developing its own particular focus and making its own unique contribution to the ecumenical movement. By tackling *apostolic tradition*, which they defined as 'the teaching, transmission and reception of the apostolic faith',[37] they were readdressing a question which the ecumenical movement had last convincingly dealt with in 1963, at the Fourth World Conference on Faith and Order in Montreal.

There are many very thought-provoking and irenical accounts of tradition in the report. For example paragraph 16 reads as follows:

> The Tradition received by the apostles itself continues an unbroken process of communication between God and human beings. Every possible human resource is employed to sustain and deepen this process: linguistic, ritual, artistic, social and constitutional. The written word of Scripture is its permanent norm. Through the sacraments of baptism and the eucharist the memory of the events whereby the Church came into being is

---

36. *Towards a Statement on the Church*, 10.
37. 'Roman Catholic–Methodist Dialogue', 107.

preserved. The living word has made a living community in which men and women converse with God and speak their faith to one another. Guided by its pastors and teachers, the Church continues to communicate with all generations, preserves its own identity and message, and is daily renewed in its obedience.[38]

But the concluding paragraph to this section is vital lest the report's strong language about tradition be misunderstood:

> In conclusion, we recall that the search for ecumenical reconciliation has revealed only too clearly the difficulty of reuniting Scripture and Tradition once they have been notionally separated. Scripture was written within Tradition, yet Scripture is normative for Tradition. The one is only intelligible in terms of the other. We do not claim to have resolved here all the ecumenical problems that arise in relation to this issue. What we have sought to do is to ask ourselves how the Christian of today can confess with Christians of all time the one true faith in Jesus Christ, the same yesterday, today and forever.[39]

This phase of the dialogue explored again the role of the Holy Spirit in the Church, linking it very closely to the role of the Word of God. In the second part of its report, entitled 'Ministry and Ministries: Serving Within the Apostolic Tradition', it explored the ordained ministry at great length and only after a great deal of consensus in understanding did it discuss what it called 'convergences and divergences'. One of the convergences had emerged earlier. It concerns the representative role of the ordained minister and reads as follows:

> Chosen from among the people, the ordained ministers represent the people before God as they bring together the prayers of the community. Entrusted with the pastoral care of the community, they act in Christ's name and person as they lead the people in prayer, proclaim

---

38. 'Roman Catholic–Methodist Dialogue', 109.
39. 'Roman Catholic–Methodist Dialogue', 109.

and explain the Word and administer the sacraments of faith.[40]

One divergence related to the sacramentality of ordination, though this seemed to be more a problem of the number of biblical sacraments than a substantial difference in interpretation of the rite which is said to be perceived by both as 'an effective sign by which the grace of God is given to the recipient for the ministry of word and sacrament'.[41] A second divergence concerned the teaching role of the ordained ministry which for Catholics is located in the college of bishops with the bishop of Rome at its head. Wesley accepted this role as he found it in the Anglican Church and exercised it himself with Methodism. How it has been exercised since and how this relates to the Catholic perception is precisely the topic of the next phase of the Methodist–Roman Catholic Dialogue which is about to begin. On the question of ordination of women, the report simply describes the position of each communion and concludes, 'Further thought will be of benefit to both traditions'.[42]

The next phase of the dialogue, in which Reverend Norman Young and Archbishop John Bathersby continued to be members, produced a report entitled *The Word of Life: A Statement on Revelation and Faith*, in 1995. In some ways this report is a commentary on a short text of scripture, 1 John 1:1–3:

> That which was from the beginning, which we have heard, which we have seen with our eyes, which we have looked upon and touched with our own hands, concerning the word of life—the life was made manifest, and we saw it and testify to it, and proclaim to you the eternal life which was with the Father and was made manifest to us—that which we have seen and heard we proclaim also to you, so that you may have fellowship with us; and our fellowship is with the Father and with his Son Jesus Christ.

---

40. 'Roman Catholic–Methodist Dialogue', 117.
41. 'Roman Catholic–Methodist Dialogue', 119.
42. 'Roman Catholic–Methodist Dialogue', 120.

Concerning *ecumenism and mission*, the report had this to say: 'Nearly thirty years of dialogue between Catholics and Methodists have revealed sufficient agreement in faith for our churches to recognise integrity and faithfulness in each other's proclamation of the Gospel.'[43] This raises the possibility of taking more seriously the ecumenical call to proclaim the gospel together. On *faith*, the report made the very helpful comment:

> In the past, Methodists tended to see the faith of Roman Catholics merely as an assent to what the church teaches, whereas Catholics sometimes thought Methodist belief to be a purely emotional personal conviction. These prejudices have been overcome. Faith is always personal but never private, for faith incorporates the believing individual into the community of faith. Therefore his or her faith is both a personal conviction and also a sharing of what is held by the 'community of the believers'.[44]

Finally, paragraphs 69 to 71 on *discernment* talk about the differences between the Roman Catholic emphasis on the teaching of the bishops in unity with the bishop of Rome and the teaching office exercised by the conferences in Methodism, and concludes in paragraph 71: 'The differences between these approaches and the implications for the communion of faith will have to be dealt with at a later stage of the dialogue between Methodists and Catholics'. It is precisely that difference which the next phase of the dialogue hopes to address. In tackling this issue, which for Catholics is that of the *magisterium*, it will be dealing with a question which has been with us since Wesley wrote in his *Letter to a Roman Catholic*: 'Is there any one point which you do not believe as well as we? But you think we ought to believe more. We will not enter into the dispute'. Wesley was making reference to the range of Catholic dogmas defined by the *magisterium*. If Wesley was unwilling to dispute this in 1749, it is good that in 1997 we no longer need to dispute it, but can dialogue about it as friends.

What then ought be our hopes for the future of this dialogue? Clearly there are many issues in the area of ministry and sacraments,

---

43. *The Word of Life: A Statement on Revelation and Faith*, 13.
44. *The Word of Life: A Statement on Revelation and Faith*, 39.

which are not yet resolved. Moreover there are issues in ecclesiology, including the role of the bishop of Rome in a future united church, that are far from resolved. At the same time, the Methodist Communion and the Catholic Church are very similar when one looks at them from the point of view of what they are trying to achieve in the lives of their members: their concern for Christian living, their common delight in the life of Christ which their members live, and their desire to share that life with others. The commission's work on the church, on apostolic tradition and on revelation and faith during the period 1986–96, and their future work on the teaching of the church, are very important for establishing a fuller shared interpretation of this life in Christ that they have in common.

What Methodists and Catholics share far outweighs those things in which they differ. These latter came about because of the divisions within the Western Christian world as a result of the Reformation. Churches have developed apart since that time. The most hopeful view of ecumenical dialogue is to see it as a process of discovering that these developments which appear so different are, in fact, both consistent with an earlier shared tradition, and are simply that tradition taking different, though not opposed, forms. Of course, this can never be presumed and it can only be the conclusion of a lengthy and careful dialogue. It would certainly not be possible to draw that conclusion about every development in every Western church. Nonetheless, those engaged in bilateral dialogues always enter with the hope of being able to achieve that goal to the extent that, under God, it is possible. It remains to be seen how far this will become possible in the present dialogue, but it is always an exercise of hope.

What is happening in dialogue is the process of each communion *recognising*[45] in the faith and life of another communion the same apostolic faith. It is a process of coming to a *recognition* that the church with which one is in dialogue is fully the same church of Jesus Christ one believes is found in one's own communion. When such *recognition* is complete, *reconciliation* is possible.

If a Christian communion were able to reach the stage of *recognising* the apostolic tradition in the very different tradition of another Christian communion, this would surely include a capacity

---

45. Compare Gerard Kelly, *Recognition: Advancing Ecumenical Thinking* (New York: Peter Lang, 1996).

to interpret positively the separation between the two communions at whatever point in history it occurred. Once again, I am convinced that a serious historical and theological study of the origins of the division between Christian communions and, in this particular case, between Methodism and the Anglican Communion, has to be part of the groundwork necessary for reconciliation between world communions. I think there may be grounds for the Roman Catholic Church to interpret the origins of Methodism in a very positive light, to see it as an authentic renewal of the Christian Church. This ought not be incompatible with its regret at the same time that this renewal occurred in a church already separated from the bishop of Rome.

Can the Methodist Church and other Protestant Churches view equally positively the particular Catholic commitment throughout history to preserve continuity in ministerial structures, sacramental dispensation, church teaching, and the role of the bishop of Rome despite the obvious slowness at times to reform these structures? This commitment has led the Catholic Church to resist church renewals which appear to jeopardise any of these commitments. The commitment to renewal and the commitment to continuity ought not to have led to the division between Protestant Churches and the Catholic Church. Both commitments are essential to the Christian Church.

Are we at a point of history where we can look together at the moments of division, share our regret, our repentance, and acknowledge that we lost something by losing communion with each other? The Catholic Church needs the continuing renewing, evangelical impulse of the Methodist Communion, and I believe the Methodist Church needs the particular commitment to continuity of the Catholic Church.

May God's renewing grace enable us to rediscover each other and to become, for God's sake, one Church again.

The Papacy: Is There a Place for the Papacy in a Future United Church

In the last paragraph of the 1995 report from the Joint Commission for Dialogue between the Catholic Church and the World Methodist Council, *The Word of Life: A Statement on Revelation and Faith*, one reads: 'In particular, future study could address the related topics of pastoral and doctrinal authority, the offices of oversight in the Church and succession in them, and the offer made by Rome of a petrine ministry in the service of unity and communion.'[1]

This paragraph follows almost immediately after two other paragraphs which describe the different understandings in the two communions of the nature and theological weight of the structures which bind local churches together in a universal communion. Catholics are said to rely on the promise they believe was given to St Peter and the other apostles. They believe this promise has been fulfilled in the apostolic succession of the college of bishops with the pope, as successor of St Peter, at its head. So for Catholics, this ministerial structure is an essential means and guarantee established by God's grace for the preservation of the continuity and unity of the Church. Methodists are said to understand apostolic tradition as preserved by a church's faithfulness to the apostolic teaching; and to see the Methodist Conferences as exercising the teaching office which decides what is faithful or not. Methodists recognise the necessity of a ministry of oversight, and some find this in the office of bishops. The bonds of communion are said to be established for them by what the statement

---

This paper was originally published in Trinity Occasional Papers, XVI/2 (December 1977): 58–71.

---

1. Methodist–Roman Catholic Joint Commission, *The Word of Life: A Statement on Revelation and Faith* (Lake Junaluska: Methodist Council, 1996), 44.

calls 'connexional structures which have to mediate the needs of local churches and the Church as a whole'.[2]

The next phase of the dialogue hopes to tackle the question of doctrinal authority in the church; but it remains a task of the future for the Joint Commission to take up directly the question of the petrine ministry in a united church. This is not to say that the dialogue has not already touched on it a number of times and already laid the groundwork for a more comprehensive treatment. Moreover, the question of the ministry of the bishop of Rome in the communion of churches is one which confronts all dialogues involving the Catholic Church. Some, like the Anglican–Roman Catholic International Commission, have already dealt with it directly,[3] and it may well touch on it again in its forthcoming statement on authority.

However all such dialogues have entered into a new context because of the offer of Pope John Paul II referred to in the paragraph from *The Word of Life* already cited. The offer is found in an encyclical of the Pope entitled *Ut Unum Sint* published in 1995. It was only his twelfth, and needs to be interpreted in the context of his previous apostolic letter on the third millennium, *Tertio Millennio Adveniente*. In that letter he expressed the following hope:

> The approaching end of the second millennium demands of everyone an examination of conscience and the promotion of fitting ecumenical initiatives so that we can celebrate the Great Jubilee, if not completely united, at least much closer to overcoming the divisions of the second millennium.[4]

Given the fact that he said this only two years ago and the year 2000 is only three years away, I believe there is an urgency behind his publication of an encyclical on ecumenism. He is trying to play his part in bringing about the vision he painted in 1994.

What has he offered, though, to make it possible? Here is what is most interesting for our topic, and is referred to in *The Word of Life*.

---

2. *The Word of Life*, 44.
3. *Anglican–Roman Catholic International Commission: The Final Report, Windsor, September 1981* (London: CTS/SPCK, 1982), 49–98.
4. 'As the Third Millennium Draws Near', in *Origins*, 24/24 (24 November 1994): 411.

> As Bishop of Rome I am fully aware, as I have reaffirmed in the present encyclical letter, that Christ ardently desires the full and visible communion of all those communities in which, by virtue of God's faithfulness, his Spirit dwells. I am convinced that I have a particular responsibility in this regard, above all in acknowledging the ecumenical aspirations of the majority of the Christian communities and in heeding the request made of me to find a way of exercising the primacy which, while in no way renouncing what is essential to its mission, is nonetheless open to a new situation.[5]

The pope goes on to refer to an exchange he had with the then Patriarch of Constantinople, Dimitrios I, in 1988, when he confessed that the papacy which should have been a service to the unity of the church sometimes 'manifested itself in a very different light' and that he prayed for the Holy Spirit to enlighten all pastors and theologians of the two communions so that they could seek together ways in which his ministry might accomplish 'a service of love recognised by all.'[6]

Finally, he called for church leaders and theologians from other churches 'to engage with me in a patient and fraternal dialogue on this subject, a dialogue in which, leaving useless controversies behind, we could listen to one another.'[7] In these two short paragraphs this encyclical has tackled the major obstacle to full communion between Catholics and all other ChristiancCommunions and has offered a new way forward through this creative invitation.

The ultimate stumbling block on the road to unity between other great Christian world communions and the Catholic Church is the role of the bishop of Rome. This was made clear in the Anglican–Roman Catholic International Dialogue and, in one way or another, in all the major dialogues involving the Catholic Church. I would like to tell a story I have told many times which illustrates this point very well. In 1982 I heard a lecture at the University of Fribourg, given by Metropolitan Damaskinos of Tranoupolis, the Greek Orthodox

---

5. John Paul II, Encyclical Letter, *Ut Unum Sint*, 'On Commitment to Ecumenism', 95.
6. *Ut Unum Sint*, 95.
7. *Ut Unum Sint*, 96.

Archbishop of Geneva. In it he described a lunch he had had in Rome with Pope John Paul II during a conference on 'the Holy Spirit.' He had been a keynote speaker with the now-deceased Roman Catholic ecumenist, Yves Congar OP, and the major Protestant theologian, Jürgen Moltmann. The conference marked the 1600th anniversary of the First Council of Constantinople and the 1550th anniversary of the Council of Ephesus. During lunch the pope remarked that it seemed to have resolved the major issue which has kept the Eastern and Western churches apart. This is the issue of the *filioque*, or the relationship of the Holy Spirit to the Father and the Son, as found in the Nicene-Constantinopolitan Creed. His conclusion was that the Churches of the East and the Roman Catholic Church ought now be able to move rapidly towards reunion. Metropolitan Damaskinos offered the opinion that there was another major obstacle keeping the two communions apart. When the pope asked what this might be, he replied: 'It's you, Holy Father.' The pope, he explained, then laughed and said he hoped that this issue might be able to be resolved as well.

Pope John Paul II's public commitment to resolving this issue establishes a new context for ecumenical dialogue on the question. At the same time it is itself only fully intelligible when one understands that it has occurred in the context of the positive fruits of a range of bi-lateral dialogues. For example, the Methodist–Roman Catholic Joint Commission, with which we began, dealt with the papacy at greatest length in its *Towards a Statement on the Church* of 1986, the product of the fourth phase of this well-established dialogue. The Joint Commission had decided that they must address this issue. Why? Their answer is simple: 'Since Catholics and Methodists have committed themselves to seeking full unity in faith, mission and sacramental life.'[8] In other words, any dialogue with the Roman Catholic Church with such a goal must eventually face the question of the ministry of the bishop of Rome.

In thirty-six paragraphs, the text devotes seven to the biblical evidence concerning Peter, and then nine to the emergence of the papal ministry in the history of the post New Testament church. Its conclusion is that 'the primacy of the bishop of Rome is not

---

8. *Towards a Statement on the Church: Report of the Joint Commission between the Roman Catholic Church and the World Methodist Council 1982–1986, Fourth Series* (Lake Junaluska: World Methodist Council, 1986), 12.

established from the Scriptures in isolation from the living tradition'.[9] Because scripture alone does not establish the papal ministry as a divine requirement for the Church, Methodists affirmed that they would judge it on its merits. When faced with the Catholic conviction that reconciliation with the See of Rome is essential to the restoration of Christian unity, the Methodist members offered the following principle by way of response: 'Methodists accept that whatever is properly required for the unity of the whole of Christ's Church must by that very fact be Go"s will for his Church'.[10] Papal primacy would need to prove its claim to be so 'properly required'.

At this point the report raises an interesting issue relevant to Pope John Paul II's request for patient and fraternal dialogue on the way he *ought to* exercise the papal ministry. It argues that some of the current functions of the pope belong to his episcopal role as local bishop in Rome or to his patriarchal role as Latin Patriarch. The report argues that if these roles were distinguished from the essence of his primatial ministry, it 'would make it easier for Methodists to reconsider whether the Bishop of Rome might yet exercise this ministry for other Christians as well as for those who already accept it'.[11] It seems that this dialogue anticipated Pope John Paul II's request for assistance in discerning how best to exercise his ministry, by nearly ten years.

The two theological issues which the report recognises especially need to be addressed are those of jurisdiction and infallibility. While it acknowledges that it is not inconceivable that at some time in the future Methodist and Catholic bishops might belong to one episcopal college with 'some kind of effective leadership and primacy'[12] attributed to the bishop of Rome, it would likely be because Methodists had accepted this role without accepting the reasons Catholics advance for it. Presumably, their reason would be that already put forward: 'whatever is properly required for the unity of the whole of Christ's Church must by that very fact be God's will for the Church'.

With regard to papal infallibility the report gives a very clear account of Catholic teaching about it. Among others it makes the following points:

---

9. *Towards a Statement on the Church,* 16.
10. *Towards a Statement on the Church,* 17.
11. *Towards a Statement on the Church,* 17.
12. *Towards a Statement on the Church,* 18.

- papal infallibility is an embodiment, like general councils, of the infallibility of the whole church;
- Christ's promise and the gift of the Holy Spirit require that the church be able to formulate matters of faith in a way beyond doubt; the pope does this within and for the whole church in very defined and limited circumstances, not every time he teaches;
- he does this as teacher and pastor of all the faithful;
- he teaches that a particular matter of faith and morals is part of divine revelation and so the teaching requires assent;
- neither the pope nor his teaching are infallible but, rather, the act of teaching, because of God preventing him from teaching error; though a particular teaching may be taught infallibly, this does not mean that it is taught in the best possible way.[13]

In response to this account, Methodists raise concerns about the claim that sinful human beings could have such a capacity to discern the truth. They then describe the locations they recognise for the Holy Spirit's guidance:

> Through reformers, prophetic figures, Church leaders and Methodist Conferences for example, as well as through General Councils. Methodist Conferences, exercising their teaching office, formulate doctrinal statements as they are needed, but do not ascribe to them guaranteed freedom from error. Nevertheless Methodists always accept what can clearly be shown to be in agreement with the Scriptures. The final judge of this agreement must be the assent of the whole People of God, therefore Methodists, in considering the claims made for Councils and for the Pope, welcome the attention which Roman Catholic theologians are giving to the understanding of the reception of doctrine.[14]

---

13. *Towards a Statement on the Church*, 19.
14. *Towards a Statement on the Church*, 19–20.

I concur wholeheartedly with this reference to the theology of 'reception'. Because of the clear teaching of Vatican I that papal dogmatic definitions are 'irreformable of themselves, not because of the consent of the church', Catholic theologians have neglected until recently the role which *reception* by the whole church plays in all authoritative teaching. The Methodist participants raised an equally interesting matter for further reflection on their side. This was Methodist doctrine of 'assurance'. They asked the question whether the Holy Spirit might not give the Church a gift of assurance in response to the teaching ministry. The final sentence of this section is particularly illuminating: 'In any case Catholics and Methodists are agreed on the need for an authoritative way of being sure, beyond doubt, concerning God's action insofar as it is crucial for our salvation.'[15] This particular sentence will, no doubt, stimulate a great deal of discussion in the next phase of the Methodist–Roman Catholic Dialogue which begins in Venice, in November 1997, and so far has as its topic precisely this: *The Teaching of the Church: Discerning the Truth of the Gospel.*

How open have other bi-lateral dialogues been to a role for the bishop of Rome in a future united Church? Agreeing in 1976 that complementary primatial and conciliar aspects to the *episcope* serving the communion of local churches was necessary at a universal level, the Anglican–Roman Catholic International Commission (ARCIC) saw the bishop of Rome as the only appropriate candidate for the primatial role.[16] This conviction went along with real questions about the petrine texts in the New Testament, papacy as of divine law, the jurisdiction of the pope, and infallibility.

The second report on 'Authority in the Church' (1981) did much to reduce Anglican concerns about these questions, though not entirely, and its last sentence is very thought-provoking: 'We suggest that some difficulties will not be wholly resolved until a practical initiative has been taken and our two Churches have lived together more visibly in the one *koinona*.'[17] They correctly point out that the experience of a petrine ministry, or the lack of it, is a real and very significant factor in understanding theological interpretations of this ministry.

---

15. *Towards a Statement on the Church*, 20.
16. *The Final Report*, 64.
17. *The Final Report*, 98.

Despite some passing references in an earlier report,[18] the Reformed–Roman Catholic Dialogue could only say in its second and latest report: 'We have begun to come to terms with the particularly difficult issue of the structure of ministry required for communion in the universal Church.'[19]

In similar words the Lutheran–Roman Catholic International Dialogue said in its first report of 1972 (Malta Report): 'In this connection, the question of papal primacy emerges as a special problem for the relationship between Lutherans and Catholics.' The specific context referred to was their treatment of 'The Gospel and the Office of the Ministry in the Church'. Interestingly enough, that first report also said:

> It was recognised on the Lutheran side that no local church should exist in isolation since it is a manifestation of the universal church. In this sense the importance of a ministerial service of the communion of churches was acknowledged and at the same time reference was made to the problem raised for Lutherans by their lack of such an effective service of unity. The office of the papacy as a visible sign of the unity of the churches was therefore not excluded insofar as it is subordinated to the primacy of the gospel by theological reinterpretation and practical restructuring.

The report went on to say: 'The question, however, which remains controversial between Catholics and Lutherans is whether the primacy of the pope is necessary for the church, or whether it represents only a fundamentally possible function.'[20] Here it touched on a particularly

18. 'The Presence of Christ in Church and World: Dialogue between the World Alliance of Reformed Churches and the Secretariat for Promoting Christian Unity: 1970–1977', in *Information Service*, 35 (1977): 24, 33.

19. 'Towards a Common Understanding of the Church: Reformed–Roman Catholic International Dialogue: Second Phase (1984–1990)', in *Information Service*, 74 (1990): 114.

20. 'Report of the Joint Lutheran–Roman Catholic Study Commission on "The Gospel and the Church", 1972 ("Malta Report")', in *Growth in Agreement: Reports and Agreed Statements of Ecumenical: Conversations on a World Level, edited by* Harding Meyer and Lukas Vischer (Geneva: WCC, 1984), 184.

difficult question in all dialogues with Catholics, their belief that many ecclesiological structures are required 'by divine law' *(de iure divino)* and have been so defined.

The question of a ministry serving the universal unity of the church was taken up again in their 1981 report, *The Ministry in the Church*. After discussing the Catholic teaching on the ministry of the bishop of Rome, the report outlined a Lutheran perspective. It made the point that the reformers held on to the view that a universal council of the church was an instrument for the expression of the consensus of all Christendom and of church unity, though they doubted that a genuinely universal and free council could still be assembled. It also seemed to Lutherans that the papacy suppressed the Gospel in practice and that this was an obstacle to Christian unity with Catholics. The teachings of the First Vatican Council confirmed their conviction.

But then the report went on to say the following:

> While the traditional controversies have not yet been completely settled, it can nevertheless be said that Lutheran theologians today are among those who look not only to a future council or to the responsibility of theology, but also to a special Petrine office, when it is a question of service to the unity of the church at the universal level. Much remains theologically open here, especially the question as to how this universal ministry in the service of truth and unity can be exercised, whether by a general council, or by a group, or by an individual bishop respected by all Christians. But in various dialogues, the *possibility* begins to emerge that the Petrine office of the Bishop of Rome also need not be excluded by Lutherans as a visible sign of the unity of the church as a whole, 'insofar as [this office] is subordinated to the primacy of the gospel by theological reinterpretation and practical restructuring'.[21]

Such openness is indicative of an entirely new theological and ecumenical context for looking at the ministry of the bishop of Rome.

---

21. 'The Ministry in the Church, 1981', *in Growth in Agreement*, 271.

This dialogue returned to the question of the papacy in its most recent report, *Church and Justification: Understanding the Church in the Light of Justification*. It expressed the hope that the dialogue will take up the question again in the context established by an ecclesiology of communion or *koinonia* which has become the dominant[22] ecclesiology in contemporary dialogues. It says this concerning the Catholic understanding of the ministry of the bishop of Rome: 'In spite of Catholic adherence to the principle of a ministry of unity in the universal church, the challenge to self-criticism cannot be ignored. The doctrine of primacy must be further developed, and primatial practice must be shaped accordingly.'[23] So the Lutheran–Roman Catholic Dialogue, like the Methodist–Roman Catholic one, also seems to have anticipated Pope John Paul II by calling for a radical rethinking of papal ministry. At the same time, it too is still open to considering such a ministry in some form or other.

Finally, the FOC of the World Council of Churches (WCC), in 1993, at its Fifth World Conference in Santiago de Compostela, Spain, asked that the primatial office, its necessity and nature, be on the agenda of any ecumenical study of the church.[24] This challenge has been taken up and the FOC is poised to tackle the question of the universal unity of the church, primacy and the ministry of the bishop of Rome. This is an extraordinary moment in the history of this mulilateral dialogue. After nearly seventy years of dialogue, thirty of which have involved the Catholic Church, a sufficient level of maturity has been reached for the question of papacy at last to be tackled.

What then are the possibilities ahead? Is there a place for papacy in a future united church? Without wanting to sound too blunt, I would have to say as a Catholic that, if a future united church were to involve us, we would need to find a place for papacy within it. The role of the bishop of Rome serving the universal unity of the church is integral to Catholic self-understanding and is believed by Catholics

---

22. Michael Putney, 'Koinonia—An Ecumenical Breakthrough', in *Themes in Interchurch Dialogue: Koinonia, Scripture, Justification* (Melbourne: Joint Board of Christian Education, 1994), 10–42.
23. 'Report on the Third Phase of Lutheran–Roman Catholic International Dialogue: "Church and Justification. Understanding the Church in the Light of the Doctrine of Justification"', in *Information Service* (1994/II–III): 149.
24. *On the Way to Fuller Koinonia, edited by* Thomas F Best and Günther Gassmann (Geneva: WCC, 1994), 251.

to be required of the church by God. It is not something we could surrender for the sake of unity, because we would find ourselves united but guilty of unfaithfulness to the apostolic tradition as we understand it. In *Ut Unum Sint*, Pope John Paul II said quite directly:

> The Catholic Church, both in her *praxis* and in her solemn documents, holds that the communion of the particular Churches with the Church of Rome, and of their Bishops with the Bishop of Rome, is—in God's plan—an essential requisite of full and visible communion. Indeed full communion, of which the Eucharist is the highest sacramental manifestation, needs to be visibly expressed in a ministry in which all the Bishops recognise that they are united in Christ and all the faithful find confirmation for their faith.[25]

Therefore, three questions arise for those dialoguing with the Catholic Church. Firstly, can they accept a role for the bishop of Rome as servant of the universal unity of the churches? Secondly, if they can accept such a role, what are the limits they would place upon it? Or would they be able to accept all that Catholics understand by it? And thirdly, can they agree with Catholics about the necessity of this ministry in the church question? This is the question of its dogmatic weight.

The first and last questions need to be distinguished when one is dialoguing with Catholics. In the accounts I have given so far, for example, of the Methodist World Communion, there are those who would permit a united church to have as part of its structure a universal ministry for the bishop of Rome, and they would do this for the sake of unity. However, they would baulk at accepting the Catholic position that this has always been required of the church and that such a requirement, of necessity, comes from God.

Since the breakdown in communion between the Eastern Churches and the Church of the West, and the breaks within the Western communion of churches at the time of the Reformation, the Catholic Church has developed a highly sophisticated theology of the ministry of the bishop of Rome, attributing to him a primacy over all the churches,

---

25. *Ut Unum Sint*, 97.

and a particular teaching authority. These definitions are part of those developments within the apostolic tradition which shape the theological consciousness of contemporary Catholics. Because these beliefs have been developed and defined at a distance from other Western Christians and from the Eastern Churches, they undoubtedly appear alien to them and would not easily appear as necessary for the church. So there is still much ground to be covered if any consensus is to be reached on these or other doctrinal questions.

Moreover, as was noted in reference to the conclusion of ARCIC, it will be very difficult to deal with such questions when other Western Christians and Eastern Christians do not have the experience Catholics have of taking for granted, day by day, a particular ministry of the bishop of Rome. No doubt all Christians, as indeed all people, have some awareness of the ministry of the bishop of Rome. But to read about what the pope has said or done in the newspapers is not the same as to have him addressing oneself as a member of the same communion.

So, in addition to the doctrinal question, which may be fairly immaterial to many ordinary Protestants and Catholics, the non-theological, psychological, historical, political, symbolic weight of the papacy will also need to be dealt with. People who have grown up believing that papacy is the work of the devil will not easily adjust to a consideration of even the possibility of a ministry for the pope in a united church simply because theologians have reached some form of doctrinal agreement. They would need to *receive*, and I use that word decidedly, the papacy into their Christian experience, their Christian consciousness, their Christian symbolic framework, and to see it as a life-giving gift, for them to welcome it as part of their future in a united church. So in addition to the three questions I listed earlier there is clearly another one: How could such a ministry be accepted by ordinary people who have no experience of it, and were raised to believe it was contrary to the gospel? This may appear to suggest that the whole question of the role of the bishop of Rome in a united church is an impossible one to resolve.

However, I have not yet addressed the question raised by Pope John Paul II himself. What changes can occur in the exercise of this papal ministry which would make it more compatible for other Christians, and which would enable its symbolic significance to be more transparent and more obviously life-giving? Which also means what changes in Catholic consciousness about and theological interpretation of the role of the bishop of Rome would need to occur for this ministry to be able to be integrated into a future united church?

I clearly don't have the answer to these questions, but I am delighted that the dialogue about them has begun. Churches and theologians around the world are beginning to come up with new models and are offering these, not only as part of the larger ecumenical conversation taking place at the moment, but especially to the Catholic Church, to provoke in it a thorough analysis of its own interpretation of the ministry of the bishop of Rome. One good recent example is in an address given by Reinhard Frieling, the Director of the Konfessionskundliche Institut in Bensheim, Germany, who is a member of the Joint Working Group (JWG) between the WCC and the Catholic Church. He delivered the address to the Catholic Theological Faculty of the University of Paderborn. It was entitled, 'Communion with, not under the Pope'. I think his title is both provocative and enlightening. He says he chose it to avoid entering into a discussion about the alternatives of either abolishing the papacy or submitting to the pope. By working with the language of communion, I believe he has located this question within its proper framework.

If Catholics were to be right about the ministry of the bishop of Rome, they could only be right because some structure is needed to preserve the universal communion of the churches, and the papacy does this better than any other. Therefore to approach the ministry of the pope in terms of that communion and to speak of communion with him, rather than under him, is to begin in the right place.

I acknowledge that when Reinhard Frieling makes the distinction between 'with' and 'under' in reference to the ministry of the pope in the communion of churches, he is using those words with a quite specific theological significance. By rejecting 'under', he is rejecting, in fact, the doctrines of universal jurisdiction and papal infallibility. He is rejecting the teaching of the First Vatican Council, and asking the Catholic Church to tolerate his rejection. One of his theses reads as follows: 'Ecclesial communion with the Pope is possible, if a common understanding of the Gospel is articulated and if the Pope does not insist that non–Roman Catholic Christians recognise the primacy of papal jurisdiction and the dogma of infallibility'.[26]

---

26. Reinhard Frieling, 'Communion With, Not Under the Pope', in *Ecumenical*

In fact, Frieling is not asking Catholics to let go of these doctrines for themselves. He envisages the possibility of Catholics continuing to accept the jurisdiction of the pope and the infallibility of his teaching office, but not demanding an acceptance of these doctrines by churches of the Reformation and indeed the Orthodox Churches; and so, being able to exist in communion with these churches despite the divergence on these questions. He is looking forward to a conciliar fellowship of churches, and a universal ecumenical council, in which the Catholic Church would participate fully and so enter into full communion with these churches, while maintaining its own understanding of papal primacy and teaching authority. Within that universal communion, the bishop of Rome would be acknowledged by others and would have a special role as promoter of unity; though this role would be a very limited one. Frieling puts forward this fresh model because, in his opinion, 'It requires no special perspicacity to see that no other church is going to accept the Catholic model of unity of faith and church unity'.[27]

I expressed my sympathy with Frieling's distinction between communion 'with' the pope and communion 'under' the pope, not because I was supporting this part of his argument. I do not do so, because I do not believe full communion is possible between churches when one considers as heretical what another holds as a dogma of faith. But I do think he is pointing to something of fundamental importance. Even for Catholics, communion with the bishop of Rome comes before any understanding of communion under him. In fact, I think Catholics would find it hard to speak of communion 'under' the pope. The authority they attribute to him, both jurisdictional and magisterial, is perceived as a ministry within the communion, not a ministry that takes him out of the communion and places him above the communion. To Catholics, Jesus Christ alone is the head of the Church. The Word of God is the only authority 'over' the Church.

The authority of bishops and the authority of the pope is an authority within the communion of churches that make up the Catholic Church. In a parish or a congregation pastors have authority as they exercise their ministry in the name of Christ. Their authority is real, but it does not place them outside the communion of the congregation or the parish. It is a ministry within it. Similarly, the ministry of the bishop of Rome in

Review (1997): 40.
27. Frieling, 'Communion With, Not Under the Pope', 39.

the college of bishops and in the Catholic Church is a ministry 'within' that communion. It can never be considered as one which would take him outside it.

Both Vatican I and Vatican II affirmed that the primacy of the bishop of Rome was a jurisdiction to be exercised for the building up of the church and for the preserving of communion among the churches. It is a quite specific kind of authority, just as his ministry is a specific form of episcopal ministry. To talk of communion 'under' the pope, without a great deal of qualification, would inflate his role within the communion, placing him in a category altogether different from that of his fellow bishops and all the other members of the church.

I believe a little known dialogue, the Joint Roman Catholic–Orthodox Committee in France, has made this point very well. In a report produced in 1990 after six years of dialogue on the topic 'The Roman Primacy within the Communion of Churches', it had this to say:

> Every primatial function—and particularly one which would be recognised in the bishop of the Church 'which presides in love' for fostering communion among sister Churches—has as its purpose the service of edification and communion among the Churches: its service is to watch over the unity of the Churches in the faith and to give expression to this faith, to witness to their communion, and not to allow the Churches to become isolated and to jeopardise the bonds of catholic communion. As such this function of a primate does not place him above the Churches but at the heart of its bonds of communion . . .
>
> However one describes the primatial responsibility, the 'honour' which is recognised in it implies real responsibility and real authority. This 'primacy' is, to be sure, *inter pares*, but it is nonetheless truly *primus*. This responsibility and power should be articulated canonically, but should never be detached from the communion among Churches and bishops which is the reason why there is a 'primatial' function and responsibility: (canonical) legislation should never be separated from the sacramental nature of the Church which legitimates it and establishes it . . .[28]

---

28. French Joint Roman Catholic–Orthodox Committee, 'The Roman Primacy within the Communion of Churches', in *One in Christ*, 29 (1993): 159.

I quoted this at length because of the importance of the dialogue between the Catholic Church and the Eastern Orthodox Churches for the question, given the history of the first millennium and the possibility of distinguishing more easily in this relationship between the three roles of the pope: the universal primate, patriarch of the West, and bishop of Rome. The report actually goes on to suggest that the supposed opposition between the primacy of honour and a primacy of jurisdiction could be seen in a new light if Rome were to define more clearly the nature and extent of its jurisdiction and were to distinguish its role in the West from its universal role.[29] This could again be seen as an anticipation of the request made by Pope John Paul II in *Ut Unum Sint* for asssistance in finding ways of exercising his ministry.

In that encyclical, Pope John Paul II himself said this about the papal ministry:

> With the power and the authority without which such an office would be illusory, the Bishop of Rome must ensure the communion of all the Churches. For this reason, he is the first servant of unity. This primacy is exercised on various levels, including the vigilance over the handing down of the Word, the celebration of the Liturgy and the Sacraments, the Church's mission, discipline and the Christian life. It is the responsibility of the Successor of Peter to recall the requirements of the common good of the Church, should anyone be tempted to overlook it in the pursuit of personal interests. He has the duty to admonish, to caution and to declare at times that this or that opinion being circulated is irreconcilable with the unity of faith. When circumstances require it, he speaks in the name of all the Pastors in communion with him. He can also—under very specific conditions clearly laid down by the First Vatican Council—declare *ex cathedra* that a certain doctrine belongs to the deposit of faith. By thus bearing witness to the truth, he serves unity.

---

29. French Joint Roman Catholic–Orthodox Committee, 'The Roman Primacy within the Communion of Churches', 160.

> All this however must always be done in communion.
> When the Catholic Church affirms that the office of the
> Bishop of Rome corresponds to the will of Christ, she
> does not separate this office from the mission entrusted
> to the whole body of Bishops, who are also 'vicars and
> ambassadors of Christ'. The Bishop of Rome is a member
> of the 'College', and the Bishops are his brothers in the
> ministry.[30]

Because the papacy is not immune to the shaping influences of its
historical context, the particular form of papacy which we inherited at
the beginning of this century was one which exercised extraordinary
authority and appeared at times to be 'above' and 'apart from' the
rest of the church. However, the teaching of Vatican I which worries
Reinhard Frieling was, in fact, *received* in a new context by the Second
Vatican Council which located the pope in the college of bishops
and located the Church of Rome in the communion of churches.
Consequently, when Pope John Paul II asks for assistance from pastors
and theologians of other communions to help him to find ways of
exercising his papal ministry, which 'while not renouncing what is
essential to its mission, is nonetheless open to a new situation', he is
referring, I believe, to the changed situation created by the ecumenical
movement and the changes already occurring in the shape of papal
ministry because of the Second Vatican Council. No-one knows
completely what reshaping or restructuring of this ministry is still
possible without undermining what is essential to the mission of the
bishop of Rome. But there is no reason to believe that any changes
would only be cosmetic or slight.

All in all, I am not worried by what may seem a major obstacle
to the restoration of full communion. I believe that, if the bishop of
Rome begins to adapt his ministry in the light of what he calls 'the new
situation', given the insights he is likely to receive from a much more
intense reflection upon his ministry in all the churches, and given an
increasing openness to work with that ministry by other Christians,
we can safely leave the future in God's hands. I believe that, through
the guidance of the Holy Spirit, Catholics will define more and more
carefully and clearly what they perceive to be essential to this ministry.

---

30. *Ut Unum Sint*, 94–5.

They may discover for themselves that aspects of papacy which they thought were essential are, in fact, historical accretions. Protestants, Anglicans and Orthodox, on the other hand, may grow more used to a ministry of the bishop of Rome and may find in it something of the life-giving ministry that Catholics find. Who knows what then may be possible. God does, and I trust that God will bring it about.

Evangelisation and Ecumenism: Is Common Witness Possible?

In the *Directory for the Application of Principles and Norms on Ecumenism*, published in 1993 by the Pontifical Council for Promoting Christian Unity in Rome, paragraphs 205 to 209 are grouped under a heading: *Co-operation and Missionary Activity*. The opening sentence of 205 reads: 'The common witness given by all forms of ecumenical cooperation is already missionary'. The point made in the rest of the paragraph is the classic one which lies at the foundation of the whole modern ecumenical movement that the divisions between Christian churches are a major obstacle to the preaching of the gospel and that ecumenical collaboration as common witness is a positive contribution to the preaching of the gospel.

The next paragraph begins with what for many Catholics would be a fairly startling claim: 'Ecumenical witness can be given in missionary activity itself'. In other words, while co-operation in all kinds of activities from worship through to welfare is an obvious positive contribution to our missionary activity, the *Directory* is going much further in suggesting that ecumenical co-operation is possible in proclaiming the gospel itself. It suggests that the basis for this ecumenical witness is our common baptism and our common patrimony of faith.

The rest of the text explores all the issues involved in such co-operation. Of particular interest for those of us who live in Australia or New Zealand would be paragraph 28 which says:

> Ecumenical co-operation is particularly necessary
> in the mission to the de-christianised masses of our

This paper was presented at a workshop at the *Hearts on Fire* Conference in Brisbane in July 1999.

contemporary world. The ability of Christians though still divided, to bear common witness, even now to central truths of the gospel can be a powerful invitation to a renewed appreciation of Christian faith in a secularised society.

In 1995, Pope John Paul II published an encyclical letter entitled *Ut Unum Sint*. This is one of the most remarkable documents of his pontificate. In a marvellous section, paragraph 84, the pope spoke of the common witness shown in the twentieth century by countless martyrs of all Christian communions who have shed their blood because of their fidelity to Jesus Christ. For him this showed that 'at a profound level, God preserves communion among the baptised in the supreme demand of faith, manifested in the sacrifice of life itself. The fact that one can die for the faith shows that other demands of the faith can also be met'. In my words, if we can be one in death, can we not be one in life, by God's grace? Pope John Paul II went on to say that he believed that the imperfect communion between our churches 'is already perfect in what all consider the highest point of the life of grace, *martyria* unto death, the truest communion possible with Christ who shed his blood and by that sacrifice brings near those who were far off (Eph 2:13)'.

This is an extraordinary example of common witness that challenges us all to take seriously our responsibility, not only to give evangelical witness by our ecumenical collaboration, but to actually co-operate ecumenically in our evangelisation. If we can die together for Jesus, surely we can speak his name together to our society.

The possibility of common witness has already been discussed in various dialogues between the Catholic Church and other Christian churches. In 1981 the Joint Working Group (JWG) between the Roman Catholic Church and the World Council of Churches (WCC) produced a report entitled *Common Witness*. I would like to quote a paragraph from it:

> When he prayed that all be one so the world might believe (John 17:21), Jesus made a clear connection between the unity of the Church and the acceptance of the Gospel. Unhappily Christians are still divided in their churches and the testimony they give to the Gospel is thus weakened. There are, however, even now many

signs of the initial unity that already exists among all followers of Christ and indications that it is developing in important ways. What we have in common, and the hope that is in us, enable us to be bold in proclaiming the Gospel and trustful that the world will receive it. Common witness is the essential calling of the Church and in an especial way it responds to the spirit of this ecumenical age in the Church's life. It expresses our actual unity and increases our service to God's word, strengthening the churches both in proclaiming the Gospel and in seeking for the fullness of unity.[1]

In describing what common witness might involve, the text emphasised two different dimensions. Firstly: 'Through proclaiming the cross and resurrection of Christ, they affirm [that is, those engaged in common witness] that God wills the salvation of his people in all dimensions of their being, eternal and earthly'. Secondly, it recognised: '[Common witness] means Christian involvement in matters of social justice in the name of the poor and the oppressed'.

Right throughout the history of the WCC there have been tensions between the different movements which brought it into being. For example, there is a tension between the Justice, Peace and the Integrity of Creation (JPIC) stream/movement/programme and the Faith and Order Commission (FOC) or Christian Unity movement/stream/programme. In their earlier forms, these two movements were present and participated in the formation of the WCC fifty years ago. However, it was only in 1961 that the International Missionary Council became part of the WCC. As someone who has been most involved in the FOC stream I have continually argued for its importance, indeed its necessity, in the WCC and the larger ecumenical movement. However, I have to say that whatever marginalisation I may have imagined had occurred for the FOC or the quest for Christian unity, such marginalisation is nothing in comparison with the marginalisation of the missionary movement within the larger ecumenical movement and the WCC. The missionary movement has always been 'the poor relation'.

---

1. 'Common Witness: Joint Working Group between the Roman Catholic Church and the WCC, 1982', in *The Ecumenical Movement: An Anthology of Key Texts and Voices*, edited by Michael Kinnamon and Brien E Cope (Geneva: WCC, 1997), 386.

Many ecumenists seem to be either focused on the world and its need for justice, peace and the protection of the environment, or on the churches and their need to come together in Christian unity. I do not deny that working for justice, peace and the integrity of creation is integral to the mission of the church and unity between the churches is crucial to its mission. However, I believe that the foundational missionary dynamic of wishing to proclaim Jesus Christ to the world very seldom comes to the forefront in ecumenical programmes or even, I fear, in the heart of many ecumenists. Everyone easily points to the Johannine text containing Jesus' prayer that we would be one so that the world might believe that it is the Father who sent him, but we are too easily sidetracked into affirming only the first part of his prayer: 'that they/we may be one'; or unconsciously concluding it only with: 'so that the world will exist in justice, peace and protective of the integrity of creation'.

In 1997, the fourth phase of the International Dialogue between the Catholic Church and some representatives or members of classical Pentecostal Churches came to a conclusion. The topic for the phase, from 1990 to 1997, was 'Evangelisation, Proselytism and Common Witness'. The report is a very interesting document because, as many would know, in parts of Latin America there can sometimes be great tensions between the Roman Catholic Church and Pentecostal Churches because of the rapid growth of the latter at the expense of the former. In paragraph 118, a kind of definition of 'common witness' emerges:

> Common witness means standing together and sharing together in witness to our common faith. Common witness can be experienced through joint participation in worship, in prayer, in the performance of good works in Jesus' name and especially in evangelization. True common witness is not engaged in for any narrow, strategic denominational benefit of a particular community. Rather, it is concerned solely for the glory of God, for the good of the whole church and the good of humankind.[2]

---

2. 'Evangelization, Proselytism and Common Witness', in *Information Service*, 97 (1998/I–II): 52.

There is no suggestion in the report, in fact the contrary, that such common witness between Catholics and Pentecostals would be easy. Later in paragraph 122 the report indicates that when it speaks of common witness it is not suggesting that there should be any compromise involved in making this possible. On the contrary, 'Common witness is not a call to indifference or to uniformity', it says. The report clearly affirms that common witness does not prevent individuals, communities or churches from witnessing to their own distinctive heritage and, indeed, witnessing separately on matters about which they disagree. 'However', as it says, 'this can be done without being contentious, with mutual love and respect'.

I think this document stands as a testimony to the fertility of the ecumenical movement through the generous loving activity of the Holy Spirit. It also stands as a challenge to Australian churches involved in the ecumenical movement. They are very often willing to bear common witness on issues of justice, but sometimes less willing to bear common witness to the gift of salvation in Jesus Christ. I believe both forms of witness are essential and integrally related.

To offer Jesus Christ to a society is to offer the way of life which he came to initiate in our world and that means to offer justice, peace and care for the environment. But common witness does mean offering Jesus Christ. Have some of us perhaps become just a little reticent about this? Is one reason for such reticence the fact that we have entered into dialogue with our culture and with other world religions? If reticence is a result of such dialogue, we have misunderstood the nature of dialogue. Authentic dialogue presupposes genuine witness. There is no value in dialoguing with 'the other' whoever that may be if we are not truly ourselves, and to be truly ourselves is to be truly Christian, to be truly disciples of Jesus Christ. In our case it means being truly convinced that he is the way, the truth and the life.

I would hope we go much further than we already have as Christian churches in our dialogue with world religions. I would hope that we have enormous respect for the gifts of our culture and the signs of the Spirit that are there before we even utter one word of the gospel. At the same time, I believe we carry within ourselves and in our communities an enormous treasure which is the knowledge and love of God revealed to us in Jesus Christ, and I would hope that we are willing to offer this gift, the greatest of all, to our society—and sometimes even to offer this gift together.

If we are so willing, and presumably many are, the question arises of how we might deal with those matters about which we disagree. One has to affirm continually that when Christian churches are involved in ecumenical collaboration, they don't in any way compromise their own conviction about the truth of the gospel as they understand it, or their perception of the kind of church structure that is asked of them in their faithfulness to the apostolic tradition of the gospel. Collaboration in evangelisation, or common witness in that sense, is not possible without serious dialogue about what can be said together and what cannot, and what will happen to people who come to faith in Jesus Christ because of our common witness and seek to be united with a Christian community. In response to this latter question, I usually argue in favour of directing people to the community of their baptism, or of their family. We ought be wary of engaging in any evangelical collaboration without some such agreement being reached between the participating churches.

This, of course, raises considerable problems for newer churches whose members are drawn almost entirely from people who belong to or who were baptised into, or whose families belong to, another church. Moreover, for some churches, the question of which church one belongs to is not of great importance. What matters is whether one has accepted Jesus Christ as one's Lord and Saviour, or whether one has been baptised in the Holy Spirit. While Catholics also would believe in the fundamental experience of conversion and transformation involved in accepting Jesus Christ into one's life and in the power of the Holy Spirit in one's life, they would also believe that this reaches its fullest expression in a church community. Moreover, they believe that it does matter to which church community one belongs because what one believes matters, and how one worships matters. Where there are disagreements, we would believe one has to speak the truth to each other in love and not settle for contradictions or oppositions as if they were of no consequence.

Evangelisation, or evangelism, with all the challenges which I have just outlined has to be an integral part of the common witness of Christian churches. But it is not all of it. Integral to bearing witness to our living the gospel is the way in which we live and the kind of world we are called to work for by the grace of God. To proclaim Jesus and not also to be willing to proclaim reconciliation with Indigenous

Australians, for example, is to proclaim a Jesus who is not the Jesus of the gospels. At the same time, to proclaim justice and peace and the integrity of creation but not Jesus is to offer only the fruits and not the source of the new life our world needs so desperately.

I would like to repeat, by way of conclusion, the point made in the paragraph first cited from the JWG: 'Common witness expresses our actual unity, increases our service of God's word, and strengthens each of our churches both in our proclamation and in our seeking of the fullness of unity with each other'. In other words, to struggle with all the issues that arise in trying to bear witness at times together will not only strengthen the witness itself, our proclamation of the gospel itself, but also our movement towards Christian unity. Not to struggle with the issues that arise around common witness is to seek Christian unity as an end in itself, forgetting the prayer of Jesus: 'Father, that we may become one so that Australia will believe that it is you who sent him'.

An Australian Catholic Comment on 'We Remember: A Reflection on the Shoah'

I do not have a memory of a particularly strong attitude of any kind towards the Jewish people or to Judaism when I was a child. This can largely be explained by the fact that I grew up in Townsville and never actually met a Jew until I was an adult in Brisbane. Nonetheless, I do remember believing that Jews must be rather obstinate people for failing even until then to accept Jesus Christ as their long awaited messiah. This obstinacy, I believed and would have been taught, was a continuation of their most fundamental failure as a people which occurred when they rejected Jesus during his lifetime and even plotted for and called for his execution. The only memories I have of the Holocaust were of considering it as the greatest of the crimes of the Nazis during the war, which more than anything proved how evil they were and how noble were the Allied soldiers who were victorious over them. I was always profoundly moved by images of the victims of the Holocaust, as I continue to be today.

My youthful, simplistic and rather negative attitude to the Jewish people and Judaism was not untypical of my other attitudes at the time, and was perhaps typical of many of my young co-religionists. I had similarly negative attitudes to Protestants of all kinds. They were guilty of rejecting the truth in their break with the Catholic Church and with the bishop of Rome. As such they were worthy targets for evangelisation and for all kinds of uncritically adopted prejudices in word and attitude. Because there were Protestants readily at hand my attitude towards them was much stronger and more active than my negative view of Jews.

This article is the text of an address given at the Great Synagogue on 28 May 1998 at a meeting between the Bishops' Committee for Ecumenical and Interfaith Relations and the Executive Council of Australian Jewry. It was later published in *Australasian Catholic Record*, 76/3 (July 1999): 343–9.

All of this changed when I entered the seminary, because I was privileged to be a student during the Second Vatican Council. The great wind of change which swept through the church also swept through my attitudes and beliefs. I became a convert to ecumenism while in my first or second year in the seminary. *Unitatis Redintegratio*, the Decree on Ecumenism, became my new teacher and guide. Since that time I have devoted much of my time and energy to the ecumenical movement. It has been a lifelong process of letting go of prejudices and growing in acceptance of 'the other', in this case 'Christian other' as friend, as brother/sister, as one's equal before God, as example of authentic religious life, and ultimately as gift in which to rejoice.

While this was happening with respect to my fellow Christians something similar had the potential to happen with respect to the Jewish people and to Judaism, and then for other great world religions. The publication of *Nostra Aetate*, the Decree on Non-Christian Religions, I accepted with the same enthusiasm. However, because I was not in any contact with Jews, or in turn with representatives of any other world religions, I did not begin the same journey of conversion which had begun for me with respect to other Christian Churches.

This journey of conversion of my heart, mind, attitudes and actions towards Jewish people and Judaism is really only now beginning so late in my life. So it is that I have greeted this document from the Vatican Commission for Religious Relations with the Jews, 'We Remember: A Reflection on the *Shoah*' as a neophyte, one eager to learn from wiser, more experienced Catholic and Jewish commentators. My own reaction was to recognise that at times the document expressed well my Catholic sentiments—when, for example, it said that the 'inhumanity with which Jews were persecuted and massacred during this century is beyond the capacity of words to convey', especially because all this was done to them 'for the sole reason that they were Jews'. The document rightly acknowledged that while bearing their 'unique witness to the Holy One of Israel and to the Torah', the Jewish people have suffered much in different times and places but the *Shoah* was the worst suffering of all.

The document also correctly noted that someone like myself, a Christian, can least of all remain indifferent to the *Shoah* because of our 'very close bonds of spiritual kinship with the Jewish people' and because of our 'remembrance of the injustices of the past'. Only six years ago, in May 1992, not far from here in the crypt of St Mary's Cathedral, Bishop Bede Heather, at the time Bishop of Parramatta and Chairman of the Bishops Committee for Ecumenical and Interfaith Relations, launched what was for the Australian Catholic Bishops' Conference a very important milestone, its *Guidelines for Catholic-Jewish Relations*. On that occasion Bishop Heather spoke of the special bond between the Catholic Church and Judaism but likewise he went on to say, after describing our shared love of the Hebrew scriptures:

> I would not want to leave the impression, however, that it is only in our common esteem for a sacred literature that we are bound together.
>
> The Church and the synagogue have also shared a history of 2000 years in Europe and in countries like ours, of culture derived from Europe. Each of us has known oppression and persecution. We have often been antagonists. The Jewish people have often suffered at our hands, as in their expulsion from Spain in 1492, recalled recently in one of the synagogues of Sydney. I trust that a fresh start has been made. The Church needs not only the ancient and sacred scriptures of Judaism but the Judaism of the present. It tells us of God's unfailing promises and reminds us of the undying quality of faith tenaciously held through persecution and oppression of the worst kind.[1]

One of the questions which arises immediately for any Catholic willing to remember such injustices of the past referred to in the Vatican document is 'the relation between the Nazi persecution and the attitude down the centuries of Christians toward the Jews'. How much is it our fault? Such a question is almost too difficult to face because of the enormity and horror of the tragedy of the *Shoah* and the fear of the ensuing shame should the verdict be that we are more guilty than we have hitherto believed. I am relieved that my church is,

---

1. 'Catholic Jewish Relations: On the Delicate Path of Faith', in *Catholic Weekly* (11 November 1992): 22.

nonetheless, trying to face the question. I am also relieved that there are many stories of Catholics in many European countries who made great sacrifices and took great risks to protect their Jewish neighbours. We have been inspired in this self-examination by the leadership of Pope John Paul II and his call in *Tertio Millennio Adveniente* for us to examine our consciences about our history before we enter into any celebration of the 2000th anniversary of the birth of Jesus Christ. He urged us to recall all the times in the past when we have sinned as a people and to acknowledge them with honesty and courage so that we might purify ourselves 'through repentance, of past errors and instances of infidelity, inconsistency, and slowness to act' (33).

When speaking to Jewish Community leaders here in Sydney on 26 November 1986 Pope John Paul II called this 'the century of the Shoah, the inhuman and ruthless attempt to exterminate European Jewry'.[2] He went on to acknowledge that thousands of survivors of the Holocaust had settled in Australia after the war. This fact, that proportionally Australia has an exceptionally high percentage of survivors, lends a particular urgency to the self-questioning of Australian Catholics about the degree of guilt we must bear for this unbelievable tragedy.

The recent Vatican document offers a number of points by way of answer to this question. Firstly it recognises that on balance the tormented history of relations between Catholics and Jews over 2000 years has been a negative one. The root cause of this negative history is located in 'erroneous and unjust interpretations of the New Testament regarding the Jewish people and their alleged culpability' which have led to hostility towards the Jewish people. In a very damning paragraph the document describes the awful history of Christian maltreatment of the Jewish people:

> Despite the Christian preaching of love for all, even for one's enemies, the prevailing mentality down the centuries penalised minorities and those who were in any way different. Sentiments of anti-Judaism in some Christian quarters and the gap which existed between the church and the Jewish people led to a generalised

---

2. Australian Catholic Bishops' Conference, Bishops Committee for Ecumenical and Interfaith Relations, *The Faithfulness of the Lord Endures Forever: Guidelines for Catholic Jewish Relations, November 1992* (Canberra: ACBC, 1992), 14.

discrimination, which ended at times in expulsions or attempts at forced conversions. In a large part of the Christian world, until the end of the 18th century those who were not Christian did not always enjoy a fully guaranteed juridical status. Despite that fact, Jews throughout Christendom held on to their religious traditions and communal customs. They were therefore looked upon with a certain suspicion and mistrust. In times of crisis such as famine, war, pestilence or social tensions, the Jewish minority was sometimes taken as a scapegoat and became the victim of violence, looting, even massacres.[3]

At an international colloquium sponsored by the International Council of Christians and Jews, and held in Rome in September 1997, Cardinal Edward Cassidy, the Australian President of the Commission for Religious Relations with the Jews, gave the Rabbi Marc H Tanenbaum Keynote Address on the topic 'The Other as Mystery and Challenge'. In that address he explored another of the foundations of this tragic 'history' and 'teaching of contempt', as it has come to be called, in Christian anti-Judaism. 'All too often in history', he said, 'and unfortunately still in our own time, *the other* has been a motive for cruel indifference or even savage treatment'.[4] In speaking of the *Shoah* he made the point that 'people turned away, for after all they were not "ours", but belonged to *the other*'.

At a symposium held at the Vatican at the end of 1997 on 'The Roots of anti-Judaism in the Christian Milieu', Father Georges Cottier OP, theologian of the pontifical household, described anti-Judaism as follows: 'By anti-Judaism we mean the collection of prejudices and pseudo-theological judgments that for a long time have circulated among the populations marked by Christianity and which have served as pretexts for the unjustifiable humiliations which the Jewish people have suffered in the course of their history'.[5]

---

3. Commission for Religious Relations with the Jews, 'We Remember: A Reflection on the *Shoah*', in *Origins*, 27 (26 March 1998): 672.
4. Cardinal Edward Idris Cassidy, 'The Other as Mystery and Challenge' (unpublished manuscript).
5. 'The Roots of Anti-Judaism', in *Origins*, 27 (13 November 1997): 367.

The crucial question which is raised in the 1998 Vatican document is the extent to which anti-Judaism and a 'teaching of contempt' contributed to the secular, racist, anti-semitism of the Nazis which led to the *Shoah*. The document asked 'whether the Nazi persecution of the Jews was not made easier by the anti-Jewish prejudices imbedded in some Christian minds and hearts. Did anti-Jewish sentiment among Christians make them less sensitive, or even indifferent, to the persecutions launched against the Jews by National Socialism when it reached power?'[6] Its answer, a crucial one for all Catholics, was that, despite all the examples to the contrary, neither the action nor the protest of Christians when they were faced with the attempted liquidation of their Jewish neighbours was what it ought to have been. So true was this that the document could say that 'this heavy burden of conscience of their brothers and sisters during the Second World War must be a call to penitence'. It went on to say: 'We deeply regret the errors and failures of those sons and daughters of the church'. Then in its concluding paragraphs it added:

> At the end of this millennium the Catholic Church desires to express her deep sorrow for the failures of her sons and daughters in every age. This is an act of repentance (*teshuva*), since as members of the church we are linked to the sins as well as the merits of all her children. The church approaches with deep respect and great compassion the experience of extermination, the *Shoah*, suffered by the Jewish people during World War II. It is not a matter of mere words, but indeed a binding commitment. 'We would risk causing the victims of the most atrocious deaths to die again if we do not commit ourselves to ensure that evil does not prevail over good as it did for millions of the children of the Jewish people ... Humanity cannot permit all that to happen again.'[7]

In its last sentence the document links anti-Judaism and anti-Semitism together: 'The spoiled seeds of anti-Judaism and anti-Semitism must never again be allowed to take root in the human heart.'

---

6. 'We Remember: *A Reflection on the Shoah*', 673.
7. 'We Remember: A Reflection on the Shoah', 674. Quotation from address of Pope John Paul II at a commemoration of the *Shoah*, in *Insegnamenti* 17/1 (1994): 897, 893.

When the International Catholic Jewish Liaison Committee met at the Vatican in March 1998, after the publication of the long-awaited document, Geoffrey Wigoder of the Israel Inter-faith Committee told Pope John Paul II that:

> It was felt that the self-criticism—for all its importance—did not go far enough and that the connection between the long history of anti-Jewish conditioning under Christian auspices and the widespread indifference and even collaboration throughout Europe during the 'Shoah' was not stated unequivocally and with sufficient clarity.[8]

Honorary Vice-President of the World Jewish Congress, Dr Gerhard Riegner, offered his own criticism:

> The document tries to exempt the church itself from any blame and charges individual Christians or 'the Christian world' of being responsible for 'the erroneous and unjust interpretations of the New Testament regarding the Jewish people and their alleged culpability which engendered feelings of hostility toward the Jews.[9]

Cardinal Cassidy tried to respond to some of these criticisms, pointing out that the use of *'the church'* in the document refers for Catholics to the inerrant mystical bride of Christ, and moreover references to *'sons and daughters'* of the church does not exclude any level of the church's membership. This is a frequent problem with Vatican references to the church itself and to the members of the church. The former is always exempted from sin which can only be found in the lives of its members. If the reader thinks 'the Church' refers to the hierarchy or to the Vatican then they will naturally be disturbed by official Catholic texts. This problem is avoided in the recent *Declaration of Repentance* of the bishops of France. Having recorded the fact that the hierarchy of the church in France during the Second World War gave an 'absolute priority' to protecting Catholics and its own institutions, and in excessive loyalty

---

8. 'International Catholic–Jewish Liaison Committee Meets at Vatican', in *Origins*, 27 (9 April 1998): 703.
9. 'International Catholic–Jewish Liaison Committee Meets at Vatican', 704.

and docility 'remained stuck in conformity, prudence and abstention' and so failed to realise that it was called to play the role of 'defender', it admitted honestly that 'ecclesiastical interests, understood in an overly restrictive sense, took priority over the demands of conscience'.[10]

In attempting to find an explanation for this failure, despite the teaching of the church about the sin of racism, the French bishops located it in the 'anti Jewish prejudices, which Christians were guilty of maintaining' which were a part of 'an animosity and ultimately a centuries-long hostility between Christians and Jews'. This hostility and prejudice, they confessed, 'stamped its mark in differing ways on Christian doctrine and teaching, in theology, apologetics, preaching and in the liturgy'. They concluded: 'It was in such ground that the venomous plant of hatred for the Jews was able to flourish.'[11] In the final paragraphs of their document, the French bishops speak directly to their Jewish neighbours:

> Today we confess that such a silence was a sin. In so doing, we recognise that the church of France failed in her mission as teacher of consciences and that therefore she carries along with the Christian people the responsibility for failing to lend their aid, from the very first moments, when protest and protection were still possible as well as necessary, even if, subsequently, a great many acts of courage were performed.
>
> This is the fact that we acknowledge today. For, this failing of the church of France and of her responsibility toward the Jewish people are part of our history. We confess this sin. We beg God's pardon, and we call upon the Jewish people, to hear our words of repentance.[12]

By all accounts, the confession of guilt of the French bishops was heard by the Jewish Community of France in a better way than the more recent Vatican document has been. However, even there, one must remember what the Catholic Jewish Liaison Committee indicated in its final communique:

---

10. 'French Bishops' Declaration of Repentance', in *Origins*, 27 (16 October 1997): 303.

11. 'French Bishops' Declaration of Repentance', 304.

12. 'French Bishops' Declaration of Repentance', 304–5.

Understanding the Vatican document on the *Shoah* as a beginning and not as an ending of the process, especially on the historical issues it raises, the International Liaison Committee as a whole expressed its commitment to continue the dialogue and to establish a joint group of historians and theologians to pursue further studies on the period of the *Shoah*, and to seek together the 'healing of memories'.[13]

As an Australian Catholic I now see the attitudes I carried as a youth, which I have never really addressed, as a less virulent form of the same anti-Judaism or 'contempt' that provided a breeding ground for the anti-Semitism which ultimately led to the *Shoah*. I am glad that Catholics in Australia never had to face the questions of conscience that our co-religionists faced in Europe, because I fear we would not have escaped with any less guilt than they have. I am also glad to be living at a time when the Catholic Church at all levels is trying to come to terms with its past failures, and to ask forgiveness for them. I wish to add my single Australian voice to so many more significant Catholic bodies to say how sorry I am that so many Catholics let you down so badly in your time of greatest need and I wish to play my part in changing the perceptions of Australian Catholics wherever it is necessary so that nothing like the *Shoah* may ever occur again.

---

13. 'International Catholic–Jewish Liaison Committee Meets at Vatican', 704. Since the meeting of 28 May 1998 at the Great Synagogue, other official responses to the Roman document have been published, for example, 'Catholics and Jews: "Creative Interfaith Dialogue"', in *Catholic International* (July 1998): 311–16; 'Heal the Wounds of Past Misunderstandings and Injustices', in *Catholic International* (October 1998): 448–53.

Baptism, Ecumenism and the RCIA

In the Decree on Ecumenism of the Second Vatican Council one reads:

> For people who believe in Christ and have been properly baptised are put in some, though imperfect, communion with the Catholic Church. Without doubt, the differences that exist in varying degrees between them and the Catholic Church—whether in doctrine and sometimes in discipline, or concerning the structure of the Church—do indeed create many obstacles, sometimes serious ones, to full ecclesiastical communion. The ecumenical movement is striving to overcome these obstacles. But even in spite of them it remains true that all who have been justified by faith in baptism are incorporated into Christ; they therefore have a right to be called Christians, and with good reason are accepted as brothers and sisters by the children of the Catholic Church (3).

My task here is to explore with you the relationship between baptism and the ecumenical movement, and the theology of communion which the Second Vatican Council used to describe it. The role of the eucharist in the ecumenical movement will then become clear.

Ecumenical Movement

Before we do anything else it is important to have a proper understanding of what we mean by ecumenism and hence what

This paper is an address given at the RCIA Conference in Toowoomba in September 2001.

is involved in the ecumenical movement. It is easy in a secular, 'post-modern' country like Australia to confuse ecumenism with the universal tolerance for others' opinions and practices which is now taken for granted as the hallmark of a modern, liberal society. Alternatively one could confuse it with what is better called 'non-denominationalism'. This latter is a relationship between Christian communities based upon a view that the differences between them can and ought be left aside or not even mentioned, for the sake of harmony in a common action or a common gathering, or even simply for living and working together as Christians.

Ecumenism is neither of these and involves so much more. It starts with the conviction that, in the beginning, Christ formed one community which became the one Church of Jesus Christ. This Church then suffered from any number of divisions throughout its history, so that today there are many churches which would view themselves as each more or less in continuity with that original Church of Jesus Christ. The task of the ecumenical movement is to restore that original unity. Consequently, ecumenism and the ecumenical movement take very seriously those things which divide churches one from another. If unity in Christ is to be restored, then the obstacles to that unity need to be overcome, whether they are obstacles in faith or order, or sometimes simply in social, political and even ethnic factors.

Ecumenism cannot afford to leave aside those things which separate Christians one from another and cannot be content with only the tolerant acceptances of these differences. This could not achieve full unity in Christ. Australians are often tempted to settle for less because our secular, 'post-modern' society approves of such solutions to ancient divisions in the community. Moreover, a 'post-modern' society sometimes does not believe that there is any point in trying to ascertain or discover which claim to the truth is valid. It is content to accept the diverse claims as somehow equally permissible, if not equally true. Very often Christians enter enthusiastically into the ecumenical movement, but the movement they have entered into is one defined by these categories which arise from our secular society rather than from the profound theological categories which are located in our Christian experience, and which have motivated the ecumenical movement from its beginning. In other words, ecumenism is a very profound Christian commitment, activity and experience.

In order to appreciate true ecumenism, one needs to recognise that it takes both love and truth seriously. Alternatively, it takes both charity and faith seriously. Too often, even within the one Church, people settle for one of these two qualities and emphasise it at the expense of the other. If one focuses almost solely on truth or faith, then one will lack that love which alone creates the restlessness and urgency to overcome the differences in faith or in perceptions of the truth that keep Christians or even Catholics divided from each other. If one focuses or commits oneself only to love and considers particular versions of the truth or of what we believe as secondary, then it is possible to enjoy very warm relationships, but relationships which are not based on a shared faith and which will eventually fall apart because of differences which will inevitably re-emerge. Alternatively, people will decide to consider the areas of difference as optional even for themselves and, consequently, begin to dismantle their Christian heritage.

For the Catholic Church ecumenism involves a deep commitment to love each other, to work with each other, to pray with each other and to commit ourselves to each other. This is the driving force to overcome the obstacles which keep us apart. At the same time, it involves a passion for the truth of Christ that each of us embraces in our confession of faith and which we believe binds us and shapes our relationship with God in Christ. The ecumenical movement requires loving truth and truthful love. It is never simply about truth or simply about love.

Ecumenism involves some pain at times because it requires courageous honesty in dealing with one's ecumenical partners. It cannot settle for avoiding the difficult issues or trying not to offend the other. The experience of ecumenical dialogue at international and national level is the opposite of this. It requires a relationship of love that can sustain very honest communication about painful differences of understanding and practice. There can be no compromise in ecumenical dialogue because the truth of Christ is at stake. The hope always is that we will discover through our dialogue that what appears to be completely opposed perceptions of the truth are, in fact, differing perspectives on the one truth, and especially that we will discover that these perspectives are not opposed but are compatible. This has happened on a great range of questions, the most recent of which was illustrated by the Agreement on Justification between the Lutheran World Federation and our own Catholic Church. We have very different ways of speaking about and dealing with the issue of justification but these differences are not necessarily opposed but, in fact, can be two perspectives on the one truth which we then can claim to share.

Ecumenical Dialogue

To appreciate the way ecumenical dialogue occurs when one takes both love and truth seriously, one can look at the two qualities which are essential for any participant in serious ecumenical dialogue or even a serious ecumenical relationship. These are the qualities of openness and fidelity. Each partner in the dialogue must be faithful to their own tradition or no real encounter will occur which can make possible a movement forward to reconcile the diverse and apparently opposed traditions. If one partner to the dialogue does not know what he or she believes about his or her tradition, then the other partner has no-one really with whom to dialogue for the sake of reconciliation.

Reconciliation between diverse and apparently opposed traditions can only come about when the partners to the relationship recognise in the other tradition the one apostolic tradition which comes from Christ, which they believe their own tradition has faithfully continued. Each partner believes that in the faith they confess they are being faithful to Christ and, therefore, in continuity with that great apostolic tradition. The aim of dialogue is for them to reach the point of recognising, in a very different and apparently opposed version of the faith, that one apostolic tradition which they believe they are professing. When recognition occurs on both sides then reconciliation becomes more possible. One can see this process of reaching a level of recognition occurring in the relationship between Lutherans and Catholics over the question of justification.

The other quality though, along with fidelity, is that of openness. If each partner is not only faithful to their tradition but open to what they will discover, then the relationship can become truly and fruitfully ecumenical. Not to be open is to settle for some kind of dogmatism that makes it impossible to progress ecumenically. At the same time what one is being open to is, on the most profound level, what the Holy Spirit will lead one to discover, not only about the other but about oneself, through the ecumenical relationship. If one is open to what the Spirit will reveal when encountering representatives of another Christian communion with their diverse ways of speaking and praying and confessing the faith, then one may not only discover that they are professing the same faith or expressing the same spirituality or living according to the same morality, but one may also discover one's own faith, one's own moral teaching, and one's own spiritual experience in a new way. The provocation of the other alerts one to one's own identity in a new and purer way.

To give an example, during the discussions on eucharist which took place in Windsor between Anglicans and Roman Catholics in the 1970s, apparently the two people who had most difficulty agreeing during the dialogue were an evangelical Anglican and a rather conservative Catholic. The rest had reached agreement about some aspect of the eucharist but these two could not, and the others stood back and watched them talk until eventually, late in the afternoon, they heard one say: 'Is that what you mean when you say such-and-such?' and when he received an affirmative reply, was able to utter, 'Well that's what I believe also'. This was a moment of enlightenment when they discovered that they shared the same faith. So while each of them was deeply and truly faithful to their tradition they were also open to what they would discover through this encounter or this meeting with another tradition, in Christ. The Holy Spirit could lead them to discover a shared way of expressing the apostolic tradition in which they could both be faithful and yet rediscover a unity which had been hidden from them. It was in this way that the Anglican–Roman Catholic International Commission produced those beautiful documents on eucharist and ministry which expressed our common faith in a new language, but yet in a way that each party could say was completely consistent with their own understanding of the gospel.[1]

This is probably enough to explain how ecumenism is a very demanding and deeply spiritual commitment and the ecumenical movement is a very profound work of the Spirit in the Christian

---

1. See Anglican–Roman Catholic International Commission, *The Final Report* (London: CTS/SPCK, 1982).

churches. It is trivialised when people think it is some kind of attempt to merge diverse Christian traditions by simply leaving aside the difficult areas or the points of conflict. It is a work of the one Christ in whom we all live, drawing together those who are already one in him on the deepest level and yet apart from each other in so many ways. On the night before he died Christ prayed that we might be one so that the world would believe that it was the Father who sent him. That prayer continues in every Christian heart because every Christian heart is united with Christ's own heart through baptism. We are one with him in every way, and so the longing that moved him to express that prayer is found in every Christian heart. The Holy Spirit through the ecumenical movement turns that longing into action, dialogue and prayer, so that step by step, divided Christians can not only individually be one with Christ but can together become fully one with him again.

Baptism

If that is what we mean by the ecumenical movement it is important to explore its relationship with baptism, because baptism is, in many ways, the source of the ecumenical movement. It is through baptism that we are made one in Christ and therefore already experience unity in some way. In the Decree on Ecumenism the relationship of baptism to the ecumenical movement is described as follows:

> Baptism, therefore, constitutes the sacramental bond of unity existing among all who through it are reborn. But baptism, of itself, is only a beginning, a point of departure, for it is wholly directed toward the acquiring of fullness of life in Christ. Baptism is thus ordained toward a complete profession of faith, a complete incorporation into the system of salvation such as Christ himself willed it to be, and finally through a complete integration into eucharistic communion (22).

We see in this quotation that baptism constitutes a 'sacramental bond' of unity. All of those who are reborn in Christ who, as St Paul says, are buried with him and rise again in him in baptism, are united to each other by the bond that this sacrament establishes. Each has received the visible sacramental rite and on the deepest and invisible level is reborn in Christ. However, when we speak of their also being incorporated into the visible Church through this baptism, which is itself a sign of their being incorporated into Christ, we acknowledge that they are incorporated into separate Christian churches. So this sacramental bond which unites them does not carry them into the full ecclesial relationship which, as the Decree noted, would require of them a common profession of faith and a common incorporation into the system of salvation willed by Christ and, finally, a complete integration into one eucharistic communion. None of these further bonds of profession of faith, sharing in the means of salvation and common eucharist, follow as a consequence when baptism is administered separately in divided Christian communities. So the sacramental bond of unity established by baptism does not of itself express the full ecclesial unity which is Christ's will for all Christians.

The ecumenical movement based on the sacramental bond of baptism draws its strength from that relationship which all Christians have to Christ and, therefore, to each other through baptism, and is precisely geared at achieving those further bonds of unity which remain lacking, despite the foundational sacramental bond of baptism. In *Ut Unum Sint* of 1995, Pope John Paul II described the foundational role of baptism in the ecumenical movement in these words:

> On the eve of his sacrifice on the cross, Jesus himself prayed to the Father for all his disciples and for all those who believe in him, that they *might be one*, a living communion. This is the basis not only of the duty, but also of the responsibility before God and his plan, which falls to those who through baptism become members of the Body of Christ, a body in which the fullness of reconciliation and communion must be made present. How is it possible to remain divided, if we have been 'buried' through baptism in the Lord's death, in the very act by which God, through the death of his Son, has broken down the walls of division? Division 'openly contradicts the will of Christ, providing a stumbling block to the world, and inflicts damage on the most holy

cause of proclaiming the good news to every creature'
(6).

In fact, the ecumenical movement may be described as a movement from the unity established by baptism to the full unity achieved in a common celebration of the eucharist or, in other words, from the real though imperfect communion achieved by a common baptism through to the full communion that is realised in the celebration of a common eucharist.

The Church as Communion

It is impossible to understand the relationship between baptism and the ecumenical movement, and eucharist and the ecumenical movement, without appreciating the profound importance of the theology of the Church as communion. Understanding the Church in this way was, in fact, at the heart of the teachings of the Second Vatican Council and has become the primary way of talking about the Church in many ecumenical dialogues since then. In *Ut Unum Sint* Pope John Paul II described this theology of communion in these terms:

> The faithful are *one* because, in the Spirit, they are in *communion* with the Son and, in him, share in his *communion* with the Father: 'Our *fellowship* is with the Father and with his Son Jesus Christ' (1 John 1:3). For the Catholic Church, then, the *communion* of Christians is none other than the manifestation in them of the grace by which God makes them sharers in his own *communion* which is his eternal life. Christ's words 'that they may be one' are thus his prayer to the Father that the Father's plan may be fully accomplished, in such a way that everyone may clearly see 'what is the plan of the mystery hidden for ages in God who created all things' (Ephesians 3:9). To believe in Christ means to desire unity; to desire unity means to desire the Church; to desire the Church means to desire the communion of grace which corresponds to the Father's plan from all eternity. Such is the meaning of Christ's prayer: '*Ut unum sint*' (9).

From this quotation it is clear that if we are to understand the Church as a communion we need to appreciate that the communion we have with each other as Christians is achieved through the grace of the communion which each of us and all of us together have with God, whereby God shares with all those who are baptised a participation in the very inner life of the Trinity. Through the Holy Spirit we are made one with the Son and thereby drawn, in the Son, into an intimate relationship with the Father. This participation in the communion of the Trinity establishes our communion with each other.

The word 'communion' therefore is a much more profound word than 'community', which has many meanings and always refers to our relationships with each other. 'Communion', on the other hand, is a relationship we have with each other because of a common participation in the very inner life of God. In the opening verses of the first letter of John we read:

> We declare to you what was from the beginning, what we have heard, what we have seen with our eyes, what we have looked at and touched with our hands, concerning the word of life—this life was revealed, and we have seen it and testified to it and declared to you the eternal life that was with the Father and was revealed to us—we declare to you what we have seen and heard so that you also may have fellowship with us; and truly our fellowship is with the Father and with his Son Jesus Christ. We are writing these things so that our joy may be complete (1 John 1:1–4).

St John says that he shares his faith with others or shares his own experience of Christ with others, so that they may have communion or fellowship with him. He has communion with the Father and with his Son Jesus Christ, and his proclamation of the gospel, which leads others to faith in that same gospel, and so to communion with him who proclaimed it, will take them into this same deeper communion which it expresses and reflects, which is communion with the triune God. This is, of course, a profound explanation of evangelisation. When we proclaim the gospel, we are inviting people into communion with God through their communion with us, by receiving the gift of faith through our proclamation.

Catholics understand ecumenism as the work of drawing Christians who share a very real communion with the triune God, but one which is imperfectly realised in their communion with each other, to a full communion with each other, so that Christ's prayer that we may be one so that the world may believe that it is indeed the Father who has sent him, will be fully answered.

I have already said that I believe that ecumenism is the movement from the communion we have through baptism to the communion we will have at one eucharistic table. This relationship between baptism and eucharist and the ecumenical movement raises many questions about our approach to eucharistic hospitality and intercommunion. This deserves our special attention.

Sharing in Sacramental Life

In *Ut Unum Sint* 46, Pope John Paul II said:

> It is a source of joy to note that Catholic ministers are able, in certain particular cases, to administer the sacraments of the Eucharist, Penance, and Anointing of the Sick to Christians who are not in full communion with the Catholic Church . . . Conversely, in specific cases and, in particular circumstances, Catholics too can request these same sacraments from ministers of Churches in which these sacraments are valid.

He went on to say: 'The conditions for such reciprocal reception have been laid down in specific norms; for the sake of furthering ecumenism these norms must be respected'. At first glance, there might appear to be a tension between the joy of the Holy Father at the beginning of this paragraph that, in fact, there can be some sharing in sacramental life, and his call at the end of the paragraph for Catholics to respect the norms that have been laid down concerning this sharing in sacramental life. But note that he says that these norms should be respected for the sake of furthering ecumenism.

Our Catholic principles of ecumenism are most obvious when dealing with this question. The principles which govern sharing in worship for Catholics are the following:

(1) Because there is a real, if imperfect communion among all Christians through their common faith and baptism, prayer and worship together ought be integral to their Christian life.

(2) At the same time, this communion between them is incomplete and this, too, must be expressed in authentic worship.

(3) So it is that Catholics do not participate fully in a common eucharist with other Christians. As the *Directory for the Application of Principles and Norms on Ecumenism* explains:

> A Sacrament is an act of Christ and of the Church through the Spirit. Its celebration in a concrete community is the sign of the reality of its unity in faith, worship and community life. As well as being signs, sacraments—most specially the eucharist—are sources of the unity of the Christian community and of spiritual life, and are means of building them up. Thus eucharistic communion is inseparably linked to full ecclesial communion and its visible expression (129).

(4) It goes on to articulate the final principle that, nonetheless, because the 'Eucharist is, for the baptised, a spiritual food which enables them to overcome sin and to live the very life of Christ, to be incorporated more profoundly in Him and share more intensely in the whole economy of the Mystery of Christ', the Catholic Church sometimes can welcome other Christians to eucharist who need its spiritual nourishment and, given their circumstances, ask it of the Catholic Church. The same applies as well to penance and the anointing of the sick for similar reasons.

Too often today people tend to believe that these Catholic principles concerning sharing in sacramental life are an indication of some failure on the part of the Catholic Church to catch up with the rest of the ecumenical movement. What is at stake here, however, is precisely the difference between the Catholic Church and some other Christian communities in their understanding of the relationship between the sacraments and the Church, especially the eucharist and the Church, and indeed of the Church itself. A Protestant approach to these questions has sometimes been understood as the ecumenical approach itself and, consequently, the Catholic, and indeed the

Orthodox approach, is somehow seen to be unecumenical. This interpretation of the issue is one which, on a popular level, even many Catholics share.

We have an enormous public relations problem here and an enormous communications gap, even with our own Catholic community. We often appear simply to be mean, or hard, or legalistic, rather than hospitable, open and inclusive. It is extremely difficult to convince people that the Catholic approach to this question flows inevitably out of its self-understanding. Our ecumenical principles flow from our understanding of the Church which is a eucharistic understanding, and more broadly a sacramental one. We could not have a different perspective on the question of admission of others to the eucharist and other sacraments without changing our understanding of the Church.

Our discipline on this matter may be able to be adjusted but it is protecting something quite fundamental in Catholic self-understanding and whatever adjustments are made, that self-understanding needs to be protected at all costs. For example, I think we can continue to reflect upon and discuss the occasions for admitting other Christians in interchurch marriages to our sacraments, without jeopardising that self-understanding. But to agree that all participants at Catholic masses from other Christian communities can receive communion, even if only on special occasions, would be to jeopardise that fundamental self-understanding.

Many issues are at stake here and many factors need to be considered. There is the question of the relationship between a commitment to the truth and a commitment to love, the relationship between fidelity and openness, the question of the boundaries of inclusion and the limits of diversity. There is most fundamentally the ecclesial significance of the eucharist, which too easily is left aside in favour of the personal dimension of eucharist and the desire of the individual, not only for the eucharist but also for inclusion in the community. The very desire of Catholics to include others in their eucharist is the fundamental ecumenical passion that arises from baptism. The question which needs to be addressed is: What has to be achieved before one can include someone in one's most fundamental self-realisation as a church? To do so too easily, too regularly, or too widely is to risk changing the definition of one's own identity.

At the same time, to be unnecessarily rigid in the application of the norms that we do have is to turn what John Paul II described as a 'joy' into a 'burden' for the Church. We have to be as creative and generous as those norms permit. If we are to protect the very ecclesiological values that are at stake, we have to somehow communicate both our joy at the possibilities that are there, our sadness at the possibilities that are not there, and our conviction that the lack of possibility arises because of the fundamental divisions among Christians and, at the same time, the unbreakable relationship between the eucharist and the Church.

This is a major task confronting the Catholic Church in many parts of the world as it engages in closer ecumenical relationships. The temptation is simply to capitulate for the sake of harmony, or because one in fact has adopted what is essentially a Protestant view of the relationship between the eucharist and the Church. When I say that, I am not suggesting such a view is not a thoroughly thought through, plausible, and inherently ecumenical point of view, but it arises out of a different understanding of the Church, and this needs to be borne in mind very seriously by all who are reflecting upon the Catholic Church's response to this matter.

One of the ways of describing a Catholic approach to ecumenism would be to say again that it is a movement from baptismal communion to eucharistic communion. We start with the communion we already share through baptism and through faith in Jesus Christ and recognise that there are degrees of this communion. Baptismal communion requires eucharistic communion of its very nature but this has been excluded by our foolishness and sinfulness which have disrupted the communion which our common baptism established. The motivation for a Catholic ecumenist to dedicate himself or herself to the ecumenical movement could be described most simply as the desire to share eucharist with one's fellow Christians.

When schism occurred in the early Church, the situation was sometimes very graphically described in terms of Christians setting up another altar, because any division among Christians became apparent at the table of the eucharist. Christians no longer communicated together because they were no longer in communion.

The naming of the local bishop and the pope in each of our Eucharistic Prayers is a continuation of the practice of the early church when the names of bishops heading churches with which one was in communion were listed in one's own Eucharistic Prayer. To go forward to receive communion during a eucharist is to receive the gift of union, not only with the sacramental body of Jesus Christ, but also with the visible ecclesial body, the Church, with which one is celebrating.

The Church of Jesus Christ is understood by Roman Catholics to be a sacramental reality and not simply a spiritual one. It is concretely, visibly, structurally, as well as spiritually, realised in a eucharistic gathering. Consequently going forward for communion would normally not be considered at a eucharist where the bishop celebrating or mentioned in the Eucharistic Prayer was not in communion with one's own bishop, because ecclesial communion would not be sufficiently realised on the visible level of church life. In fact, the existence of separate altars would itself be seen as a manifestation of division rather than of communion.

More general intercommunion on the part of Roman Catholics would risk trivialising for them their perception of the ecclesial dimension of eucharistic communion and the division remaining between Christian communions. For them, eucharistic intercommunion presupposes and represents ecclesial communion. The two are inseparable. To share in the eucharist with other Christians as the norm is to be in full communion.

The efforts of Catholics to overcome Church divisions through dialogue and collaboration are precisely aimed at making it possible once more for divided Christians to celebrate one eucharist together. For Catholics, the ecumenical goal is simply one eucharist. This is what drives them forward ecumenically. If they were able without significant ambiguity to share eucharist with other Christians, all that really matters would have been achieved. There would be nothing of significance left to do. From that point the ecumenical movement would become purely an administrative or bureaucratic negotiation. Because they believe they cannot share more generally with other Christians, so they are committed to ecumenical dialogue and collaboration. Put simply, they are ecumenists because they want to share eucharist with other Christians.

Seeking Full Communion

If this is the relationship between baptism, eucharist and the ecumenical movement on the larger scale, what then of the individual

Christian who seeks full communion with the Catholic Church in anticipation or prior to the realisation of full communion between the Catholic Church and his or her own Christian community? In the Decree on Ecumenism this journey of the individual is distinguished from the ecumenical movement in this way: 'However, it is evident that the work of preparing and reconciling those individuals who wish for full Catholic communion is of its nature distinct from ecumenical action. But there is no opposition between the two, since both proceed from the marvellous ways of God' (4). The *Directory for the Application of Principles and Norms on Ecumenism* takes up this paragraph and acknowledges that every Christian has the right for 'conscientious religious reasons' (99) freely to decide to come into full Catholic communion. It then refers to the *Rite of Christian Initiation of Adults* as the place where one can find the formula for receiving such persons into full Catholic communion. It emphasises that there must be a clear distinction between catechumens and those who are received into full communion but are already baptised.

The entry of other Christians into the Catholic Church raises the question of the relationship between ecumenism and evangelisation. Can a Church which is involved in ecumenical relationships or, more broadly, in interfaith relationships, still engage in evangelisation? The Catholic Church has a very broad understanding of evangelisation. It is not limited to explicit proclamation of the gospel which would be more akin to what Protestants call evangelism. Evangelisation for Catholics involves the whole mission of the Church, which is a participation in the divine work of drawing the whole of creation into communion with God and all human beings into communion with each other and with the rest of creation. Everything we do to share in this work of God is indeed a work of evangelisation. Central though to our work of evangelisation is the actual sharing with others of our own personal relationship with God in Jesus Christ. If one truly believes, then one will always bear witness to one's belief by one's way of life and, where appropriate, by one's words.

Obviously evangelisation in the sense of an intentional activity directed at members of other Christian churches so that they might change their allegiance and seek the full communion of the Catholic Church would be incompatible with an ecumenical relationship. But this does not mean that within the ecumenical relationship the Catholic party is not still at the same time always bearing witness to his or her Catholic identity. Likewise an ecumenical relationship is not incompatible with both parties believing quite independently that their church is the most complete or the most perfect realisation of the Church of Jesus Christ as he intended it. Such a theological stance must be distinguished from the foolish claim that one's holiness is greater than another's. This has always been acknowledged in the ecumenical movement.

The One Church of Jesus Christ

The controversy at the end of 2000 over *Dominus Iesus*, a document of the Congregation for the Doctrine of the Faith, on the 'unicity and salvific universality of Jesus Christ and the Church' would indicate that there is a great deal of confusion at present concerning this matter which is really one of the Catholic understanding of the relationship of the Church of Jesus Christ to the various Christian communities. This understanding emerged at the Second Vatican Council and remains unchanged today. Nothing is served by pretending that it is not integral to the Catholic approach to ecumenism. There may be a value in looking at it again, despite the issues it can raise for some.

The Catholic Church's description of its relationship with other Christian communities is based on two principles. Firstly, as the *Directory* explains:

> Catholics hold the firm conviction that the one Church of Christ subsists in the Catholic Church 'which is governed by the successor of Peter and by the Bishops in communion with him'. They confess that the entirety of revealed truth, of sacraments, and of ministry that Christ gave for the building up of his Church and the carrying out of its mission is found within the Catholic communion of the Church. Certainly Catholics know that personally they have not made full use of and do not make full use of the means of grace with which the Church is endowed. For all that, Catholics never lose confidence in the Church. Their faith assures them that it remains 'the worthy bride of the Lord, ceaselessly renewing herself through the action of the Holy Spirit until, through the cross, she may attain to that light which knows no setting' (17).

Secondly, at the same time, the Catholic Church recognises that these same essential elements of the Church of Jesus Christ are found in different degrees in all other churches. This is the foundation for both the communion which already exists, and for the ecumenical movement which is aimed at deepening this communion. Pope John Paul II affirmed again this very important Catholic conviction in *Ut Unum Sint*:

> Indeed, the elements of sanctification and truth present in the other Christian Communities, in a degree which varies from one to the other, constitute the objective basis of the communion, albeit imperfect, which exists between them and the Catholic Church.
> To the extent that these elements are found in other Christian Communities, the one Church of Christ is effectively present in them (11).

This latter affirmation of the effective presence of the one Church of Christ in all Christian communities to one degree or another is very important. The task of ecumenical dialogue, from a Catholic point of view is, as has been noted, to move from not being able to recognise all the essential elements and hence the Church of Christ in its fullest realisation in other ecclesial communities, to being able to so recognise it and hence to be able to be reconciled and, therefore, finally to celebrate one eucharist.

Entering Full Communion

Given the witness of Catholics to their own identity and their own belief about the Christian tradition and the one Church of Jesus Christ, it sometimes occurs that individuals from other Christian communities seek full communion with the Catholic Church. A similar movement of Catholics into other Christian Churches sometimes occurs because of personal or family reasons, and sometimes because they believe that these other Christian Churches are more faithful to the vision of Christ, the will of Christ, for the Church.

What then of those who seek to become Catholics? How ought they be treated and how does their movement into the Catholic Church relate to the entry of unbaptised persons into the Church through the RCIA? For those who are interested in this topic I recommend a small publication, *One at the Table: The Reception of Baptised Christians*.[2] We need to recognise at the outset that there are three groups of people who might seek entry into the Catholic Church. There are catechumens, who are seeking baptism and experiencing conversion to Jesus Christ, to his way of life and to his Church in the complete sense of the word. Then there are candidates who are already baptised but have received only minimal catechesis or have minimal involvement in a church or even a Christian life in any way. The third group are those who, in fact, have been involved in the life of another Christian Church, who are baptised and catechised in a reasonably complete way, but are seeking to enter into the full communion of the Catholic Church.

These two groups of candidates must be distinguished. Kathy Brown concludes her article entitled 'Expanding the Limits of Initiation' by saying that: 'Those who have come to us seeking to become Catholic and already have been living a deeply committed life of faith have challenged us to recognise that not everyone belongs in the catechumenate or its adapted process for baptised, uncatechised candidates'.[3] I repeat her words: 'not everyone belongs in the catechumenate'. As to how such Christians should be treated and how they would relate to those journeying through the RCIA are some of the matters dealt with in the articles in *One at the Table*. The liturgical rite for such candidates is the *Rite of Reception into the Full Communion of the Catholic Church*. Rita Ferrone describes this as a 'humble rite, intentionally modest in its character and aims'[4] and she lists some of the ways in which it reflects the Church's ecumenical attitude which has emerged since the Second Vatican Council:

- An abjuration of heresy is no longer required of candidates.
- Conditional baptism is very narrowly circumscribed, and may not be celebrated publicly or with solemn rites.

---

2. Ronald A Oakham, *One at the Table*: *The Reception of Baptised Christians* (Chicago: Liturgy Training Publications, 1995). See also Anne Y Roester, 'The Reception of Baptised Christians: A Short Course in Vatican II Ecclesiology and Ecumenism', in *Worship*, 75 (2000): 130–49.
3. Kathy Brown, 'Expanding the Limits of Initiation', in *One at the Table*, 3–19.
4. Rita Ferrone, 'Reception in Context: Historical, Theological and Pastoral Reflections', in *One at the Table*, 21–41.

- In view of the close relationship between the Catholic and the Orthodox churches, no rite of any kind is required for Orthodox candidates.
- The Rite of Reception may be celebrated within the Mass for Christian Unity.
- Triumphalism is to be avoided.
- Ecumenical sensitivity is allowed to dictate a more modest than usual approach to the celebration of the rite, limiting the participants to a few friends and family members.
- Anything that discounts the Christian identity of candidates and therefore equates them with catechumens is to be 'absolutely avoided'.
- The readings chosen for the Rite of Reception, if the readings of the day or of the Mass for Christian Unity are not used, are passages well loved by all Christians, rather than controversial or 'Roman' passages.
- The presider's invitation to the candidate's profession of faith emphasises pastoral and spiritual themes of free choice, thoughtful reflection and guidance by the Spirit.
- The profession of faith contains no more than what is strictly necessary.
- If the candidate is accustomed to praying the doxology at the end of the Lord's Prayer, the doxology can be added when the rite is celebrated outside of mass (within mass, of course, the doxology is included already).

At the heart of the Rite of Reception is the Profession of Faith, which is an incorporation of the individual believer into the faith of the Catholic Church, which those assembled would profess with him or her. This embracing of the Catholic tradition as encapsulated in its formula of faith then makes it possible for the candidate to join the other Catholics at the table of the eucharist, which seals this entry into the full communion of the Catholic Church. In most cases the candidate would also be confirmed after their Profession of Faith because the Catholic Church is unable at this point of history to recognise the ordained ministry of Western Christian churches and hence the Sacrament of Confirmation administered within those

Christian churches. This does not, of course, apply to the Orthodox churches.

Rita Ferrone points out rather interestingly that three movements are involved in the reception of a candidate of another Christian church into the full communion of the Catholic Church. She suggests the first movement is the candidate seeking participation or a sharing in some of the distinctive gifts that are found within the Catholic Church. In my experience they have sought the eucharist or the sacraments or the fullness of the Catholic tradition or an authoritative teaching office. The second movement is their bringing with them the spiritual richness of their own tradition. This is sometimes not sufficiently acknowledged by those preparing such candidates. I can remember speaking in class quite some years ago about the need to be very sensitive to and respectful of the spiritual and faith formation that candidates had received in their former churches or traditions, and to recognise these as great gifts they brought with them. At this stage, somebody in the class became very teary because, as it developed, he had entered the Church some years before and had felt somehow that he was disowning his past, and no-one had acknowledged his previous religious tradition. For the first time he felt free to rejoice in it and even to grieve about the loss of some aspects of it. I often have to deal with Anglicans who have become Catholics and who regret very much that they have left behind the great musical heritage of the Anglican Communion. The third movement Rita Ferrone speaks of is the movement to holiness or conversion that is always involved in a major change in one's religious life. This needs to be attended to very sensitively by all those walking with the candidates.

Joseph Favazza's article on reconciliation as second baptism is a very challenging one.[5] I think his writing on the sacrament of penance has been one of the most enlightening of the past few years, and his suggestion that what we ought to do with baptised and catechised believers who seek to enter the full communion of the Catholic Church is to reconcile them, is, I think, a very thought-provoking suggestion. Our problem, as he points out, is that we have such a diminished understanding of the value of the sacrament of penance and its rites of reconciliation that this suggestion can easily appear as somewhat unusual.

---

5.   Joseph A Favazza, 'Reconciliation as Second Baptism', in *One at the Table*, 43–58.

The Approach of the Catholic Church to Ecumenism

If I am to speak of *The Approach of the Catholic Church to Ecumenism*, I think I can do no better than begin with the homily of Pope John Paul II on 25 January 2001. He was preaching at the concluding liturgy of the Week of Prayer for Christian Unity in Rome, in the Basilica of St Paul Outside the Walls. The scripture reading was from the fourteenth chapter of St John's Gospel, containing Jesus' proclamation, 'I am the way, and the truth, and the life'. Pope John Paul saw these words of Jesus as an answer to the questions that fill the human heart, and especially the hearts of young people: questions about truth, about the road that one should take, about how we can overcome the power of death with life, and so on.

Ecumenism and Witness

The pope then went on to affirm that the task of Christians in the contemporary world is to propose again this proclamation of Jesus 'with all the power of their witness'. He concluded, 'Only in this way can the men and women of today discover that Christ is the power and the wisdom of God (cf 1 Cor 1:24), that he is the fulfilment of every human longing'. He was also convinced that the ecumenical movement of the twentieth century has 'the great distinction of clearly re-affirming the need for this witness'. The link he drew here between witness and ecumenism is no more than the link Christ himself drew in the seventeenth chapter of St John's Gospel when he prayed that we might be one so that the world would believe that it is the Father who sent him.

This is a previously unpublished paper.

157

The Present Ecumenical Situation

While affirming that unity which Christians already share through their faith, Pope John Paul II did not shy away from acknowledgement, in that same homily, of the painful divisions which still exist. With respect to these divisions, he made a very important observation which is too often missed by tired ecumenists or impatient parishioners. I would like to quote him in full:

> It would be less than honest to disguise or ignore them. But they should not lead us to mutual recriminations or discouragement. The pain resulting from misunderstanding or mistakes must be overcome by prayer and penance, by signs of love, by theological investigation. The questions which remain open are not an obstacle to dialogue; rather, they ought to be seen as an incentive to frank and charitable discussion. The question remains: *Quanta est nobis via?* How long until our journey comes to an end? It is not ours to know the answer, but we are encouraged by hope, knowing that we are being led by the presence of the Risen One and the inexhaustible power of his Spirit, always capable of new surprises (cf. *Novo millennio ineunte*, n. 12).

Ecumenism and the Life of the Church

In an address given around the same time to an audience in Rome of bishops associated with the Focolare movement, the Holy Father called 'the ecumenical way' 'the Church's way'—something he had already said in his encyclical of 1995, *Ut Unum Sint*. This is a very evocative description of the Catholic Church's understanding of the centrality of ecumenism to its life and mission. I am reminded of a much earlier statement of the pope which he made in an address to the Roman curia in June 1985. Each year he delivers an address to the curia about some fundamental aspect of the Church's life. In that year he spoke about ecumenism. The points he made have served well since that time as a key for interpreting the precise way the Catholic Church understands the place of ecumenism in its life and mission. He said on that occasion:

> The search for unity and ecumenical concern are a necessary dimension of the whole of the Church's life. Everything can and must contribute to it. I have already asked on more than one occasion that the re-establishment of unity among all Christians must be considered a pastoral priority. We are committed together with our brothers and sisters of the other churches and ecclesial communities in the ecumenical movement.

This statement and the more recent phrase 'the ecumenical way is the Church's way' tell us that ecumenism is not simply a pastoral activity of the Church alongside other activities, and one which could be entrusted to some individuals or agencies only. Likewise it is not something that a local church might or might not become involved in. It is, rather, fundamental to the Church's identity. As Pope John Paul indicated, it is a necessary dimension of the whole of the Church's life.

Each of those words is extremely important. It is 'necessary'. In other words, not only is it not optional, it is an imperative arising from the very nature of the Church itself. It demands of us a response. 'It is a dimension of the Church's life.' In other words it is not only a task, or a ministry, or a particular mission, or responsibility: it is interior to the Church itself. The very existence, nature, and life of the Church has an ecumenical dimension. Moreover the pope says that this dimension is true of 'the whole of the Church's life'. And again, 'everything can and must contribute to it'. There is no moment of the Church's existence; there is no place where it exists; there is no aspect of its life; there are no members of it; there are no ministries within it; there are no activities of it; there are no decisions it makes, missions it undertakes, policies it formulates, relationships it establishes, tasks it undertakes or goals it seeks, that do not have an ecumenical dimension. If Pope John Paul II made this claim in 1985, one understands how easily he could say in 2001 'the ecumenical way is the Church's way'.

In order to understand why it is that Pope John Paul II would express in such terms the Catholic approach to ecumenism, the best resource available is his own encyclical letter *Ut Unum Sint* which he signed on the feast of the Ascension, 25 May 1995. In his apostolic letter *Novo Millennio Ineunte* on 'the beginning of the new millennium', he said of the phrase *ut unum sint* and so of Christ's prayer for Christian unity:

> The invocation *ut unum sint* is, at one and the same time, a binding imperative, the strength that sustains us, and a salutary rebuke for our slowness and close-heartedness. It is on Jesus' prayer and not on our own strength that we base the hope that even within history we shall be able to reach full and visible communion with all Christians (48).

The other most important exposition of the approach of the Catholic Church to ecumenism which has been formulated is the *Directory for the Application of Principles and Norms on Ecumenism*. It was published by the Pontifical Council for Promoting Christian Unity, and approved by Pope John Paul II on 25 March 1993. It becomes clear in those documents that at the foundation of a Catholic approach to ecumenism is a theology and spirituality of communion (*koinonia*).

Theology of Communion

In *Ut Unum Sint* Pope John Paul II spoke of the Church as a communion, in these words:

> The faithful are *one* because, in the Spirit, they are in *communion* with the Son and, in him, share in his *communion* with the Father: 'Our *fellowship* is with the Father and with his Son Jesus Christ' (1 Jn 1:3). For the Catholic Church, then, the *communion* of Christians is none other than the manifestation in them of the grace by which God makes them sharers in his own *communion*, which is his eternal life. Christ's words 'that they may be one' are thus his prayer to the Father that the Father's plan may be fully accomplished, in such a way that everyone may clearly see 'what is the plan of the mystery hidden for ages in God who created all things' (Eph 3:9). To believe in Christ means to desire unity; to desire unity means to desire the Church; to desire the

Church means to desire the communion of grace which corresponds to the Father's plan from all eternity. Such is the meaning of Christ's prayer: '*Ut unum sint*' (9).

If this is the communion that Christ wills, then the Holy Father could say earlier in the same encyclical concerning the division which exists among Christians:

> How is it possible to remain divided, if we have been 'buried' through Baptism in the Lord's death, in the very act by which God, through the death of his Son, has broken down the walls of division? Division 'openly contradicts the will of Christ, provides a stumbling block to the world, and inflicts damage on the most holy cause of proclaiming the Good News to every creature' (6).

In other words, for Catholics, the universal visible communion of the Church is willed by God. At the same time they recognise that Christians through the ages have damaged that communion to varying degrees by their foolishness and sinfulness; even though the communion we share has never been completely destroyed, because of our common faith and baptism. On their foundation, then, we are all called to work to restore full communion.

The *Directory* described this imperative as follows:

> No Christian, however, should be satisfied with these forms of communion. They do not correspond to the will of Christ, and weaken his Church in the exercise of its mission. The grace of God has impelled members of many Churches and ecclesial Communities, especially in the course of this present century, to strive to overcome the divisions inherited from the past and to build anew a communion of love by prayer, by repentance and by asking pardon of each other for sins of disunity past and present, by meeting in practical forms of cooperation and in theological dialogue. These are the aims and activities of what has come to be called the ecumenical movement (19).

Given this theology of communion/*koinonia*, we can see why the search for unity is a necessary dimension of the church's life. Because of the real but incomplete communion which we have with each other through our common baptism and faith, we are always and everywhere related to each other. This relationship is not as complete as it is with my fellow Catholics, in my case, but it is just as real. Therefore everything we are and do affects that relationship. It cannot be avoided because it is a relationship in Christ. Ecumenism is simply the name we give to the positive expression of a relationship inherent in our very identity.

Also, given this theology of communion, we can see why the goal of the ecumenical movement is always described by Catholics as the realisation of full communion among Christians, and that for them this communion will be manifest in the celebration of one eucharist. Sharing one faith, bound together in one life and mission, served by ministers recognised by all, all Christians will share in the one eucharist of Jesus Christ. Such a restoration of full communion can only come about through a continuing relationship of collaboration and dialogue whereby churches reach the stage of being able to recognise the one apostolic faith in the faith of the other, and the Church of Jesus Christ in its fullness in the other. Only then could they be fully reconciled with the other.

For Catholics, such reconciliation and full communion welcomes the continuance of all the spiritual, theological, ministerial and apostolic diversity consistent with mutual recognition. As the *Directory* says:

> This unity which of its very nature requires full visible communion of all Christians is the ultimate goal of the ecumenical movement . . . this unity by no means requires the sacrifice of the rich diversity of spirituality, discipline, liturgical rites and elaborations of revealed truth that has grown up among Christians in the measure that this diversity remains faithful to the Apostolic Tradition (20).

Diversity is an essential dimension of the Church and a restored communion would retain all the diversity of Christian traditions consistent with mutual recognition of the *one* apostolic faith and the *one* Church of Jesus Christ.

The One Church of Jesus Christ

The controversy at the end of last year (2000) over *Dominus Iesus*, a document of the Congregation for the Doctrine of the Faith, on the 'unicity and salvific universality of Jesus Christ and the Church' would indicate that there is a great deal of confusion at present concerning the Catholic understanding of the relationship of the Church of Jesus Christ to the various Christian communities. This understanding emerged at the Second Vatican Council and remains unchanged today. Nothing is served by pretending that it is not integral to the Catholic approach to ecumenism. There may be a value in looking at it again, despite the issues it can raise for some.

The Catholic Church's description of its relationship with other Christian communities is based on two principles. Firstly, as the *Directory* explains:

> Catholics hold the firm conviction that the one Church of Christ subsists in the Catholic Church 'which is governed by the successor of Peter and by the Bishops in communion with him'. They confess that the entirety of revealed truth, of sacraments, and of ministry that Christ gave for the building up of his Church and the carrying out of its mission is found within the Catholic communion of the Church. Certainly Catholics know that personally they have not made full use of and do not make full use of the means of grace with which the Church is endowed. For all that, Catholics never lose confidence in the Church. Their faith assures them that it remains 'the worthy bride of the Lord, ceaselessly renewing herself through the action of the Holy Spirit until, through the cross, she may attain to that light which knows no setting' (17).

Second, at the same time, the Catholic Church recognises that these same essential elements of the Church of Jesus Christ are found in different degrees in all other churches. This is the foundation for both the communion which already exists, and for the ecumenical movement which is aimed at deepening this communion. Pope John Paul II affirmed again this very important Catholic conviction in *Ut Unum Sint*:

> Indeed, the elements of sanctification and truth present in the other Christian Communities, in a degree which varies from one to the other, constitute the objective basis of the communion, albeit imperfect, which exists between them and the Catholic Church.
> To the extent that these elements are found in other Christian Communities, the one Church of Christ is effectively present in them (11).

This latter affirmation of the effective presence of the one Church of Christ in all Christian communities to one degree or another is very important but it is not always appreciated as being central to a Catholic understanding of other ecclesial communities. The task of ecumenical dialogue, from a Catholic point of view, is to move from not being able to recognise all the essential elements and hence the Church of Christ in its fullest realisation in other ecclesial communities, to being able to so recognise and hence to be reconciled and, therefore, finally to celebrate one eucharist. The agreement with the Lutheran World Communion on Justification and the ARCIC reports illustrate just how far we have travelled on this journey of mutual recognition and all our recent dialogues indicate just how committed we are to going much further.

Purification of Memories

There are many different ways of describing what a commitment to ecumenism would involve on a practical level for the Catholic Church and perhaps for any other Christian community. Pope John Paul II has once again inspired a renewed reflection by his homily at the close of the Week of Prayer for Christian Unity in Rome last month (January 2001). He situated the ecumenical movement in the context of the millennium which has just begun and of which he has spoken so powerfully in his most recent Apostolic Letter *Novo Millennio Ineunte*. In his homily, as I indicated in the beginning of this address, he saw the duty of all Christians as one of bearing a common witness in this new millennium. He then described the most fundamental task in that perspective as a purification of our memories. 'In the second millennium we were hostile and divided; we condemned and fought one another. We must forget the shadows and the wounds of the past and strain forward towards the coming hour of God (cf Phil 3:13).'

It seems to me that the Holy Father has touched on something we too easily forget in the ecumenical movement. Because we have moved from a relationship of hostility to one of friendship and collaboration over this past century, and for Catholics especially since the Second Vatican Council, we too easily neglect the healing that still needs to take place in our relationships. During the celebration of the Year of Great Jubilee, Catholics around the world were invited to reflect on their failures of the past and to seek forgiveness from God and those whom they had offended. Pope John Paul II did this himself on the first Sunday of Lent, in St Peter's Basilica, in a very powerful liturgy of repentance. The bishops of Australia attempted something similar with a 'Statement of Repentance' on Ash Wednesday, in which we expressed our repentance for, among other things, our failures with respect to other Christians in the previous two centuries of Australian history.

I was amazed, at the time, by the reaction to our Statement of Repentance in the Australian community. People were surprised that we would be willing to acknowledge that we had failed, and that we would genuinely seek forgiveness of others. They rightly warned us that true repentance required not just words but a change of heart, and a change in performance as well. No doubt we have not achieved anywhere near a complete conversion, but we have begun.

I wonder whether Christian communities have adequately dealt with our common past of pain and hostility. There still seem to be areas of history and theology which we avoid because they will resurrect some of the pain of the past. For example, very few international or national dialogues have been willing to actually tackle the question of the Reformation, and to deal with the differing interpretations of that event within our respective Christian traditions. Perhaps we don't want to hurt each other again, because we have hurt each other in the past. The recent controversy surrounding *Dominus Iesus* also illustrates just how easily we can still misunderstand each other. I believe Pope John Paul II is right in urging us to deal with the past precisely because it is the future that matters; and again, the future for us has to be a future of common witness, for the sake of the world. We will never do that effectively as long as the conflicts of the past remain unreconciled.

Degrees of Communion

The next task which the pope placed before us in his homily was 'to develop a spirituality of communion (*koinonia*), on the model of the Trinity'. As he said 'We need to live and practise that communion which, though not yet full, already exists between us. Leaving behind distrust, we must meet, know one another better, learn to love one another, and work together fraternally as much as possible'. That is a huge agenda. I am reminded there of a quotation from the late Cardinal Mercier of Malines: 'In order to unite with one another, we must love one another; in order to love one another, we must know one another; in order to know one another, we must go and meet one another'.

In the recent meeting of Anglican and Roman Catholic bishops from thirteen countries which was convened in Mississauga near Toronto in May last year, and which was attended by Bishop John Cunneen, a final document was produced entitled *Communion in Mission*. Both of those words are very important and echo the theme of Pope John Paul II's homily in Rome: 'We are called to common witness and so we have to develop our spirituality of communion'. He spoke of our need to live and practice the communion which exists between us. The Mississauga document developed the same theme rather extensively while acknowledging very frankly the differences and points of tension which exist between Anglicans and Catholics. It argued that, when one uses the language of 'degrees of communion' between different Christian communities, one must acknowledge that because of the dialogue and collaboration which has existed over the past thirty years, a new degree of communion has been reached between Anglicans and Catholics which needs to be acknowledged by both communities and allowed to find concrete expression in the daily life of those communities. While full communion has not yet been reached, we are in no way in the situation we were thirty years ago, and it is time that the new relationship between our two

Christian communities was obvious and, to use the language of Pope John Paul II, a dimension of the whole of the life of our respective communities.

What was stated by Anglicans and Catholics in Canada last year will no doubt begin to bear fruit in practical ways in the life of the Anglican and Catholic communities around the world, especially through the establishment of a Joint Unity Commission. On the Catholic side this is being chaired by Archbishop Bathersby of Brisbane, which has delighted us very much. This approach could also be the way forward, I believe, in the relationship between all Christian communities. The diverse churches and ecclesial communions have differing relationships with each other, that is, differing degrees of communion. But too seldom the way in which that degree of communion has been deepened over the past century, and especially the past thirty or forty years, has been acknowledged and taken seriously in the life and mission of the respective communities. As the pope concluded in his homily in Rome, different communities need to 'work together fraternally as much as possible'.

The 'as much as possible' in this exhortation depends upon the degree of communion which has been reached. But unless that degree of communion is recognised, acknowledged and allowed to impact on every dimension of the respective community's life, there is no possibility that the communities will work together with any ease, let alone do so 'as much as is possible'. Collaboration in work, ministry and mission flow out of the degree of communion which exists. Unless the degree of communion is explored, rejoiced in, celebrated liturgically, profoundly appreciated and lived, then any collaboration will lack a foundation in our spirituality and will too easily be seen as simply a human strategy, or a convenient exercise, or, perhaps worst of all, 'simply the right thing to do'.

Fidelity and Openness

Pope John Paul II called this whole spirituality of communion and what flows from it 'the dialogue of charity'. He went on in his homily to suggest that this needs to be complemented by, and indeed would not be genuine without, a 'dialogue of truth': 'Overcoming our differences involves serious theological study. We cannot gloss over those differences; we cannot alter the deposit of faith.' Ecumenism requires love and truth, openness and fidelity. If one places an emphasis solely upon the dialogue of charity or the role of love and openness in ecumenical relationships, there is a danger that one will create just one more new community, perhaps called an ecumenical one, where collaborative, harmonious relationships are achieved by leaving aside the doctrinal matters which divide Christians one from the other, and which will inevitably reassert themselves unless one settles for a doctrine-free Christianity. This is particularly attractive in a post-modern, Western society where openness and inclusion are so highly valued and tolerance is regarded as the hallmark of a decent human being. If, on the other hand, an ecumenical relationship is based only on fidelity to the truth as one perceives it, without any dialogue of charity or experience of love between the partners, no community at all will be able to be created. The partners will stand apart from each other, each remaining faithful to their tradition but unable to cross the divide which separates them.

To put it simply, ecumenism, and especially ecumenical dialogue, requires of us loving truth and truthful love. Love without a commitment to truth will lead to a too easy compromise which will not carry the churches into full Christian unity. A commitment to the truth without love will lead to dogmatism and intransigence and will delay Christian unity forever. Utter openness to the other, with utter fidelity to one's own tradition, is the way forward for the committed ecumenist. Indeed in some ways it is only in meeting the other in complete openness, while remaining faithful to one's own identity, that one discovers one's own identity in its full profundity. The meeting of hearts and minds that can come between dialogue partners who have both qualities of utter faithfulness and utter openness is the meeting which takes the movement towards Christian unity a step forward.

Ecumenism and Prayer

The final comment made by Pope John Paul II about the tasks that make up the work of ecumenism was a very important one. He said 'It is not up to us to create unity'. He went on to say:

> unity is the Lord's gift. And so we must pray, as we have done during this week, that we may be given the Spirit of unity. At every celebration of the Eucharist the Catholic

Church prays: 'Look not on our sins but on the faith of
your Church, and grant us the peace and unity of your
Kingdom.' Prayer for unity is a part of every Eucharist.
It is the soul of the whole ecumenical movement (cf. *Ut
unum sint*, n. 21).

The Christian community can do nothing to further the unity of
the Church without the grace of God. It is always and everywhere
an instrument of God and never an agent in its own right. Prayer
is the means whereby Christians recognise the trinitarian source of
their existence and their mission and, in recognising it, draw upon
it. Right from the beginning of the ecumenical movement, prayer for
unity has been one of the most fundamental characteristics of that
movement. However, in more recent times it has tended to be taken
for granted.

The Week of Prayer for Christian Unity in Australia, for example,
no longer captures the imagination as it used to and hence fewer
people come to fewer ecumenical services during that week.
Individual Christians praying and even dedicating their lives as a
spiritual offering for the unity of the churches seem to be more the
characteristic of the early years of the ecumenical movement than
they are of today. Obviously, this is a broad statement and there are
many exceptions.

People talk, I believe quite incorrectly, of an ecumenical winter or
of a slowing down of the ecumenical movement. If there is a loss of
interest or passion for ecumenism the cause may well lie in a failure to
tap the spiritual roots of the ecumenical movement and to act instead
as if it is simply a human work. As the latter, its achievements will be
too slow in coming and too hard to plan for it to sustain enthusiasm.
Too often today action for Christian unity or common Christian
action for justice and peace is paramount and prayer is simply an
addendum. This surely deserves attention as pointing to something
more than a minor lapse in one aspect of ecumenical activity. It rather
represents a profound gap between ecumenical activity and its source,
between activity and spirituality.

To quote again Jesus' prayer in St John's Gospel:

As you, Father, are in me and I am in you, may they also
be in us, so that the world may believe that you have sent

me. The glory that you have given me I have given them, so that they may be one, as we are one, I in them and you in me, that they may become completely one, so that the world may know that you have sent me and have loved them even as you have loved me (John 17: 21–23).

If all Christians live in Christ, in the communion of the Holy Spirit, then that prayer to the Father will be one of the gifts which Christ gives to them through their union with him.

If human hearts are united with the heart of Christ because of this intense communion established by the Holy Spirit, through faith and baptism, and deepened through the eucharist, then the prayer of Christ's heart will gradually become the prayer of every Christian heart. Action for Christian unity ought to flow from this divine prayer for unity rather than the other way round.

Conclusion

I would like to conclude by quoting Pope John Paul II again. This time from *Novo Millennio Ineunte* of 6 January 2001:

> Christ's prayer reminds us that this gift needs to be received and developed ever more profoundly. The invocation '*ut unum sint*' is, at one and the same time, a binding imperative, the strength that sustains us, and a salutary rebuke for our slowness and closed-heartedness. It is on Jesus's prayer and not on our own strength that we base the hope that even within history we shall be able to reach full and visible communion with all Christians.
>
> In the perspective of our renewed post-Jubilee pilgrimage, I look with great hope to the *Eastern Churches*, and I pray for a full return to that exchange of gifts which enriched the Church of the first millennium. May the memory of the time when the Church breathed with 'both lungs' spur Christians of East and West to walk together in unity of faith and with respect for legitimate diversity, accepting and sustaining each other as members of the one Body of Christ.

A similar commitment should lead to the fostering of ecumenical dialogue with our brothers and sisters belonging to the *Anglican Communion* and the *Ecclesial Communities born of the Reformation*. Theological discussion on essential points of faith and Christian morality, cooperation in works of charity, and above all the great ecumenism of holiness will not fail, with God's help, to bring results. In the meantime we confidently continue our pilgrimage, longing for the time when, together with each and every one of Christ's followers, we shall be able to join whole-heartedly in singing: 'How good and how pleasant it is, when brothers live in unity!' (Ps 133:1).

A Catholic Understanding of Ecumenical Dialogue

In an article published in 2004, 'The Nature and Purpose of Ecumenical Dialogue', Cardinal Walter Kasper wrote of the concerns and even the anger of many other Christians after the publication of *Dominus Iesus* by the Congregation for the Doctrine of the Faith in 2000. The issues raised by a number of statements in *Dominus Iesus* have already been discussed many times.[1] However, Cardinal Kasper described a more worrying, because more fundamental, consequence of the document:

> The question arose: Is real dialogue possible for a church and with a church which claims to have the absolute truth in an infallible way? For dialogue presupposes openness towards other positions and an encounter of equals. So the question was, and for many still is: Is this document not a sign that the Catholic Church understands ecumenism only as simple return of the separated brethren into the fold of the Catholic Church and thus she withdraws from the spirit and the precepts of the Second Vatican Council and relinquishes the concept of dialogue?[2]

This paper was originally published in *Ecclesiology*, 2/2 (2006): 179–94.

1. *Sic et Non: Encountering Dominus Iesus*, edited by Stephen J Pope and Charles Hefling (Maryknoll: Orbis, 2002); Francis A Sullivan SJ, 'The Impact of *Dominus Iesus* on Ecumenism', in *America*, 183/13 (28 October 2000): 8–11; Kilian McDonnell, 'The Unique Mediator in a Unique Church: A Return to Pre-Vatican II Theology', in *Ecumenical Trends*, 29/11 (December 2000): 1–7; John T Ford, '*Dominus Iesus*: Retrenchment or Reminder?', in *Ecumenical Trends*, 29/11 (December 2000): 7–12.
2. Walter Kasper, 'The Nature and Purpose of Ecumenical Dialogue', in *That They May All be One: The Call to Unity Today* (London: Burns & Oates, 2004), 34–5.

Despite the anxiety of some, there can be no moving back from the Catholic Church's engagement in ecumenical dialogue. Even though it embraced it later than others, dialogue with other Christians is of the essence of the Church as Catholics understand it. The Church is a communion participating in the life of the triune God. Because of this, dialogue with all parties and certainly with other Christians is integral to its very nature. This was clear from the first statement of the Catholic Church on ecumenism and has only become more obvious in the subsequent decades.

Decree on Ecumenism

21 November 2004 marked the fortieth anniversary of the promulgation by the Second Vatican Council of its Decree on Ecumenism (*Unitatis Redintegratio*). This 'magna carta' for the entry of the Roman Catholic Church into the modern ecumenical movement committed it to engaging in ecumenical dialogue; and it is perhaps this dialogue which has been most conspicuous about it since that time.

In the fourth paragraph of the Decree, the bishops of the council described the ecumenical movement which they saw occurring around the world as 'under the influence of the grace of the Holy Spirit'. They urged 'all the Catholic faithful to recognise the signs of the times and to take an active and intelligent part in the work of ecumenism'.[3] Already for Catholics ecumenism was seen as something to which the Holy Spirit who dwells within all Christian communities was directing them. Initially the bishops described dialogue as occurring 'between competent experts from different churches and communities', and attributed to it a rather limited goal of simply gaining thereby 'a truer knowledge and more just appreciation of the teaching and religious life of both communions'.[4]

But in the same paragraph the Decree began to map the contours of a more theological understanding of ecumenical dialogue:

> Catholics must gladly acknowledge and esteem the truly Christian endowments from our common heritage which are to be found among our separated brethren . . .

---

3. Vatican Council II, Decree on Ecumenism, *Unitatis Redintegratio*, in *Vatican Council II: The Conciliar and Post Conciliar Documents*, edited by Austin Flannery OP (Northport: Costello, 1992), 4.
4. Decree on Ecumenism, 4.

And again:

> anything wrought by the grace of the Holy Spirit in the
> hearts of our separated brethren can contribute to our
> own edification. Whatever is truly Christian is never
> contrary to what genuinely belongs to the faith: indeed
> it can always bring a more perfect realisation of the very
> mystery of Christ and the Church.[5]

Here the bishops affirmed as early as 1964, and so right from the
beginning of Catholic engagement, that the relationship into which
they were leading the Catholic Church was one in which it would
receive gifts from other Christians because of the presence and
activity of the Holy Spirit within them; and that, through dialogue,
the Holy Spirit could lead Catholics themselves to something more
perfect spiritually and ecclesially.

Later in the Decree the bishops spoke of participants in dialogue
meeting 'on an equal footing',[6] which was both a practical requirement
and again an acknowledgement of an openness to the other and a
readiness to receive from them. Another very important contribution
of the Decree to ecumenical dialogue was the celebrated text on what
is called the 'hierarchy of truths'.

To begin with, the Decree rejected 'false irenicism' and required
that Catholics reveal their full faith to their dialogue partners, which
alone can ensure a profound and unrestricted encounter of equals in
the Holy Spirit. Then after asking them to explain themselves 'more
profoundly' in ways which would assist understanding, the bishops
went on to say:

> When comparing doctrines with one another, they
> should remember that in Catholic doctrine there exists
> an order or 'hierarchy' of truths, since they vary in their
> relation to the foundation of the Christian faith. Thus
> the way will be opened whereby this kind of 'fraternal
> rivalry' will incite all to a deeper realization and a clearer
> expression of the unfathomable riches of Christ.[7]

---

5. Decree on Ecumenism, 4.
6. Decree on Ecumenism, 9.
7. Decree on Ecumenism, 11.

This text is indicative of an attitude on the part of the bishops not only of not compromising the fullness of Catholic faith but also of expressing it differently for the sake of 'the other'; and of seeking the truth of Christ with the dialogue partner. Already a conversion both of mind and of heart was being asked of Catholics, which would have irreversible consequences for Catholic theology. The goal was from the beginning always one of coming closer to Christ with the other who also belongs to him. This was fundamentally not about negotiation with others but about Christ and his claim upon both parties.

Ecumenical Directory (1970)

In 1970 the Catholic Church published a formal account of its understanding of and commitment to dialogue. In its *Directory Concerning Ecumenical Matters: Part Two: Ecumenism and Higher Education* published by the then Secretariat for Promoting Christian Unity, there was a section on 'Dialogue Between Christians in Higher Education'. This repeated the need for fidelity to one's own faith, commenting that without it 'dialogue is reduced to a conversation in which neither side is genuinely engaged'.[8] Dialogue cannot really happen without faithfulness on the part of those involved. Secondly, it indicated again that spiritual conversion can occur for those engaged in dialogue if they had, as it said, 'a mind open and ready to base life more deeply on one's own faith because of a fuller knowledge derived from dialogue with others, who are to be reckoned as sharing with us the true name of Christian'.[9] They foresaw Catholics becoming better Catholics, in the sense of closer to Christ as Catholics, because of the deeper appropriation of their faith which would come about by dialogue with others.

Thirdly, it developed more fully its rejection of 'false irenicism' by seeing the goal of dialogue as unity based on greater fidelity to the gospel, the conversion already spoken of, and not on a 'facile accommodation to the demands of the age'.[10] Already they could

---

8. *Directory Concerning Ecumenical Matters: Part Two: Ecumenism in Higher Education*, in *Vatican Council II: The Conciliar and Post Conciliar Documents*, 524, 76(d).

9. *Directory Concerning Ecumenical Matters*, 76(b).

10. *Directory Concerning Ecumenical Matters*, 524, 76(c).

see that there is a cultural or purely natural motivation for Christian unity which would compromise their commitment to the gospel rather than deepen their response to it.

It also emphasised that ecumenical dialogue is 'never a mere exchange between persons and institutions, but of its very nature engages the whole Church'.[11] Dialogue is intensely personal and evokes the conversion already mentioned but it is always ecclesial as well. The dialogue partners are representatives of their respective communions and are one of the most intense points of encounter between communions. It is a rather grand claim to describe the role of those involved in dialogue as engaging 'the whole Church', but to forget this is to risk the whole purpose of drawing communions closer to each other by their together drawing closer to Christ, who is always the ultimate dialogue partner.

Reflections and Suggestions Concerning Dialogue (1970)

In August of that same year, 1970, the secretariat published a document entitled 'Reflections and Suggestions Concerning Ecumenical Dialogue'. One new insight of this document was its rejection of a doctrinal indifferentism which would claim that 'before the mystery of Christ in the Church, all positions are equivalent' (IV, 2a). Again this appears to be an acknowledgement of the relativism of the day, and perhaps a Catholic distancing from a too-easy denominationalism in which confessional identity and ecclesial tradition cease to be precious gifts which one brings to the ecumenical table.

It presumed that 'those who take part recognise one another as existing in Christ' and so are able 'through the Holy Spirit to hear their brethren tell them of the marvellous works of God' and to recognise 'a certain communion'[12] existing between them. This trinitarian foundation in an ecclesiology of communion was really the basis for all other conditions for dialogue and pointed in the direction of a genuinely theological understanding of dialogue. It was the foundation for ecumenism already mapped out in the Decree on Ecumenism.

---

11. *Directory Concerning Ecumenical Matters*, 524, 76(d).
12. 'Reflections and Suggestions Concerning Ecumenical Dialogue', in *Vatican Council II: The Conciliar and Post Conciliar Documents*, 543, (IV, 2d).

When speaking of the methods of dialogue the document asked Catholic participants to put 'aside the tendency to define by opposition, which generally results in certain positions becoming overstressed or unduly hardened'. It described this as 'a purifying process' and said that 'the warping from which our respective theologies suffer can only be corrected at this price'.[13] This was a very important acknowledgement not just practically but also theologically. It was an admission that the theology of the Catholic Church had been warped because of its separation from other Christians, and again the way forward was one of conversion or purification.

The secretariat spoke of dialogue leading to the discovery not just of truths which are held in common—and of truths which might have become obscured in this or that community as a result of the divisions and which have been better preserved in another communion—but also of new insights which could be discovered only through the process of dialogue. This represented a theological recognition that Christian division diminishes both parties and actually hinders their grasp of the gospel. Wounded by separation, separated Christians' grasp of the truth of the gospel is impoverished until dialogue opens up new understandings for them. Clearly ecumenical dialogue was recognised as a requirement for Catholics not just as their Christian duty, but as essential for the full flowering of their Christian identity and their understanding of Christ and his gospel.

Ecclesiam Suam (1964)

In 2004 the Catholic Church also celebrated the fortieth anniversary of Pope Paul VI's first encyclical which was entitled *Ecclesiam Suam*. Pope John Paul II said of this encyclical of his predecessor that it indicated 'the path of an inspired ecclesial journey towards the third millennium'.[14] In particular he said of its third section on dialogue: 'For the ecclesial community, the method of dialogue is becoming the way in which to work to bring the Lord's comforting message of salvation everywhere'.[15]

---

13. 'Reflections and Suggestions Concerning Ecumenical Dialogue', 548, (V, 2b).
14. 'Spread the Good News Through Dialogue', in *L'Osservatore Romano* (11–18 August 1999): 1.
15. 'Spread the Good News Through Dialogue', 1.

For Pope Paul VI, and later Pope John Paul II, dialogue was always a *dialogue of salvation* because it was a way of communicating the great gift of salvation which we have received. It was modelled on the dialogue of salvation between God and human beings.

> This relationship, this dialogue, which God the Father initiated and established with us through Christ in the Holy Spirit, is a very real one, even though it is difficult to express in words. We must examine it closely if we want to understand the relationship which we, the Church, should establish and foster with the human race.[16]

Pope Paul VI spoke in terms of four concentric circles of dialogue. In the first circle were all people of the world. In the second were the representatives of the other great world religions and in the third were all Christians. In the last circle were members of the Catholic Church itself. In speaking of dialogue with other Christians, the pope did not reflect in any systematic way upon the ecumenical movement but he did acknowledge that his own papal ministry was seen by many as a 'stumbling block'[17] to Christian unity, and hoped that through dialogue it would be able to be seen as a service to unity. He foreshadowed here the bold step which would be taken in this regard by Pope John Paul II twenty-five years later.

The order of these concentric circles was reversed by the Pastoral Constitution of the Church in the Modern World, *Gaudium et Spes*, in the following year at the very end of the Second Vatican Council, beginning with dialogue within the Church and ending with the dialogue with the world. The larger dialogue with the world could not be successful unless the Catholic community were one of dialogue. Ecumenical dialogue then became the next important requirement for the mission of the church.[18] Both *Ecclesiam Suam* and *Gaudium*

---

16. Paul VI, Encyclical Letter, *Ecclesiam Suam*, 'Paths of the Church' (Boston: St Paul Books and Media, 1964), 33.
17. *Ecumenical Documents I: Doing the Truth in Charity: Statements of Pope Paul VI, Popes John Paul I, John Paul II, and the Secretariat for Promoting Christian Unity 1964–1980*, edited by Thomas F Stransky and John B Sheerin (New York: Paulist Press, 1982), 270.
18. Pastoral Constitution on the Church in the Modern World, *Gaudium et Spes*, in

et Spes indicate how integral dialogue is to the life and mission of the Catholic Church even if this has still to be understood and adequately implemented.

Ecumenical Directory (1993)

The new Ecumenical Directory of 1993 harvested previous publications on the ecumenical activity of the Catholic Churches, and updated then in some instances. In its section on 'Ecumenical Dialogue' it repeated what had already been said in other documents, but it did contribute something of great importance when referring to the evaluation of the results of dialogue by Catholic Church authorities. It required that 'the members of the People of God, according to their role or charism, must be involved in this critical process,'[19] which it called one of 'reception'. They were to exercise their *sensus fidei* in this process, so that ultimately there would be a universal consent to the results of the dialogue. It recognised that assistance would need to be given for this to happen because there would be 'new insights in to the faith, new witnesses to the truth, new forms of expression' (179).[20] Once again the profound ecclesial weight attributed to ecumenical dialogue and the openness to new gifts of the Spirit in their results is immediately obvious.

Ut Unum Sint (1995)

In his extraordinary encyclical of 1995, *Ut Unum Sint*, Pope John Paul II carried further the teaching of the Decree on Ecumenism and intensified it for the Catholic Church. One very interesting contribution to contemporary ecumenical reflection was the pope's listing of matters still needing further dialogue thirty years after the promulgation of the Decree on Ecumenism:

> (1) the relationship between Sacred Scripture, as the highest authority in matters of faith, and Sacred

---

Vatican Council II: The Conciliar and Post Conciliar Documents, 1000.

19. Pontificium Consilium ad Christianorum Unitatem Fovendam, *Directory for the Application of Principles and Norms on Ecumenism* (London: CTS Publications, 1993), 79.

20. *Directory for the Application of Principles and Norms on Ecumenism*, 79.

Tradition, as indispensable to the interpretation of the Word of God; (2) the Eucharist, as the Sacrament of the Body and Blood of Christ, an offering of praise to the Father, the sacrificial memorial and real Presence of Christ and the sanctifying outpouring of the Holy Spirit; (3) Ordination, as a Sacrament, to the threefold ministry of the episcopate, presbyterate and diaconate; (4) the Magisterium of the Church, entrusted to the Pope and the Bishops in communion with him, understood as a responsibility and an authority exercised in the name of Christ for teaching and safeguarding the faith; (5) the Virgin Mary, as Mother of God and Icon of the Church, the spiritual Mother who intercedes for Christ's disciples and for all humanity.[21]

Pope John Paul II then went on to ask of the Catholic Church and other Christian communions that they take up the task of 'receiving' the results of the dialogues which have already achieved so much. He called for a serious examination of the reports of dialogues in the comprehensive manner already outlined in the *Directory* and emphasised the need to assess the results in terms of their congruence with the apostolic tradition. What we see in *Ut Unum Sint* is both a recognition that the total doctrinal patrimony of each communion must be dealt with in any relationship of dialogue; but at the same time, that all agreements need to be received with the hope that they can now be part of a common patrimony. Moreover, acceptance can never be purely a natural response but must be a deep, honest acceptance in faith based upon a recognition of the congruence of the agreement with the apostolic tradition as adhered to by each communion.

In that same encyclical, the pope gave a very good example of the role of dialogue when he invited church leaders and theologians from other Christian communions 'to engage' as he said, 'with me in a patient and fraternal dialogue on this subject [the ministry of the bishop of Rome], a dialogue in which, leaving useless controversies behind, we could listen to one another, keeping before us only the will

---

21. John Paul II, Encyclical Letter, *Ut Unum Sint*, 'On Commitment to Ecumenism' (Vatican: Libreria Editrice Vaticana, 1995), 90.

of Christ for his Church and allowing ourselves to be deeply moved by his plea "that they may all be one . . . so that the world may believe that you have sent me" (Jn 17:21).[22] The first results of this new and unique dialogue are still being evaluated.[23] Finally perhaps his most widely quoted contribution to the Catholic perception of dialogue was something which he saw as consistent with the teaching of Pope Paul VI in *Ecclesiam Suam*: 'Dialogue is not simply an exchange of ideas. In some way it is always an "exchange of gifts"'.[24]

The Nature and Purpose of Ecumenical Dialogue

In 2004 the Joint Working Group between the Roman Catholic Church and the World Council of Churches (WCC) produced a new report entitled 'The Nature and Purpose of Ecumenical Dialogue'.[25] This provides many additional theological and practical insights into ecumenical dialogue given the much longer period of engagement by the Catholic Church in such dialogue.

Its description of dialogue begins appropriately with John 17:21, Christ's prayer for unity so that the world may believe. It called dialogue 'a spiritual experience', a 'listening and speaking to one another in love'. The aim of dialogue is an understanding of each other 'in a deep way' as a result of communicating one's ecclesial experience to each other, and entering into the other's experience and seeing the world through their eyes. Its metaphor was 'walking with the other' in 'pilgrimage' and its biblical image was that of the disciples on the road to Emmaus:

> Dialogue entails walking with the other; pilgrimage is an apt metaphor for dialogue. Dialogue represents a word—neither the first nor the last—on a common journey, marking a moment between the 'already' of our past histories and the 'not yet' of our future. It images

---

22. *Ut Unum Sint*, 107.
23. Peter Lüning, 'Universal Episkopé and the Papal Ministry: Responses to *Ut Unum Sint*', in *One in Christ*, 39/1 (October 2004): 24–36.
24. *Ut Unum Sint*, 36.
25. 'The Nature and Purpose of Ecumenical Dialogue', in *Joint Working Group between the Roman Catholic Church and the World Council of Churches, Eighth Report, 1995–2005* (Geneva: WCC, 2005).

> the disciples' conversation on the road to Emmaus, recounting the wonders the Lord has worked during a journey culminating in the recognition of the Lord in the breaking of bread at a common table.[26]

It then continued with this spiritual rather than merely practical description of dialogue by affirming that 'Dialogue is more than an exchange of ideas. It is a mutual gift exchange', echoing thereby the sentiment of Pope John Paul II in *Ut Unum Sint*.

In its account of what it called 'the theological foundations of dialogue', this report has produced the richest account yet of dialogue in terms of a trinitarian ecclesiology of communion. For the Joint Working Group (JWG): 'Ecumenical dialogue reflects analogically the inner life of the Triune God and the revelation of His love'.[27]

A Catholic Theology of Dialogue

In the light of all these various documents it is possible to recognise the emergence of a theology of dialogue, at least in outline, and indeed a spirituality of dialogue, which has its basis in a trinitarian ecclesiology, or an ecclesiology of communion. This is consistent with the fundamental ecclesiology of the documents of the council and, in particular, of the Decree on Ecumenism. A biblical basis for this ecclesiology can be found in St John's Gospel and many other places in the New Testament, and it is congruent with the spiritual experience of those involved in serious ecumenical dialogue. One cannot properly understand dialogue unless one understands the relationship which exists between the dialogue partners precisely because they are already one in Christ. Some biblical texts which are often quoted in ecumenical contexts indicate just how profound is the theological foundation for ecumenical dialogue.

John 17:20–21

The most often quoted text within the ecumenical movement is John 17:20–21: 'I ask not only on behalf of these, but also on behalf of those who will believe in me through their word, that they may all be one.

---

26. 'The Nature and Purpose of Ecumenical Dialogue', 76.
27. 'The Nature and Purpose of Ecumenical Dialogue', 77.

As you, Father, are in me and I am in you, may they also be in us, so that the world may believe that you have sent me'. Jesus prayed quite simply that all would be one and described that unity in terms of his own relationship with the Father.

It would be a mistake when talking about unity between the churches or the unity within any one Christian community to start with or focus primarily upon the relationship of Christians with each other. The unity that Christians are called to, established in, or formed into involves a very particular kind of relationship. It is not only modelled on the kind of relationship that Jesus has with his Father, or indeed the Second Person of the Trinity has with the First Person of the Trinity, but involves a participation by Christians in that very same relationship. As he said: 'May they be in us' and again later: 'that they may be one, as we are one, I in them and you in me, that they may become completely one'. There is a mutual indwelling of Jesus in the Father and the Father in him and of believers in him, and he in them, so that they dwell in the very inner life of God where Father and Son are one with the Holy Spirit. The unity Christians have with each other arises from this prior unity they have through Christ, whereby they are drawn into the heart of the triune God.

Any effort to work for unity between Christian communions, and all ecumenical dialogue, has as its foundation this unity which is a pure gift of the risen Lord who died so that Christians might experience it. It is called elsewhere than in these texts of St John *koinonia*/communion. Whatever we may observe among Christians which could be called 'community' is but a visible expression of this deeper common participation in the very life of the triune God, or communion.

The profound depth of this relationship between Christians is what endures despite their divisions; and it supplies the only sure foundation for ecumenical dialogue. All the efforts of Christians to stay apart cannot entirely resist the divine communal embrace which holds them together and constantly creates a hunger for the full realisation of communion. It creates a longing, usually unacknowledged, for the gift of the other which alone will fill up what is lacking in any one separated Christian's experience of communion within the triune God. Dialogue is simply the conversation which gives voice to this longing, and initially enables it to become apparent to the participant.

As such it is always an intensely spiritual experience. It occurs in the Spirit. To engage in dialogue is no more than to respond to the Holy Spirit. It is an inevitable consequence of our Christian existence in the triune God, though it is often delayed by human sinfulness and that even for centuries.

The commencement of an ecumenical dialogue is the beginning of a surrender to the triune God in whom both parties dwell despite their separation. The experience of dialogue is one of human resistance to each other and to God being overcome by the divine love which will inevitably unify Christians, even if they know not when, how or with whom.

John 14:25–26

Another important text for understanding the experience of dialogue is John 14:25–26: 'I have said these things to you while I am still with you. But the Advocate, the Holy Spirit, whom the Father will send in my name, will teach you everything, and remind you of all that I have said to you'.

Christians engaged in dialogue have to be men and women of the truth; and Jesus is the truth. The Spirit will never lead them in any direction other than to him. The Spirit will never lead them to think something contrary to what he has taught; and the Spirit will find ways of revealing to them what is God's will, even when they are resistant. One can conclude from these fundamental affirmations that the Spirit has never revealed to Christians different truths. Because God respects their different cultures, languages and histories, the Spirit will have revealed the one truth to them in different forms. Sometimes too the Spirit will have revealed to one or another a new insight into the truth which is meant as a gift for all, even if the gift is first received by one divided from another. Perhaps, too, the Spirit is hindered from revealing 'everything' because of the barriers which divisions have created in the hearts and minds of Christians.

Sadly, the different forms the one truth has taken through the working of God's Spirit have been interpreted as opposed truths, not because of conflicts inherent in the different versions of the one truth, but because of conflicts, sometimes sinful, between languages, cultures and people. So instead of allowing the one truth which is Christ to unite them despite their differences, Christians have succumbed to their differences, and so torn apart the one truth of Christ. After all the divisions of the past, they are now left with divided versions of the truth, of the gospel, of the tradition, which they have made into opposed truths. Ecumenical dialogue seeks to reconcile these by trying again to recognise the one truth of Jesus Christ, the Word of God, the apostolic tradition, in these diverse and divided forms. Mutual recognition is the precondition for mutual reconciliation.[28]

However this is not easy. Each Christian community finds its certainty or its confidence about the truth in different ways: from the scriptures themselves; from the living tradition of the Church; from the authoritative teaching of the governing bodies of the Church; from the discernment of the truth among all the faithful; from theologians and from scholars; from saints and mystics; through the signs of the times; in the silence of their own hearts. They put together those various sources of authority or certainty in different ways. They weight them differently. But in one way or another, most are present in most Christian communities.

Tolerance and inclusion may be respectable goals for Christians but they are also called to believe what Christ has taught them. Therefore while Christians may be tolerant of all members of the human community, and especially their fellow Christians, they have boundaries laid down by what they believe about Christ which inhibits their having the same relationship with everyone. They cannot share their Christian fellowship in the same way with everybody.

Two hallmarks of the Christian community are truth and love. Christians are people who stand for the truth which is Jesus Christ and they are people whose love is their own sharing in his passionate love for all whom God has created. If they were only people of the truth, then they would have no capacity to touch the heart of each other or to accept what others have to offer them, because they would easily become intransigent or dogmatic or utterly exclusive. If they were only people of love, then they would easily cease to stand for anything and there would ultimately be no boundary between them and the world. When speaking of dialogue in the ecumenical context, one is not describing a meeting of persons in which no-one holds to anything with utter conviction, or, on the other hand, in which no-

---

28. See Gerard Kelly, *Recognition: Advancing Ecumenical Thinking* (New York: Peter Lang, 1996).

one is free to say they believe something is true and consequently something else seems to be false. In fact, genuine dialogue requires the capacity to do precisely that. Those engaged in dialogue have to be people of truthful love and of loving truth.

In his article already referred to, Cardinal Kasper made the same point:

> A distinction is often made between the dialogue of love and the dialogue of truth. Both are important, but neither can be separated; they belong together. Love without truth is void and dishonest; truth without love is hard and repelling. So we must seek the truth in love, bearing in mind that love can be authentic only when it is an expression of truth.[29]

Another way of saying this would be that partners in dialogue have to be truly open and yet truly faithful. If they are only open to the other, or to their culture, then they can easily lose themselves in the other or in their culture. If they are only faithful, then they will not recognise Christ among his other disciples and they will not recognise signs of the Spirit struggling to build up the Church of Jesus Christ outside their own Christian community. But if they are faithful while at the same time being open, then the Spirit can work in them and indeed their openness and their faithfulness are already his work in them.

But to be faithful while being open is a very demanding task. It is a profoundly Christian challenge. Too easily Christians bind themselves up in the truth as they have perceived it within their own communities, their own families or their own selves. This gives them a particular position vis-à-vis God and the rest of the world, and they hold on to it with great tenacity. The risk of being open to others and their ideas or experiences can be too great because it might jeopardise this truth to which they hold with such conviction.

Alternatively, Christians may be so open that the truth of Christ is watered down and eventually their Christian identity fades to some extent. It is very hard to be equally faithful with the same tenacity and equally loving with the same generosity of spirit as those are who exemplify but one side of this dual calling of the Christian.

---

29. 'The Nature and Purpose of Ecumenical Dialogue', 44.

Dialogue is the patient, painstaking determination to hear the other with complete openness and to reveal one's own deepest self to the other, not just one's best rhetoric. True dialogue is the lifelong task of the Christian in relationship with others in his or her own community and with other Christian Churches.

Unless one is open to the other in dialogue at every level of one's being and not just intellectually, there is no possibility of any major development through the encounter. One develops a much more profound understanding of one's tradition when one is questioned or challenged by a dialogue partner, because one is thereby forced to review one's fidelity to the Word of God or the apostolic tradition. In fact, in Christian dialogue, one is ultimately open to what the Holy Spirit will lead both parties to discover, about the other and, indeed, about themselves, and above all about the Word of God. As both Pope Paul VI and Pope John Paul II have indicated, dialogue is not simply as an exchange of ideas, but in some way it is always an exchange of gifts.

The results of ecumenical dialogue between the Catholic Church and so many other world communions are indicators of the extraordinary fruitfulness of genuine dialogue when both of these virtues are exercised. The signing of the Joint Declaration on the Doctrine of Justification by the Catholic Church and the Lutheran World Federation on 31 October 1999, and the move for the World Methodist Council to become a party to this agreement, is a marvellous example of such fruitfulness.

John 15:12–15

A further text which is relevant to any discussion of ecumenical dialogue is John 15:12–15:

> This is my commandment, that you love one another as I have loved you. No one has greater love than this, to lay down one's life for one's friends. You are my friends if you do what I command you. I do not call you servants any longer, because the servant does not know what the master is doing; but I have called you friends, because I have made known to you everything that I have heard from my Father.

A very apt description for the Church and for each of our Christian communities would be 'the friends of Jesus'. The love Christians are called to have is not so much the love they might have for their own particular friends, but the love for all of his friends. Indeed, through faith and baptism, he is living in his friends and to love them as his friends is in fact to love him whom one finds in them. Because Jesus is claiming the hearts of so many as his friends, they cannot really walk away easily from his other friends.

However they see the members of other Christian communities, Christians have to see them as friends of Jesus. They ought to have an expectation of discovering him in the lives and witness of those who are 'other' than ourselves, whenever they meet them. The openness that they need to have to 'the other' in Christian dialogue is not simply their openness to them: it is an openness to him whom they will find in them. He is there among, and indeed living in, his friends.

Some people believe that the ecumenical movement is grinding to a halt, that it is going backwards, or that we have entered a winter or a darkness at this present point of history. The evidence to the contrary is too great, even of major developments in the ten years from 1996 to 2005. Early dialogues were exciting because they involved getting to know each other and discovering that prejudice blinded Christians to all kinds of truths about their dialogue partners who were far less threatening or different to them than they might have believed.

That easy, exciting period is past. It was like a honeymoon in a marriage, or the first flush of a friendship, when one falls in love to some extent with one's new friend. Another stage follows when one realises that friendship, like marriage, is a long-term relationship, and that friendships need to deepen by moving gradually to deeper levels of acceptance and understanding. At times, it also means that friends have to challenge each other when they do not believe the other is being their best possible selves, and to forgive each other when they fail, or offend.

No-one has any right *ever* simply to walk away from another Christian within their own community or from another Christian community. They may have to pause and say they cannot walk with the other in the same way at this point of their common journey because of what the other is saying or doing, but they need to add that they will wait for them and for a future reunion when they can recommence their journey together. Their friendship is in some ways 'on hold'. They are not deserting them. To do so would be to desert some of Christ's friends and they don't have the right to do that.

Obviously there are degrees of difficulty in a relationship, and there can even be the possibility of a rather definitive separation when some appear to the eyes of others to have themselves rejected Christ. In doing so they have rejected those with whom he is united as well. But if one can recognise the others still as belonging to him in some way, then they continue to be, no matter how difficult the relationship, united to oneself as well. Discerning this correctly is very difficult and requires enormous patience. Historically, Christians have seldom had such patience in their dealings with each other, and have far too easily accepted separations as definitive. If the separation or the apparent definitiveness is too easily accepted, the separation will involve as well a separation in some way from Christ because it will involve rejecting some whom he loved and in whom he lived.

Therefore, it is helpful sometimes to speak of estranged friends or alienated friends who hopefully will one day be good friends again. The five hundred years of division among Christian communities since the Protestant Reformation was not a final break which Christians are now attempting to repair so that they can start completely anew together. Their separate histories were histories lived in Christ himself. Separated they were and long lasting, but they were really only temporarily separated. Christ could never let such a break be permanent or irrevocable. It was ever only a matter of time. They may have forgotten that they were both his friends, but he did not, and hence the modern ecumenical movement.

Jewish–Catholic Relations Today in the Light of Forty Years of *Nostra Aetate*

Last year Pope Benedict XVI visited the synagogue in Cologne when he was in that city for the gathering of Catholic young people from all around the world for World Youth Day 2005. He drew attention to the fact that Cologne was the oldest site of a Jewish Community on German soil, dating back to Roman times, and acknowledged that relations between the Jewish and Christian Communities since that time had been complex and often painful. This history involved the expulsion of the Jews from Cologne in the year 1424. He then referred to 'the darkest period of German and European history' when 'an insane racist ideology, born of neo-paganism, gave rise to the attempt, planned and systematically carried out by the regime, to exterminate European Jewry'. Seven thousand named individuals died in the *Shoah* from Cologne alone, though the real figure was surely much higher.

In that context, Pope Benedict referred to the fortieth anniversary of the promulgation of *Nostra Aetate* in which he said there opened up 'new prospects for Jewish–Christian relations in terms of dialogue and solidarity'.[1] I would like to take his reflections as a starting point for a similar reflection on the Australian situation. In Cologne he noted that *Nostra Aetate* 'recalls the common roots and the immensely rich spiritual heritage that Jews and Christians share. Both Jews and Christians recognise in Abraham their father in faith . . . and they look to the teachings of Moses and the Prophets'.[2] *Nostra Aetate*, quoting St Paul, affirmed that Christians are convinced that with respect

This paper was presented at the celebration of Jews and Catholics in Sydney on 26 March 2006 to mark the 40th anniversary of *Nostra Aetate*.

1. 'A Papal Visit to Cologne Synagogue', in *Origins*, 35/12 (1 September 2005): 207.
2. 'A Papal Visit to Cologne Synagogue', 207.

to the Jewish people, 'the gifts and the call of God are irrevocable'. Pope Benedict also quoted a statement by the German bishops as had Pope John Paul II before him that because of the Jewish roots of Christianity, 'whoever meets Jesus Christ meets Judaism'.

We have come to take for granted this positive affirmation in *Nostra Aetate* of the relationship between Jews and Christians and it is on the basis of that relationship so described that Jews and Catholics have in the past forty years come together in Australia on many different levels for dialogue and collaboration, and to attempt to address the dark and tragic elements in the historical relationship between Jews and Catholics. One major moment in that relationship here in Australia was the launch by Bishop Bede Heather in the crypt of St Mary's Cathedral in May 1992 of the Australian Catholic Bishops' Conference, *Guidelines for Catholic–Jewish Relations*. On that occasion, Bishop Heather spoke of the special bond between the Catholic Church and Judaism which, for him, as a scripture scholar, expressed itself most powerfully in a shared love of the Hebrew Scriptures, but he went on to say:

> I would not want to leave the impression, however, that it is only in our common esteem for a sacred literature that we are bound together. The Church and the synagogue have also shared a history of 2000 years in Europe and in countries like ours, of culture derived from Europe. Each of us has known oppression and persecution. We have often been antagonists. The Jewish people have often suffered at our hands, as in their expulsion from Spain in 1492, recalled recently in one of the synagogues of Sydney. I trust that a fresh start has been made. The Church needs not only the ancient and sacred Scriptures of Judaism but the Judaism of the present. It tells us of God's unfailing promises and reminds us of the undying quality of faith tenaciously held through persecution and oppression of the worst kind.[3]

---

3. Bede Heather, Launch of *Guidelines for Catholic–Jewish Relations*, St Mary's Cathedral Crypt, Sydney, 2 November 1992, 4.

Those guidelines addressed such matters as the way Judaism ought be referred to in preaching and teaching, enactments of Passover meals by Christians, co-operation in social action, and theological dialogue.[4]

Earlier there was the occasion in 1986 when Pope John Paul II spoke to Jewish Community leaders, again in Sydney. He spoke of last century as 'the century of the Shoah, the inhuman and ruthless attempt to exterminate European Jewry'.[5] In 1998, the Holy See through its Commission for Religious Relations with the Jews, attempted to deal with this most tragic and monumental of moments in the relationship between Christians and Jews, in its document 'We Remember: A Reflection on the *Shoah*'.

One way in which we attempted to address this directly ourselves here in Australia was through a meeting of the Bishops' Committee for Ecumenical and Interfaith Relations and representatives of the Council of Australian Jewry, at which I delivered a paper entitled 'An Australian Catholic Comment on *We Remember: A Reflection on the Shoah*'. In my concluding paragraph I spoke as follows:

> As an Australian Catholic I now see the attitudes I carried as a youth, which I have never really addressed, as a less virulent form of the same anti-Judaism or 'contempt' that provided a breeding ground for the anti-Semitism which ultimately led to the *Shoah*. I am glad that Catholics in Australia never had to face the questions of conscience that our co-religionists faced in Europe, because I fear we would not have escaped with any less guilt than they have. I am also glad to be living at a time when the Catholic Church at all levels is trying to come to terms with its past failures, and to ask forgiveness for them. I wish to add my single Australian voice to so many more significant Catholic bodies to say how sorry I am that so many Catholics let you down so

---

4. Bishops' Committee for Ecumenical and Interfaith Relations, Australian Catholic Bishops' Conference, *The Faithfulness of the Lord Endures Forever: Guidelines for Catholic–Jewish Relations*, November 1992.

5. John Paul II, 'Address to Representatives of the Jewish Community', in *The Pope in Australia: Collected Homilies and Talks* (Homebush: St Paul, 1986), 57.

badly in your time of greatest need and I wish to play my
part in changing the perceptions of Australian Catholics
wherever it is necessary so that nothing like the *Shoah*
may ever occur again.[6]

Australian Catholics also regularly participate in services
remembering the *Shoah*, not least of all in Sydney in the crypt of St
Mary's Cathedral. Moreover, one of the things we have said on more
than one occasion at the meetings of the Australian Catholic Bishops'
Committee and representatives of the Council of Australian Jewry
is that we recognise our responsibility to stand beside the Jewish
Community in Australia whenever there are manifestations of anti-
Semitism in the Australian community. I hope that we will learn to
do that well and never fail to do it when it is called for.

In his address to the synagogue in Cologne, Pope Benedict went
on to say:

> We must come to know one another much more and
> much better. Consequently, I would encourage sincere
> and trustful dialogue between Jews and Christians,
> for only in this way will it be possible to arrive at a
> shared interpretation of disputed historical questions,
> and, above all, to make progress towards a theological
> evaluation of the relationship between Judaism and
> Christianity. This dialogue, if it is to be sincere, must not
> gloss over or under-estimate the existing differences: in
> those areas in which, due to our profound convictions in
> faith, we diverge, and indeed precisely in those areas, we
> need to show respect for another.[7]

At our last meeting of the Australian Catholic Bishops' Conference
with representatives of the Council of Australian Jewry, we addressed
two topics which enabled us to start the journey towards the
'theological evaluation' of our relationship of which the pope spoke.
One was a paper on evangelisation which I delivered and the other

---

6. 'An Australian Catholic Comment on *We Remember: A Reflection on the Shoah*',
   in *Australasian Catholic Record*, 76/3 (July 1999): 349.
7. 'A Papal Visit to Cologne Synagogue', 207.

was a paper on Zionism which Peta Pellach delivered. In my paper I reflected upon a document signed by 172 Jewish scholars mainly from the United States, on 10 September 2000, which was entitled 'Dabru Emet: A Jewish Statement on Christians and Christianity',[8] and then on a statement entitled 'Reflections on Covenant and Mission',[9] which was produced on 12 August 2002 from a consultation sponsored by the National Council of Synagogues in the USA and Delegates of the Bishops' Committee on Ecumenical and Inter-Religious Affairs of the United States Catholic Conference. Both of these documents have provoked a considerable amount of discussion and even controversy in our respective communities, but they have touched on some very important theological questions which as yet have not been adequately addressed in dialogue on any level in our Catholic–Jewish relationship.

Cardinal Walter Kasper, the President of the Commission for Religious Relations with the Jews would not have been unaware of this latter paper when he himself addressed the question of mission in an important address in Boston on 6 November of that same year. In that address he said:

> But whilst Jews expect the coming of the Messiah, who is still unknown, Christians believe that he has already shown his face in Jesus of Nazareth, whom we as Christians therefore confess as the Christ, he who at the end of time will be revealed as the Messiah for Jews and for all nations . . .
>
> This does not mean that Jews in order to be saved have to become Christians; if they follow their own conscience and believe in God's promises as they understand them in their religious tradition they are in line with God's plan, which for us comes to its historical completion in Jesus Christ.

---

8. 'Dabru Emet: A Jewish Statement on Christians and Christianity', in *Gesher*, 2/4 (October 2001): 44.
9. US Catholic–Jewish Dialogue, 'Reflections on Covenant and Mission', in *Origins*, 32/13 (5 September 2002): 218–24.

He went on to say:

> The question of mission belongs in this larger context
> and cannot be dealt with in isolation from it because for
> Christians mission in its full sense is nothing less than
> a consequence of our belief in Jesus as the Christ. For
> missionary activity is much more than targeting Jews or
> others for conversion and seeking new candidates for
> baptism. . .
>
> For Christians this includes giving testimony of Jesus
> the Christ to all and in all places; for Christians this is
> the mandate of Jesus Christ himself (Matt 28:19). They
> cannot renounce doing so without renouncing to be
> Christians. Yet giving this testimony is undertaken
> differently in relation to Jews with respect to Gentiles.
>
> . . . the question of mission can only be solved in
> the wider context of the overall Christian theology of
> Judaism. Here we are only at the beginning and still
> far from a definitive understanding. The long period of
> anti-Judaistic theology cannot be overcome in only forty
> years. 'Nostra aetate' was only the beginning of a new
> beginning.[10]

Catholics recognise that God's promise to Jewish people is irrevocable
and that Judaism continues to flourish as a living, religious community
that has not been simply superseded by Christianity no matter what
theologians may have said for much of our history. At the same time,
we must acknowledge also our own deep conviction of the unique
and universal significance of Jesus Christ for the salvation of the
human race and our inevitable witness to him in all our relationships.
This theological question is not yet answered, as Cardinal Kasper said
so well in 2002.

In a recent address to the Association of Jewish Studies in
Washington, Bishop Sklba, the new Chairman of the United States
Bishops' Committee on Ecumenical and Interreligious Affairs,
summed up the theological question in this way:

---

10. Walter Kasper, 'The Commission for Religious Relations with the Jews: A Crucial
 Endeavour of the Catholic Church', Boston College, 6 November 2002, 7–8.

On the one hand, Christian theology must avoid blatant supersessionism, which would invalidate Paul's teachings regarding the irrevocability of God's gifts. On the other hand, we Christians must be faithful to our own convictions regarding the redemptive mission of Jesus of Nazareth.

... How is Jesus definitive for us, while still respecting the inherent inner autonomy and salvific vitality of Judaism?

It seems important for us as Christians to avoid a simple scenario of two parallel traditions of divine election, mutually tolerant but virtually ignoring each other's inner logic and identity. While not proselytizing, Christians today would still feel the need to imitate the Apostle Paul and to invite Jewish colleagues to understand the logical development we find when reading the Scripture of Israel. A respectful invitation is faithful to our Christian sense of continuity and development. Conversely, faithful members of the Jewish covenant should invite Christians to appreciate the joyful gift of Torah, rather than a burden, as it is so often portrayed in an erroneous and stereotypical fashion by Christian apologists.

For us, therefore, it is a question of developing a new Christology that can express our Christian convictions, bridge our two traditions in an authentically Jewish fashion and still respect the vitality of contemporary Judaism in the modern world. This delicate and patient work of theological inquiry is the work of reconciliation.[11]

So one can say that at this point of history, the relationship between Catholics and Jews would profit by a more serious endeavour to deal with theological questions which are raised for both of us by Jesus Christ. This theological reflection and dialogue has not yet taken place at all sufficiently in Australia.

---

11. Bishop Sklba, 'New Beginnings: Catholic–Jewish Relations after 40 Years', in *Origins*, 35/31 (19 January 2006): 513.

Moreover, a major re-education program still needs to be taken up by the Catholic Church in Australia on a grassroots level which would deal with such issues as how Catholics ought to speak in a new way about Jews in their preaching and teaching, using and interpreting the scriptures differently, dealing with questions such as enactments of Passover meals, passion plays, Mel Gibson's film, etc. Because most Catholic communities in Australia have no or little experience of Jews, this work has not been done sufficiently or very widely. One recent example is the textbook edited by Maurice Ryan of the Australian Catholic University entitled 'Jewish–Christian Relations'.[12] It contains ten chapters addressing very important topics, including interviews with Rabbi John Levi and Cardinal Cassidy entitled 'Christians and Jews: Progressive or Regressive', and an article by Rabbi John Levi entitled 'Judaism Today'.

In addition to the guidelines of our own Bishops' Conference, there have been wonderful documents produced by the Commission for Religious Relations with Jews of the Holy See, by the United States Catholic Bishops' Conference and by others around the world which would help the Australian Catholic community to carry forward this very important project. Examples of helpful documents from the Holy See and the US Bishops' Conference would be:

> 'Notes on the Correct way to Present Jews and Judaism in Preaching and Catechesis in the Roman Catholic Church' (Commission, 1985),
> 'Jews and Judaism in the Liturgies of Lent and Holy Week' (USCC, 1985),
> 'Criteria for the Evaluation of Dramatisations of the Passion' (USCC, 1988),
> 'God's Mercy Endures Forever: Guidelines on the Presentation of Jews and Judaism in Catholic Preaching' (USCC, 1988),
> 'The Jewish People and their Sacred Scriptures in the Christian Bible' (PBC, 2001).

---

12. *Jewish–Christian Relations: A Textbook for Australian Students*, edited by Maurice Ryan (Ringwood: David Lovell, 2004).

The Victorian Council of Christians and Jews has produced valuable resources as well, such as:

> 'Rightly Explaining the Word of Truth' (1995),
> 'Re-reading Paul: A Fresh Look at His Attitude to Torah and Judaism' (1999).

This does not mean that we ought not continue to deal with the equally important questions that were raised by Peta Pellach in her paper concerning the religious significance of the land of Israel for Jews, and the cluster of socio-political questions that this raises for all people in the contemporary world. It also does not imply any neglect of the continuing question of racism and anti-Semitism, and of the honest acknowledgement of the responsibility which can be attributed to Catholics at different levels in the Church and in different places for the *Shoah* and for other crimes against Jews throughout history.

Towards the very end of his address in the synagogue in Cologne Pope Benedict turned to speak of the future and the tasks that lie ahead. He said:

> Our rich common heritage and our fraternal more trusting relations call upon us to join in giving an evermore harmonious witness, and to work together on the practical level for the defence and promotion of human rights and the sacredness of human life, for family values, for social justice and for peace in the world.[13]

On 28 February 2006 the bilateral commission meeting of the Holy See's Commission for Religious Relations with the Jews and the Chief Rabbinate of Israel's Delegation for Relations with the Catholic Church produced a document on respect for human life, particularly taking a stand against 'active euthanasia (so-called mercy killing)', which it described as 'the illegitimate human arrogation of an exclusive divine authority to determine the time of a person's death'.[14] This is a

---

13. 'A Papal Visit to Cologne Synagogue', 207.
14. Catholic-Jewish Bilateral Commission Meeting, 'A Rejection of Active Euthanasia and a Reaffirmation of the Value of Life', in *L'Osservatore Romano*, 11 (15 March

good example of the kind of witness about which Pope Benedict was speaking in the Cologne synagogue.

The final paragraph of the short statement from this meeting began with a reference to abuses of religion, its symbols, holy sites and houses of worship:

> At the same time, such abuses and the current tensions between civilisations, demand of us to reach out beyond our own bi-lateral dialogue which has its unique compelling character. Thus we believe that it is our duty to engage in and involve the Muslim world and its leaders in respectful dialogue and co-operation. Furthermore, we appeal to world leaders to appreciate the essential potential of the religious dimension to help resolve conflicts and strife and call on them to support inter-religious dialogue to this end.[15]

More recently, on March 16 (2006), Pope Benedict addressed a delegation of the American Jewish Committee. He began by saying: 'In many ways this distinguishes our relationship as unique among the religions of the world. The Church can never forget that chosen people with whom God entered into a holy covenant (cf *Nostra Aetate*, n. 4)'. Then he concluded in a very similar vein to his comments in Cologne:

> Judaism, Christianity and Islam believe in the one God, Creator of heaven and earth. It follows, therefore, that all three monotheistic religions are called to cooperate with one another for the common good of humanity, serving the cause of justice and peace in the world. This is especially important today when particular attention must be given to teaching respect for God, for religions and their symbols, and for holy sites and places of worship. Religious leaders have a responsibility to work for reconciliation through genuine dialogue and acts of human solidarity.

2006): 9.
15. 'A Rejection of Active Euthanasia and a Reaffirmation of the Value of Life', 9.

This kind of cooperation is also happening here in Australia. There is a dialogue/conversation sponsored by the National Council of Churches in Australia involving Jews, Christians and Muslims which likewise meets here in Sydney, to name but one example.

Much remains to be done but much has been done. Jews and Catholics stand today in their relationship in Australia in a vastly different place to where they did forty years ago because of *Nostra Aetate*. I thank God for that and look forward to what is yet to come as we move on from 'the beginning of the new beginning'.

Receptive Catholic Learning through Methodist–Catholic Dialogue

Introduction

For his year 2000 *Père Marquette Lecture in Theology*, Geoffrey Wainwright took as his topic 'Is the Reformation Over?'[1] He identified five different ways in which one could press this claim, evocatively captured in the following questions: (1) Has the Catholic Church turned Protestant? (2) Has Protestantism poped? (3) Were they mere misunderstandings? (4) Does doctrine (still) matter? (5) Are matters now settled? Or, less provocatively expressed:

> The idea might be that the Roman Catholic Church has now, for good or ill, accepted the proposals by which Luther launched the Reformation. Alternatively, it could be . . . that Protestant truth has sold out to Rome, or . . . that Protestantism is on the point of being welcomed back into the Catholic fold. A third, and more irenical possibility, would be that the unfortunate mutual 'misunderstandings' of the sixteenth century have at last been cleared up. Or again, the sixteenth-century controversies may be thought ... to have since become irrelevant or at least no longer church-dividing. Fifth and finally, it might be considered that genuine and substantial differences, which were insoluble when they first arose, can now be reconciled and overcome through the discovery

This paper was published in *Receptive Ecumenism and the Call to Catholic Learning: Exploring a Way for Contemporary Ecumenism*, edited by Paul D Murray (Oxford: Oxford University Press, 2008), 122–33.

1. See *Is the Reformation Over? Catholics and Protestants at the Turn of the Millennia* (Milwaukee: Marquette University Press, 2000).

> of new insights . . . or . . . the recovery of more original
> perceptions that antedate the Reformation.[2]

None of these proposals would justify the claim that the Reformation is completely over but each of them affords a way of reviewing developments in the state of ecumenical relationships since the Catholic Church officially embraced the ecumenical movement at the Second Vatican Council. As to why none of them could claim a complete resolution of Reformation divisions, Wainwright concluded that the most basic and comprehensive issue still needing to be dealt with was 'the nature, identity and location of the church, the question of fundamental ecclesiology'.[3]

Related to this, I would suggest that for as long as our starting point is with our historical relationship to each other as brought about by the Reformation, then we will never be able to answer definitively questions such as 'Is the Reformation over?' or 'Are our divided churches finally able to accept each other in the embrace of full communion?' The desired reconciliation will never be achieved simply by looking back or looking at each other as divided. In contrast, along with others here, I believe that Pope John Paul II's description of dialogue as 'not simply an exchange of ideas' but as in some ways 'always an "exchange of gifts"' (*Ut Unum Sint*, 28) gives us a new starting point for describing our present relationships and thereby indicates a possible way to future reconciliation.

Further, this exchange of gifts should not be viewed thinly in terms of some potentially enriching ecclesial practices or elements which might simply be added on to the fundamental gift of deepened understanding that should always occur through dialogue. Obviously, such a practical exchange does already occur. We receive from each other not just new insights into the gospel but even new ways of perceiving ourselves or the way in which we and others stand within the apostolic tradition. One startling example of this occurred through the dialogue between the Catholic Church and the Assyrian Church of the East which led to the recognition of the latter's eucharist despite its lacking an explicit proclamation of the words

---

2. *Is the Reformation Over? Catholics and Protestants at the Turn of the Millennia*, 9–10.
3. *Is the Reformation Over? Catholics and Protestants at the Turn of the Millennia*, 61.

of institution.[4] Again, other very practical changes occur because of our ecumenical engagement. One need only think, for example, of the biblical and liturgical renewals that have been shared between Christian communions. However, the exchange of gifts to which Pope John Paul II referred, developing the teaching of Pope Paul VI in his 1964 encyclical *Ecclesiam Suam*, describes a more profound exchange and deeper relationship than the practical alone. It is the nature of this more profound exchange that I would like to explore.[5]

Dialogue, Exchange, and Deepened Communion in Christ

In a 1970 document of the then Secretariat for Promoting Christian Unity, it was presumed that 'those who take part [in ecumenical dialogue] recognise one another as existing in Christ' and so are able 'through the Holy Spirit to hear their brethren tell them of the marvellous works of God' and to recognise 'a certain communion' existing between them.[6] The document could then speak of dialogue leading not just to the discovery of truths held in common, or truths which have been obscured because of separation, but also the discovery of new insights indicative of the unique, divinely grounded fruitfulness of the relationship of dialogue.[7]

In a more recent document produced by the Joint Working Group (JWG) between the Roman Catholic Church and the World Council of Churches (WCC), one reads:

> Dialogue entails walking with the other; pilgrimage is an apt metaphor . . . Dialogue represents a word—neither the first nor the last—on a common journey, marking a moment between the 'already' of our past histories and the 'not yet' of our future. It images

---

4. See Robert F Taft SJ, 'Mass without the Consecration? The Historic Agreement on the Eucharist between the Catholic Church and the Assyrian Church of the East, Promulgated 26 October 2001', in *Liturgical Renewal as a Way to Christian Unity*, edited by James F Puglisi (Collegeville: Liturgical Press, 2005), 199–226.
5. See Paul VI, *Ecclesiam Suam*, 'The Church in the Modern World' (London: Catholic Truth Society, 1979 [1965]), particularly nn. 78–85.
6. 'Reflections and Suggestions Concerning Dialogue', 15 August 1970, *Vatican Council II: The Conciliar and Post Conciliar Documents*, edited by Austin Flannery, 535–53, at 543.
7. 'Reflections and Suggestions Concerning Dialogue', 547–8.

the disciples' conversation on the road to Emmaus, recounting the wonders the Lord has worked during a journey culminating in the recognition of the Lord in the breaking of bread at a common table.[8]

Dialogue, then, looks not only to the past but also to the future. It is always a process of discovery of the divine presence and activity in the other and so always opens each partner to receiving a new gift from the Lord.

I draw attention to these texts because they point to a way of viewing dialogue which starts from the common participation of the dialogue partners in Christ, their common sharing in the leading of the Holy Spirit, and their communion in the very life of the triune God. If one perceives this deeper relationship as occurring not only for individuals but also for ecclesial communities, then one can look at Christian communions that may have been divided over many centuries of acrimony with the eyes of a faith that makes one expectant of discovering in them some version of all of those elements which one believes Christ wills for his church and which one believes are found in one's own ecclesial communion. Indeed, one can look at them in the faith-filled expectation that some aspects of the full richness of the Church of Christ may be more evident in other communions than in one's own.

This positive and hope-filled perception of inter-ecclesial relationships has only become possible because of the new context created by the ecumenical movement, which can itself be seen as a movement of conversion. In this perspective, ecclesial communities grow toward each other as they grow closer to Christ. Already having some level of relationship with each other through their common immersion into Christ and so into the life of the triune God, they are drawn to reclaim their relationship with each other in him and to discover the developments within each other which have occurred both because of him and because of the Spirit who was sent by the Father to remind all his followers of what he has said. This 'living memory' of the church, which is the Holy Spirit, is a living memory that has existed in different communions. Because it is the memory of

---

8. 'The Nature and Purpose of Ecumenical Dialogue: A JWG Study', in *Information Service*, 117 (2004): 206.

the same Christ, and it is the same Spirit who is keeping it alive; what each communion which strives to be faithful will grow to understand and endeavour to put into practice will be the same gospel, the same apostolic tradition, and the same requirements for the full realisation of the Church of Christ.

In other words, contemporary dialogue between Christian communions involves a process of discovering in the other what the Holy Spirit has done to conform them to Christ and his wishes for the church. The exchange of gifts then becomes an exchange not just of other insights, other ways of living the gospel, and other ways of remaining faithful to those which have developed in one's own communion. Beyond all of this, it can also involve an exchange of those gifts which are yet to develop as fully in one's own communion or which may be present only very embryonically but yet belong to Christ's vision for his church.

Methodist–Catholic Dialogue—A Case in Point

To look specifically at the Methodist–Catholic Dialogue over the past forty years is to discover a very good illustration of this way of seeing the relationship between divided Christians and the potential for a new way of reconciling them. In the opening chapter of *The Grace Given You in Christ*, the latest report of the Methodist–Catholic Dialogue, an attempt is made to explore the new context which exists for a mutual reassessment by Methodists and Catholics.[9] Such a reassessment needs to include a new understanding of the past which would not only be guided by contemporary historical research but would also be the result of the openness created through decades of dialogue, collaboration and prayer. The report contains the following key insights:

> Neither Methodists nor Catholics should regard their separation as acceptable. Some may believe that certain separations were necessary in the past for the sake of

---

9. The Joint Commission for Dialogue between the World Methodist Council and the Roman Catholic Church, *The Grace Given You in Christ: Catholics and Methodists Reflect Further on the Church* (Lake Junaluska: World Methodist Council, 2006).

the gospel. Others may view all separations as failures
... which have obscured the unity of Christ's Church. In
2003 the Archbishop of Canterbury said of the divided
histories of the Church of England and the Methodist
Church of Great Britain, 'Wesley came to the point
where he believed that he and his followers could only
be fully obedient to Jesus Christ if they took the risk of
separation. No-one can easily pass judgement on this
costly decision, and no-one is seeking to do so; what
we can be sure of is that by God's direction it bore fruit
in witness and transforming service to the Kingdom of
God in this nation and far beyond.' Similarly, the separate
histories of Methodism and the Roman Catholic Church
can show how God has worked in both of them for the
fulfilment of the divine purpose ... (§13).

Later, taking up a reflection of Pope John Paul II, we find:

The separations of the last five hundred years cannot
simply be condoned even if they cannot simply be
condemned and blame apportioned. Reflecting on why
the Holy Spirit had permitted all the divisions between
Christians, Pope John Paul II noted: 'Could it not be
that these divisions have been a path continually leading
the Church to discover the untold wealth contained in
Christ's Gospel and in the redemption accomplished by
Christ? Perhaps all this wealth would not have come to
light otherwise ...'[10]

In the light of this, *The Grace Given You in Christ* continues:

A review of past history suggests that God has led each
of our churches in new ways that came through the
separations. Catholics can recognise that God has used
Methodism, both in its beginning and throughout its
history, to develop gifts which eventually ought to bless

---

10. *The Grace Given You in Christ*, §14, citing Pope John Paul II, *Crossing the Threshold
of Hope*, edited by Vittorio Messori (London: Jonathon Cape, 1994), 153.

all Christians everywhere. Similarly, Methodists can recognise that God has been at work in the Catholic Church's preservation of important traditions and in its pursuit of fresh presentations of the Gospel for the benefit of all Christian believers.

The most recent phase of the dialogue has in fact endeavoured to harvest the work of previous phases and, in the light of what has been achieved, to deepen and extend the recognition that each communion is able to offer the other. A deliberate attempt has been made to describe the elements of each communion which represent to the others' eyes, genuine elements of the Church of Christ. This recognition cannot at this point in history be imagined as being complete. It is, nevertheless, of an extraordinary depth and breadth which none would have imagined even a few decades ago. We are each able to acknowledge that the relationship is radically different to that which existed when the dialogue began and can now speak easily of the gifts we have received and hope further to receive.

Of course, one properly faces here the obvious fact that all members of the communion do not share this new level of mutual recognition. This is a practical problem which confronts all dialogues and which needs always to be dealt with by both partners: how the different levels of the church, its leaders, theologians, ordinary women and men can all move together through increasing levels of relationship and mutual recognition.

In this regard, in *The Grace Given You in Christ* it is acknowledged that there are some core elements of each communion that are equally precious to both, such as the quest for holiness, the commitment to mission and the recognition that life in Christ is one lived in communion or 'connexion'. In addition, of course, both communions share a fundamental trinitarian faith and a fundamental centring on the person of Jesus Christ, the Word incarnate. We recognise too that in regard to the Reformation controversy concerning co-operation with God's grace, Catholics and Methodists are largely of one mind. This became obvious in Seoul in 2006 when Lutherans and Catholics were able to sign a new agreement concerning justification with the World Methodist Council. On these points at least, if full communion were to be restored between Methodists and Catholics, far from this diminishing or even challenging respective identities, it would serve only to enhance these fundamental characteristics of ecclesial life which are already so central to each communion.

Equally, beyond these points already held in common, it is acknowledged that there are also gifts to be exchanged which can only be received through this new relationship. On the one hand, Catholics should be able to see that there are elements that the Holy Spirit has led Methodists to grasp in ways that are exemplary for all communions. Examples explored in *The Grace Given You in Christ* and also treated very fully in the 2001 Brighton Report are the Methodist understanding of lay ministry based on baptism and of the priesthood of all believers.[11] This leads Methodists in practice to give lay people a very significant place in ecclesial governance. On the other hand, there is the Catholic understanding of ordination as a sacrament and its sacramental understanding of the ministry, authority and ecclesial significance of those who are ordained. What could cause a certain polarisation between Methodists and Catholics, with the priesthood and authority of the ordained being defended over against the priesthood and authority of the faithful can, it is hoped, become in a mutual exchange of gifts an enrichment to both. In one sense, this could be an example of a 'clash' of gifts, or an exchange of gifts which requires that one gift be modified in order to make room for the other to be received.

Again, in dialogue over the decades both parties have come to describe the particular attributes and dimensions of the church to which they have steadfastly adhered in language increasingly acceptable to the other party because there is no longer any need to define them over against the other. In this redefinition, which takes place continually in ecumenical dialogue, the true gift which was perhaps hidden by polemical language over the centuries begins to emerge and can be welcomed, although not uncritically, by the other as indeed a gift of the Spirit. This takes time, a long time, and when there is an apparent 'clash' in the gifts themselves dialogue over time is the only way forward. As the true character of the other's gift emerges, it should threaten less and less the gift being offered. It may well be

---

11. *Speaking the Truth in Love: Teaching Authority among Catholics and Methodists* (Lake Junaluska: World Methodist Council, 2001).

that it is only through such dialogue that the Holy Spirit can lead each of us to recognise the limitations in our current interpretations of our respective gifts and so to corresponding possible adaptations in our ecclesial lives which may have appeared unthinkable some decades ago or only as a capitulation to the different or opposed other. In contrast, at this point such an adaptation may rather be seen as the proper adjustment necessary for the reception of a gift from God through the other.

Lest it be assumed to the contrary, however, it should be noted that this process does not require that an element which Catholics recognise to be more developed in Methodism than in their own communion ought, therefore, simply to be adopted on the automatic assumption that it is necessarily a work of the Spirit. Likewise, there are many gifts which the Catholic Church would like to offer Methodism which Methodism may, despite forty years of dialogue, still find hard to recognise as unalloyed gifts. For its own part, the particular gift of lay participation in ecclesial governance and, hence, in authoritative decision-making, is a gift which the Catholic Church would discern very carefully given its own understanding of the unique role of the ordained ministry. But precisely because of this dialogue, it is called before God to do this discerning. Fellow Christians have, in Christ, asked us to do so. I do not wish to discuss this question in detail here but there are many elements which could be brought into the discussion, such as various examples in the history of the undivided Church and the consultative bodies called for by the Second Vatican Council, the significance of which is undermined when they are described as 'only' or 'just' consultative.

This remains a question for further dialogue: a dialogue based on the positive premise of seeking to find the gift hidden within the Christian experience of another communion which may at first sight appear as unacceptable but which can emerge through the unveiling that takes place in dialogue as a gift which comes from Christ and is meant for all. When this happens, the receiving party will normally have already found within itself some traces of the gift in question precisely because it is integral to Christ's wishes for the church—or at least a 'space' or lack within their own ecclesial experience which requires such a gift to fill it and complete it.

Reflecting such a spirit, in *The Grace Given You in Christ*, the Methodist participants were able to say the following concerning gifts they were increasingly open to receiving from the Catholic Church: 'At a basic level, the diversity in unity of the Roman Catholic Church is one such element; another is its concrete expression of the universality of the Church'. And specifically, 'Whilst treasuring the Wesleyan emphasis on the sacrament of the Lord's Supper, Methodists would benefit from a more developed theology of the Eucharist, such as can be found in Roman Catholic teaching' (§111). They also identified some Catholic devotions which they might be willing to adopt in the future and even addressed the question of 'veneration of Mary . . . subject to continuing dialogue about the later Marian dogmas' (§111). More generally, they added: 'Greater awareness of the communion of the saints and the Church's continuity in time, the sacramental use of material things and sacramental ministry to the sick and dying are also ecclesial elements and endowments that Methodists might profitably receive from Roman Catholics'. Again, after acknowledging a renewed appreciation of the whole of church history rather than only those extraordinary moments when they perceived the Holy Spirit as acting, they were able to make the following comments about episcopacy:

> Accordingly, Methodists acknowledge the episcopal college and the historic succession of bishops within the Roman Catholic Church to be a sign (though not necessarily a guarantee) of the unity of the Church in space and time . . . Historically, *episcopé* in Methodism has mostly been exercised corporately, even in those parts of the world where Methodism is endowed with bishops. However, Methodists increasingly recognise the value of *episcopé* properly exercised by individuals within the context of a collegial ministry of oversight. Thus Methodists are open to receiving from Roman Catholics fresh insights into the exercise of individual forms of *episcopé* for the building up of the Body of Christ (§112).

Finally, they were able to express openness to the gift of the ministry of the bishop of Rome:

Methodists around the world responded positively to Pope John Paul II's invitation to engage in dialogue about the exercise of the Petrine ministry of the Bishop of Rome (*UUS* 96). In the light of the present crisis of authority in the Christian Church, Methodists may come to value a Petrine ministry at the service of unity. In particular, with proper safeguards, Methodists may be prepared to receive a Petrine ministry exercised collegially within the college of bishops as a final decision-making authority in the Church, at least insofar as essential matters of faith are concerned (§113).

In turn, Methodists hoped that Catholics might be able to welcome some of their ecclesial elements and endowments as gifts to be received with thanksgiving. They began by inviting Roman Catholics to consider 'how their own appreciation of the spiritual gifts bestowed upon lay people may be informed by Methodism's fruitful experience of the spiritual empowerment of lay people for ministry and mission' (§115). They then focused specifically on the ministry of women who, in the movement's early years and again more recently, 'have made a full contribution to the mission and ministry of Methodism' (§116). So it is that Methodists 'do not restrict any ministry or office in the Church to either men or women, believing that to do so would be contrary to God's will as they discern it in obedience to the Scriptures'. With this, they invited Roman Catholics to consider 'how the Methodist experience and practice of ordained ministry might contribute to their own understanding of the Church's ministry' (§116). In the light of their own flexible and pragmatic approach towards ecclesial structures borne out of their commitment to mission, they also invited Catholics to consider 'how greater flexibility and pragmatism might enhance their own missionary activity' (§117). Again, alongside these more ecclesiological elements, the Methodists also focused on the characteristic spiritual gifts of their tradition:

[A] significant feature of the historic mission of Methodism has been an emphasis on the crucial importance of personal experience of Jesus Christ and his redeeming love. However else it may be described,

> the Church is a community of Christians whose personal
> experience of Jesus Christ compels them to join with
> other Christians in worship, fellowship, mission and
> service in the world. Methodists invite Roman Catholics
> to consider how this same emphasis, and the forms that
> it takes, might contribute to their own pastoral ministry
> and mission (§118).

In turn, after reflecting on the consequences of their own commitment
to Christian unity, they asked whether the commitment of Catholics
to ecumenism might influence 'their own understanding of their
particular identity, and their willingness to distinguish between what
is essential and what is changeable' (§119). From this they went on
to discuss their own 'characteristic ethos in worship and spirituality'
and concluded by inviting Roman Catholics to consider how these
same ecclesial elements and endowments might enhance their own
worship and spirituality. Given that these gifts and, likewise, those
being offered by Catholics to Methodists would not all be recognised
easily or by all as truly gifts of Christ, it is fair to say that the agenda
for future dialogue has come to clear definition in *The Grace Given
You in Christ*.

The Wesleys, Holiness and Connexionalism

One gift of Methodism which stands out for me from my ten years'
experience in this dialogue is the gift of John and Charles Wesley
themselves. They were extraordinary Christian men. In speaking of
them and of the Methodist movement in his homily at Ponte Sant'Angelo
Methodist Church in Rome on 22 June 2003 in a celebration to mark
the 300th anniversary of the birth of John Wesley, Cardinal Kasper
spoke of their being 'characterised by a desire to make known the
love of Christ, to reform the inner life of the church, to encourage
participation in the celebration of the Eucharist, to foster Christian
education, to serve the poor, to impassion professed Christians into
articulate witness for Christ's sake'.[12] In that same homily he compared
the imprint that John Wesley left on Methodism to that of St Ignatius
on the Jesuits and went on to say: 'In like manner, just as you continue

---

12. 'The 300th Anniversary of the Birth of John Wesley: Cardinal Kasper's Statements',
　　in *Information Service*, 114 (2003), 184.

to turn to the ministry of John Wesley for inspiration and guidance, we can look to see and find in him the evangelical zeal, the pursuit of holiness, the concern for the poor; the virtues and goodness which we have come to know and respect in you'.[13] Later that year, a letter from Cardinal Kasper was read during the liturgy marking the 225th anniversary of Wesley's Chapel, City Road, London. In that letter he explained that by means of his homily at Ponte Sant'Angelo he had hoped to contribute to a Catholic 'reassessment' of Wesley. He saw this reassessment as rich with possibilities given the new context created by the Methodist–Catholic dialogue.[14]

Were John and Charles Wesley members of the Catholic Church, they would certainly be on the list of those whose causes would be put forward for canonisation. I look forward to a day when in the Litany of the Saints in the ordination ceremony of a bishop we would sing together 'Saints John and Charles Wesley, pray for us'. One can rejoice also in the hymns that flowed from their pens, especially that of Charles, which have already enriched the Catholic Communion and certainly challenged it to accept the gift not just of these hymns, but of hymn singing itself as a form of prayer and spiritual enrichment which has clearly proved its worth in the Methodist tradition. Of these hymns, Cardinal Kasper said in the message referred to, that they have been the means for members of the Catholic Church to discover some of the insights of John and Charles Wesley into the call to holiness.[15]

Linked to this, Methodists believe that holiness is the basis for the Church's unity and communion. Methodism emerged because of the desire in the hearts of John and Charles Wesley and others to preach scriptural holiness to the people of England and Ireland and in a special way to the poor working men and women. Indeed, Methodism was primarily a renewal movement within the Church of England which sought to foster social and personal holiness in response to the proclamation of the gospel. It grew apart from the Church of England without major conflict over the gospel or the faith but, positively speaking, because of this commitment to evangelism and holiness.

---

13. 'The 300th Anniversary of the Birth of John Wesley: Cardinal Kasper's Statements', 184.
14. 'The 300th Anniversary of the Birth of John Wesley: Cardinal Kasper's Statements', 185.
15. 'The 300th Anniversary of the Birth of John Wesley: Cardinal Kasper's Statements', 185.

Just as the Church of England in that day, so the Catholic Church today, needs to ask itself how true it is to claim that holiness is a major pastoral goal for the preaching of its clergy and the pastoral life of its parishes? There have been and still are many like John and Charles Wesley within the Catholic Church who endeavour to make these the Church's priorities. The Methodist Communion bears this gift in abundance, and the Catholic Church would be blessed enormously were it to receive it.

In this regard, one of my major learnings from ten years of dialogue with the Methodist Church is the discovery of the fundamental difference between Catholic and Methodist understandings of the holiness of the Church. What is true of Methodists would also be true of many other Christians. Catholics are determined to protect the holiness of the Church from those who would say the Church itself is sinful. They distinguish between the Church as the Body and sacrament of Christ which cannot but be holy and the holiness or sinfulness of its members.[16]

Other Christians do not always make this distinction because of the evidence of sinfulness and distortion or corruption which they perceive at all levels and in all aspects of the Church including its teaching. Their fundamental commitment to reform or renewal seeks to change this and to bring genuine holiness to every aspect of the Church's life. There is also a reluctance to canonise any structure, aspect or teaching of the Church because of the frailty, fallibility and sinfulness of the human members of the Church who are responsible for what it does or says. The Catholic principle—which relies on the certainty of the divine presence and activity in sacraments, teaching, and ministerial activity on account of the Church being the Sacrament of Christ's presence and activity in the world—can too easily lead to a neglect of the human contribution which can distort as well as enhance the communication of the divine presence and activity.

The emphasis in *Lumen Gentium* on the universal call to holiness (*LG* 8) and the recognition that the Church is holy but always in need of purification and renewal (*LG* 39–42) are very important

---

16. See Karl Rahner, 'The Church of Sinners' (1947), in *Theological Investigations*, vol 6, translated by Karl-H Kruger and Boniface Kruger (London: Darton, Longman & Todd, 1969), 253–69; Karl Rahner, 'The Sinful Church in the Decrees of Vatican II' (1965), in *Theological Investigations*, vol 6, 270–94.

insights for the Church which are, as yet, insufficiently explored for their potential to bring about a change in priorities for the Catholic Church. The emphasis in the ministry of Pope John Paul II upon the witness of saints and martyrs and their authority is also a sign of a Catholic reaffirmation of the fundamental call to holiness. The gift of Methodism and other Christian churches may be both a rediscovery of holiness as an essential mark of the Church and an admission that no matter how holy the teaching, sacraments and ministerial structures of the Church, they are inadequate without a constant renewal by the Holy Spirit bringing genuine scriptural holiness into all of these aspects of the Church's life.

Finally, a gift of enormous importance for the Catholic Church as it grows in an ecclesial spirituality of communion is the Methodist experience of always 'living in connexion', and hence of ensuring that structures of communion are such that pastors and people, congregations and larger regions, all people on every level of ecclesial life take each other into consideration and actually care about each other, seek each other's wisdom and serve each other's needs. Methodists obviously do this imperfectly but they have structures which ensure that communion is lived and not just loved. Catholics have a beautiful rhetoric about communion, collegiality, participation and collaboration which is variously realised in the daily life of the Church. For their own part, Methodists have a practice of connexion or communion which challenges Catholics the more fully to live what they confess. It would be a worthy gift indeed if Methodists were to help Catholics to establish other structures of collaboration and mutual accountability which ensured that communion was much more than an ideal on every level of the Church's life and in every place.

Conclusion

It is easier to recognise the validity and the value of an exchange of gifts when one is talking about such gifts of renewal or new theological insights, which are the regular fruit of dialogue. It becomes harder, however, when one speaks of the way a Church structures its ministry and the way in which authority is exercised in a communion, or the doctrinal weight that a Church gives to some of its teachings which may not be part of the teaching of another Christian communion.

There can be no rushing this particular process of learning, receiving and giving. Nor should there be any delay. It cannot be carried out by theologians and Church leaders alone but must draw upon the experience of ordinary men and women of each communion who live the life of Christ daily in ordinary human situations and therefore test the authenticity of the claims of theologians and Church leaders about what Christ wills for his Church. At the same time, this is always undertaken in the hope that Christ who dwells in each communion is drawing each to grow more like his vision for his one Church and that our only task is to seek him in the other and so to discover the gifts that he has in store for us if only we can finally see.

Ecumenism and Inter-Religious Relations with Benedict XVI

In his inaugural homily on 24 April 2005, Pope Benedict XVI took up one of the themes of his predecessor. Before Pope John Paul II died, he frequently drew our attention to those texts in the gospels which refer to a miraculous catch of fish. The disciples had been fishing all night but because Jesus told them to, they put out into the deep and caught a miraculous catch of fish. They were astounded by this and in awe of Jesus, and he in turn called them to their mission no longer to catch fish from the sea, but to catch people for the gospel.

Pope Benedict reflected on the image of the unbroken nets filled to overflowing with fish and the fact that the account ends with the joyful statement: 'although there were so many, the net was not torn' (John 21:11). He went on to say:

> Alas, beloved Lord, with sorrow we must now acknowledge that it has been torn! But no—we must not be sad! Let us rejoice because of your promise, which does not disappoint, and let us do all we can to pursue the path towards the unity you have promised. Let us remember it in our prayer to the Lord, as we plead with him: Yes, Lord, remember your promise. Grant that we may be one flock and one shepherd! Do not allow your net to be torn, help us to be servants of unity![1]

I found this gloss or extension of one of Pope John Paul II's favourite themes a most illuminating insight into the thought of Pope Benedict

---

This paper was presented at a public gathering at Australian Catholic University in Canberra on 27 February 2007.

---

1. 'The Inauguration Homily', *Origins*, 34/46 (5 May 2005): 737.

XVI. He turned it around to emphasise in his first mass as pope that the net is torn. We are not one flock, we are not anymore one single net full of fish. His prayer in his homily was that the Lord would not allow the net to be torn, but would help us to be servants of unity. In itself, his homily was enough to convince me that he would continue the amazing commitment of Pope John XXIII, Pope Paul VI and Pope John Paul II by being himself a servant of that unity.

Two days later he spoke to the representatives of other Christian communities who were present for his inaugural mass. He repeated to them that same phrase *duc in altum*, 'put out into the deep', which was in some ways the last will and testament of Pope John Paul II to the Church. He then seemed to apply this phrase to the very work of Christian unity to which he had already committed himself in his homily. He went on to say:

> the path towards the full communion desired by Jesus
> for his disciples implies a concrete docility to what
> the Spirit says to the Churches, courage, gentleness,
> firmness and hope to reach the end. It implies, above all,
> insistent prayer with only one heart, to obtain from the
> good shepherd the gift of unity for his flock.[2]

He asked those who were present to join with him in giving the example of spiritual ecumenism, 'which in prayer realises our communion without obstacles'.[3]

Pope Benedict did not make a particular reference to the representatives of other world religions in the homily of his first mass, but he did address them at the gathering of representatives of other religions and other Christian communities. He said to them: 'I offer warm and affectionate greetings to you and to all those who belong to the religions that you represent'.[4] He then went on to say that he was particularly grateful for the presence of members of the Muslim community, and expressed his appreciation for the growth of dialogue between Muslims and Christians, both at the local and

---

2. 'New Pope's Ecumenical and Interreligious Commitments', in *Origins*, 35/1 (19 May 2005): 3.
3. 'New Pope's Ecumenical and Interreligious Commitments', 4.
4. 'New Pope's Ecumenical and Interreligious Commitments', 4.

international levels. He continued: 'I assure you that the Church wants to continue building bridges of friendship with the followers of all religions, in order to seek the true good of every person and society as a whole.'[5] He then particularly focused on the need 'to come together and foster dialogue' as 'a valuable contribution to building peace on solid foundations'. He stressed that it was 'imperative to engage in authentic and sincere dialogue, built on respect for the dignity of every human person, created, as we Christians firmly believe, in the image and likeness of God (cf Genesis 1:26–27)'.[6]

Just as interesting however as these most significant initial statements of Pope Benedict was what he had said about his ecumenical commitment beforehand in his address to the cardinals gathered for his inaugural mass.

> Fully conscious, therefore, at the beginning of his ministry in the Church of Rome, which Peter bathed with his blood, his present Successor aims, as a primary commitment, to work without sparing energies for the reconstitution of the full and visible unity of all the followers of Christ. This is his ambition, this is his imperative duty. He is aware that for this, manifestations of good sentiments are not enough. There must be concrete gestures that penetrate spirits and move consciences, leading each one to that interior conversion that is the presupposition of all progress on the path of ecumenism.
>
> Theological dialogue is necessary. Also, in-depth knowledge of the historical reasons for choices made in the past is perhaps indispensable. But what is urgent in the main is that 'purification of the memory,' so many times recalled by John Paul II, which alone can dispose spirits to receive the full truth of Christ. It is before him, supreme Judge of every living being, that each one of us must place himself, in the awareness of one day having to render an account to him of what one has done or not

---

5. 'New Pope's Ecumenical and Interreligious Commitments', 4.
6. 'New Pope's Ecumenical and Interreligious Commitments', 4.

done for the great good of the full and visible unity of all his disciples.

The present Successor of Peter lets himself be challenged in the first person by this request and is prepared to do all that is in his power to promote the fundamental cause of ecumenism. In the footsteps of his Predecessors, he is fully determined to cultivate every initiative that might seem appropriate to promote contacts and understanding with representatives of the diverse churches and ecclesial communities. To them, indeed, he also sends on this occasion the most cordial greeting in Christ, the only Lord of all.[7]

In that same address he spoke of the representatives of other religions as follows:

In undertaking his ministry, the new Pope knows that his task is to make the light of Christ shine before the men and women of today, not his own light but that of Christ.

Conscious of this, I turn to all, also to those who follow other religions or who simply seek an answer to the fundamental questions of life and have not yet found it. I turn to all with simplicity and affection, to assure them that the Church wishes to continue to engage with them in an open and sincere dialogue, in search of the true good of man and of society.

I invoke from God the peace and unity for the human family and declare the readiness of all Catholics to cooperate for a genuine social development, respectful of the dignity of every human being.

I will spare no efforts and devotion to continue the promising dialogue undertaken by my venerable Predecessors with the various civilizations, so that from reciprocal understanding conditions will flow a better future for all.[8]

---

7. 'The New Pope's First Speech', in *Origins*, 34/45 (28 April 2005): 724.
8. 'The New Pope's First Speech', 724–5.

In his first trip outside of Rome to the Italian Eucharist Congress in Bari on 29 May 2005, during a beautiful homily on 'The Eucharist, Sacrament of Unity', Pope Benedict referred to Bari as 'a city that preserves the bones of St Nicholas, a land of encounter and dialogue with our Christian brothers of the East', and repeated there the commitment he had made already including his call for 'concrete acts that penetrate souls and shake consciences', which he had spoken of to the cardinals.

He went on to say: 'I ask you all to set out with determination on the path of that spiritual ecumenism that through prayer opens the doors to the Holy Spirit, who alone can create unity'.[9]

Given these commitments made at the beginning of his pontificate we can now ask, two years later, how he has carried them forward. I could say without the slightest hesitation that he has done everything anyone could have hoped for in the field of ecumenical engagement. He has met delegation after delegation of representatives of other world communions including the representatives of the World Methodist Council whom I was privileged to accompany to a meeting with him in December 2005. On each occasion he not only articulated a similar commitment and affirmed what had been achieved: he also did so with enormous warmth and encouragement for those who are involved in ecumenical relations between different world communions. Perhaps most significantly he gave time to prayer with, discussion with, and a private meal with Archbishop Rowan Williams, the Archbishop of Canterbury, on 23 November 2006 during a very troubled time for the Anglican Communion. In their joint declaration they 'celebrated the good which has come from four decades of dialogue' for which they expressed thanks to God. At the same time they said it was 'necessary to acknowledge publicly the challenge represented by new developments which, besides being divisive for Anglicans, present serious obstacles to our ecumenical progress'.[10]

Similarly in his meeting with the Pontifical Council for Promoting Christian Unity in December 2006, he encouraged, supported and inspired those who are committed to this aspect of the Church's mission.

---

9. 'The Eucharist, Sacrament of Unity', in *Origins,* 35/6 (23 June 2005): 87.
10. 'Joint Declaration: Pope, Canterbury Archbishop', in *Origins,* 36/26 (7 December 2006): 406.

I would like now to point to certain themes that have continually emerged in his statements. The most obvious is that of spiritual ecumenism, as most recently in his homily at St Paul's Outside the Walls on 25 January 2007 for the end of the northern hemisphere Week of Prayer for Christian Unity. We will discover in our own week of prayer from Ascension to Pentecost that it has as its theme 'he even makes the deaf hear and the mute speak (Mark 7:37)'.

He said very beautifully on that occasion:

> Listening to the Word of God is a priority for our ecumenical commitment. Indeed, it is not we who act or who organize the unity of the Church. The Church does not make herself or live of herself, but from the creative Word that comes from the mouth of God.
>
> To listen to the word of God together; to practice the *lectio divina* of the Bible, that is, reading linked with prayer; letting ourselves be amazed by the newness of the Word of God that never ages and is never depleted; overcoming our deafness to those words that do not correspond with our prejudices and our opinions; to listen and also to study, in the communion of believers of all ages; all these things constitute a path to be taken in order to achieve unity in the faith as a response to listening to the Word.[11]

He went on to link this spiritual ecumenism with proclamation of the Word or evangelisation:

> Anyone who listens to the Word of God can and must speak and transmit it to others, to those who have never heard it, or who have forgotten it and buried under it the thorny troubles and deceptions of the world (cf Mt 13:22).
>
> We must ask ourselves: have not we Christians become perhaps too silent? Do we not perhaps lack the courage to speak out and witness as did those who witnessed

---

11. 'Our World Awaits the Common Witness of Christians', in *L'Osservatore Romano* (31 January 2007): 5.

the healing of the deaf-mute in the Decapolis? Our world needs this witness; above all, it is waiting for the common testimony of Christians.[12]

Finally he moved to the theme of ecumenical dialogue:

> Therefore listening to the God who speaks also implies a reciprocal listening, the dialogue between the Churches and the Ecclesial Communities. Honest and loyal dialogue is the typical and indispensable instrument in the quest for unity . . . in dialogue we listen and communicate; we confront one another and, with God's grace, it is possible to converge on his Word, accepting its demands that apply to all.
>
> The Council Fathers did not expect listening and dialogue to be helpful for ecumenical progress alone, but they added a perspective which refers to the Catholic Church herself: 'From such dialogue' the conciliar text states, 'will emerge still more clearly what the situation of the Catholic Church really is' (*Unitatis Redintegratio*, n. 9).[13]

This final statement illustrates his profound understanding of ecumenical dialogue, which involves an encounter at the deepest level with other Christians that does not leave oneself unaffected. He also affirmed the need for doctrine to be presented in its entirety without compromise, but also that the way in which it is expressed should further dialogue and not be a hindrance. He added that ecumenical dialogue involves 'evangelical fraternal correction and leads to a reciprocal spiritual enrichment in the sharing of authentic experiences of faith and Christian life'.[14]

Pope John Paul II had often spoken of ecumenical dialogue as not just an exchange of words or ideas, but as a mutual exchange of gifts, and this theme was explored in the most recent phase of the Methodist–Roman Catholic Dialogue when it produced a report

12. 'Our World Awaits the Common Witness of Christians', 5.
13. 'Our World Awaits the Common Witness of Christians', 5.
14. 'Our World Awaits the Common Witness of Christians', 5.

'The Grace Given You in Christ: Catholics and Methodists Reflect Further on the Church'. This was presented at the assembly of the World Methodist Council in Seoul in 2006.[15] That report endeavours to explore the degree to which our two communions are able to recognise the Church of Jesus Christ in each other and what we share as far as the apostolic faith and ecclesial life is concerned. But most interestingly, it then explores what gifts we would like to receive from the other, and what gifts we would like to give to the other. In that sense it is a very significant watershed report from our dialogue. It was inspired in its structure by Pope John Paul II's call to a mutual exchange of gifts which is echoed in some way by Pope Benedict's reference here to a 'reciprocal, spiritual enrichment in the sharing of authentic experiences of faith and Christian life'.

I was rather thrilled to hear in his address to the Pontifical Council the following reference: 'I would like to mention in particular the "Joint Declaration of the Doctrine of Justification" which was achieved in the dialogue with the Lutheran World Federation and the fact for its own part, the World Methodist Council gave its assent to this Declaration'.[16] Along with the publication of our report 'The Grace Given You in Christ', the signing of a document affirming the inclusion of the World Methodist Council in a three-way agreement with the Lutheran World Federation and the Catholic Church in Seoul, Korea, was one of the major milestones of the ecumenical movement in 2006.

Pope Benedict returned in his homily on 25 January 2006 to spiritual ecumenism, the need to 'tirelessly implore the help of God's grace and the enlightenment of the Holy Spirit', and he summed up his reflections by linking that prayer again to witness. Spiritual ecumenism and evangelisation are intimately linked because the former is based on listening to the Word of God and the latter upon sharing the Word of God with others.

One can see that the pope has continued to repeat in an inspiring, warm-hearted and enthusiastic way his commitment to ecumenical

---

15. 'The Grace Given You in Christ: Catholics and Methodists Reflect Further on the Church: Report of the International Commission for Dialogue between the Roman Catholic Church and the World Methodist Council', in *Information Service*, 123 (2006/III–IV).

16. 'Shaping the "Changing Ecumenical Situation"', in *L'Osservatore Romano*, 48 (29 November 2006): 3.

engagement on the part of the Catholic Church and to connect the themes of spiritual ecumenism, evangelisation and dialogue. The promise he seemed to offer on the first days of his pontificate of concrete gestures that would further the cause of Christian unity have not been realised in a dramatic way, but are obvious in the regular and enthusiastic commitment he reveals on every possible occasion to doing what he can to further the ecumenical cause. At the meeting of the Pontifical Council at the end of last year we spoke about what possibilities there might be for him to make other gestures. One of the things discussed was his making it clear that he wished to carry forward Pope John Paul II's call to other Christian communions to help him to find ways of exercising his ministry, which while remaining faithful to the apostolic tradition as we understand it, would enable it to be recognised and accepted as a service of unity for others.

One of the matters that did cause some concern during the year 2006 was the dropping of the title 'Patriarch of the West' from the list of the titles of Pope Benedict XVI in the *Annuario Pontificio*. On 8 June, the Ecumenical Patriarchate of Constantinople put out a document raising their concerns about this. Already on 22 March the Pontifical Council for Promoting Christian Unity had felt obliged to publish an explanatory statement. The former made the point that the unity of the Church cannot be conceived as a sum of culturally distinct Churches, but as a unity of local, geographically determined, Churches. They saw the removal of the title 'Patriarch of the West' as perhaps leading to the absorption of clearly distinct geographical ecclesiastical jurisdictions by the Universal Church, which would then consist only of Churches distinguished on the basis of their culture, confession, or rite. The one Church they said must, from an ecclesiological point of view, be considered to be the unity of full local Churches.

The Pontifical Council itself pointed out that the term 'West' currently refers to a cultural context not limited only to Western Europe, but including North America, Australia and New Zealand, thereby differentiating itself from other cultural contexts. The term 'West' does not describe an ecclesiastical territory, nor could it be adopted as the definition of a patriarchal territory. If they wished to give the term 'West' a meaning applicable to ecclesiastical juridical language, it could only be understood in reference to the Latin Church.

It would then describe the bishop of Rome's special relationship with the Latin Church and could express the special jurisdiction he has over her. But the Catholic Church had found episcopal conferences were the best canonical structure for the needs of the Latin Church, rather than a patriarchate. They concluded that it is not a very clear title and that it had become obsolete over history and practically unusable.

At the same time, the Pontifical Council said very clearly that dropping the title did not alter in any way the recognition of the ancient Patriarchal Churches, nor should it be seen as implying a new claim; rather it was an attempt to be historically and theologically realistic. Finally, they thought renunciation of the claim could in fact prove useful to ecumenical dialogue.[17] Given that one of his former staff at the Congregation for the Doctrine of the Faith had written a book very critical of this title, Cardinal Ratzinger, now Pope Benedict XVI, would have been very aware of its ambiguities or limitations, and would have therefore chosen not to use it rather than use a title which might be inadequate. Happily, despite this the Orthodox–Catholic Dialogue finally resumed in September last year (2006) after being in abeyance for six years and many attribute this to the respect Orthodox leaders have for the new pope.

As to his relationships with other world religions, I would be happy firstly to make the claim that his relationship with Judaism carries on the tradition of Pope John Paul II. He is generally perceived by Jews as wishing to continue the relationship of friendship and respect that developed under Pope John Paul II and is equally willing to deal with the harsh and tragic realities of history for which we are far from blameless.

It was interesting in Cologne during the World Youth Day celebrations that the most significant event not on the actual World Youth Day program was his visit to the synagogue, which is said to belong to the oldest Jewish Community in Germany, dating back to Roman times, and which had been all but wiped out during the terrible days of the Holocaust or the *Shoah*. During that visit he spoke of the 'previously unimaginable crime' which claimed 11,000 victims officially, but probably many more. He linked the Nazi rejection of

---

17. 'Orthodox React to Dropping of Papal Title', in *Origins*, 36/6 (22 June 2006): 93–5.

God and their contempt for human life, and repeated the Church's condemnation of anti-Semitism adding: 'It is a particularly important task, since today, sadly, we are witnessing the rise of new signs of anti-Semitism and various forms of a general hostility towards foreigners. How can we fail to see in this a reason for concern and vigilance?'[18] The fact that he is German and could address them as the leader of the Catholic Church in the German language added great significance to the visit.

This visit was received much more serenely than his visit on 28 May 2006 to Auschwitz during his visit to Poland. There he took up in his address his theme the questions: 'Where was God in those days? Why was he silent? How could he permit this endless slaughter, this triumph of evil?'[19] He argued that those who had engaged in such terrible evil as was obvious at Auschwitz had 'wanted to kill God' by destroying Israel. His passion and the profundity of his thought is obvious in the following sentences:

> Deep down those vicious criminals, by wiping out this people, wanted to kill the God who called Abraham, who spoke on Sinai and laid down principles to serve as a guide for mankind, principles that are eternally valid. If this people, by its very existence, was a witness to the God who spoke to humanity and took us to himself, then that God finally had to die and power had to belong to man alone—to those men who thought that by force they had made themselves masters of the world.
>
> By destroying Israel, by the Shoah, they ultimately wanted to tear up the taproot of the Christian faith and to replace it with a faith of their own invention: faith in the rule of man, the rule of the powerful.[20]

Some Jews criticised him afterwards for, among other things, not asking for forgiveness for the *Shoah* and for not condemning anti-Semitism. His reflection was far more theological and spiritual than socio-political. It was profound and typical of his genius. On his return

---

18. 'A Papal Visit to Cologne Synagogue', in *Origins*, 35/12 (1 September 2005): 207.
19. 'The Pope's Visit to Auschwitz', in *Origins*, 36/4 (8 June 2006): 50.
20. 'The Pope's Visit to Auschwitz', 51.

to Rome he did address some of their concerns in his reflections at a public audience.

On 25 July that same year he came under fire from some Israeli and Jewish sources for not mentioning Israel in a reference to recent terrorist attacks after the Angelus prayer on 24 July in Rome. The meeting in Cologne and other meetings with Jewish representatives in the Vatican have reaffirmed the overwhelming positive reception of Benedict XVI's contribution to Jewish–Catholic relations.

A small number of the Muslim community in Cologne, which is largely Turkish, also visited him at his residence during the celebrations of World Youth Day. This was a very different kind of meeting and illustrates very well the vastly different relationship the Church has with each of these religions, the differing agendas and priorities in the relationships. This difference, I think, has become even clearer with Benedict XVI. He said to them on that occasion: 'I am profoundly convinced that we must not yield to the negative pressures in our midst, but must affirm the values of mutual respect, solidarity and peace'. He went on to repeat what he had said on 25 April after his inauguration that he wanted 'to continue building bridges of friendship with the followers of all religions, in order to seek the true good of every person and of society as a whole'. He spoke of the pages of history which record battles and even wars that have been waged with both sides invoking the name of God, as if fighting and killing the enemy could be pleasing to God. He argued that remembering these sad events should fill everyone with shame because we know only too well what atrocities have been committed in the name of religion and therefore concluded:

> the lessons of the past must help us to avoid repeating this same mistake. We must seek paths of reconciliation and learn to live with respect for each other's identity. The sense of religious freedom, in this sense, is a permanent imperative and respect for minorities is a clear sign of true civilisation.[21]

---

21. 'Terrorism Discussed in Cologne Meeting with Muslims', in *Origins*, 35/12 (1 September 2005): 208.

Clearly he spoke in a way very conscious of the tensions that have arisen in relationships between Muslims and Christians around the world and for the Western world as it copes with so-called Islamic terrorists and so on. However, he did end his address very positively as follows:

> Inter-religious and inter-cultural dialogue between Christians and Muslims cannot be reduced to an optional extra. It is in fact a vital necessity, on which in large measure our future depends. Young people from many parts of the world are here in Cologne as living witnesses of solidarity, brotherhood and love. They are the first fruits of a new dawn for humanity. I pray with all my heart, dear Muslim friends, that the merciful and compassionate God may protect you, bless you and enlighten you always. May the God of peace lift up our hearts, nourish our hope and guide our steps on the paths of the world.[22]

Two actions of Pope Benedict XVI have raised concern among representatives of other world religions. One of them was the appointment of the Cardinal Prefect of the Pontifical Council for Culture as also the Cardinal Prefect for the Pontifical Council for Inter-religious Dialogue. Because Cardinal Poupard thereby replaced Archbishop Michael Fitzgerald, who had rightly developed an international reputation in inter-religious relations, the change in the headship of the Pontifical Council was particularly dramatic. In order to understand this one needs to note that there has been a consistent theme in Pope Benedict's addresses concerning the relationship between religion and culture. It seems clear that, as far as he is concerned, the relationship of the Catholic Church to other world religions must take this into account. He often speaks of the relationship between faith, reason and culture and sees the relationship between the three differently, depending on the religion he is dealing with.

In an interview given by Cardinal Poupard, the new Prefect of the Pontifical Council for Inter-religious Dialogue, he addressed

---

22. 'Terrorism Discussed in Cologne Meeting with Muslims', 209.

this particular aspect of Pope Benedict's approach. He said that Pope Benedict made it clear that religion can 'neither be separated from nor identified with culture'. He then quoted Monsignor Sabbah, the Latin Patriarch of Jerusalem, who had said that 'ruptures between believers of different religions in most cases have cultural causes rather than theological ones'—what Monsignor Sabbah called 'the shock of mutual incomprehension'. Cardinal Poupard therefore argued that to encourage inter-religious dialogue on the level of culture does not mean that its significance is being diminished. He himself argued that the obstacles in the way of dialogue between religions today are mainly cultural.[23]

The second incident which caused concern specifically to Muslims was Pope Benedict's address at the University of Regensburg on 12 September last year, entitled 'Faith, Reason and the University: Memories and Reflection'. This was an example of Pope Benedict returning to the university halls where he had lectured in the past and delivering again a stimulating, academic address on a crucial question confronting the Church and the world at this point of history. In that address he quoted from a book which he had recently read by Professor Theodore Khoury of Münster who in turn quoted the Byzantine Emperor Manuel II Paleologus, in dialogue with an educated Persian on the subject of Christianity and Islam.

The emperor is quoted as saying in the dialogue: 'show me just what Mohammed brought that was new, and there you will find things only evil and inhuman, such as his command to spread by the sword, the faith he preached'.[24] The pope acknowledged in his lecture that the emperor had expressed himself forcefully, and was more interested in the argument of the emperor as to why the spreading of faith through violence is unreasonable. Violence is incompatible with the nature of God and the nature of the human soul.

The decisive argument to which Pope Benedict pointed was that: 'not to act in accordance with reason is contrary to God's nature'.[25] He then went on to argue that Muslims and Christians, because of the different relationship between faith and reason, perceive God differently. This is a very serious paper and well deserving of

---

23. Originally published in *La Croix*, 4 July 2006.
24. 'The Regensburg Academic Lecture', in *Origins*, 36/16 (28 September 2006): 249.
25. 'The Regensburg Academic Lecture', 249.

attention. In his address to the Roman curia in December last year, he outlined what was the true argument of his paper rather than the more discussed reference to Islam.

> In Regensburg the dialogue between the religions was only marginally touched on and in a twofold perspective. Secularized reason is unable to enter into a true dialogue with the religions. It remains closed to the question of God, and this will end by leading to the clash of cultures. The other perspective concerned the affirmation that the religions must encounter one another in the common task of putting themselves at the service of the truth and thus, of the human being.[26]

As to why he used the quote in question and whether he was aware or unaware of the likely political and social consequences of it remains unclear. As to who helped him prepare it and who advised him again is clouded in mystery. Archbishop Coleridge himself pointed out in the press that this incident would have alerted the pope 'to just how infinite the possibilities of misunderstanding can be and how woeful some of the misreporting is'. What is clear though is that Pope Benedict took decisive steps to remedy the pain he caused in the hearts of some Muslims and to mollify those who were angrily reacting because of what he said. On 16 September Cardinal Bertone, the Secretary of State, issued a statement that the Holy Father 'sincerely regrets that certain passages of his address could have sounded offensive to the sensitivities of the Muslim faithful and could have been interpreted in a manner that in no way corresponded to his intentions'.[27] He also met with ambassadors from Islamic countries and affirmed with them his commitment to good relations with Islam and his 'total and profound respect' for Islam, which was particularly appreciated by the thirty-eight Muslim scholars who wrote an open letter to him hoping to enter into dialogue with him about the errors they saw in his address. He went on to say at that meeting:

---

26. 'Themes of the Pope's 2006 Travels', in *Origins*, 36/31 (18 January 2007): 493.
27. 'Quotation in Papal Speech Stirs Muslim Reaction', in *Origins*, 36/16 (28 September 2006): 247.

Inter-religious and inter-cultural dialogue is a necessity for building together this world of peace and fraternity ardently desired by all people of good will. In this area, our contemporaries expect from us an eloquent witness to show all people the value of the religious dimension of life. Likewise, faithful to the teachings of their own religious traditions, Christians and Muslims must learn to work together, as indeed they already do in many common undertakings, in order to guard against all forms of intolerance and to oppose all manifestations of violence; as for us, religious authorities and political leaders, we must guide and encourage them in this direction.[28]

The text of his Regensburg lecture as finally published by the Holy See on its website also expands Pope Benedict's actual reference to the emperor to the much more critical 'he addresses his interlocutor with a startling brusqueness, a brusqueness that we find unacceptable'.

One could also point to Pope Benedict's message to the twentieth inter-religious gathering for peace in Assisi on 4–5 September, just before his trip to Germany, as another example of a papal intervention which enhances the Church's commitment as he said 'to dialogue between people of different cultures and religions'.[29]

Finally, Pope Benedict's more recent visit to Turkey involved ecumenical and inter-religious encounters which established very clearly and once and for all his deep commitment to the Catholic Church's ecumenical and inter-religious relationships.

In his own reflections on that trip he spoke of his visit to Turkey offering him the opportunity, as he said, 'to show also publicly my respect for the Islamic religion'.[30] He spoke of 'a dialogue to be intensified with Islam' and described the Muslim world as facing the challenges of the Enlightenment which Christians had already been obliged to face, and to which the Second Vatican Council

---

28. 'The Castel Gandolfo Meeting of the Pope and Muslim Leaders', in *Origins*, 36/17 (5 October 2006): 262.
29. 'Message to Assisi Prayer Meeting for Peace', in *Origins*, 36/17 (5 October 2006): 265.
30. 'Themes of the Pope's 2006 Travels', 493.

was a response. While affirming the positive contributions of the Enlightenment, such as human rights and especially the freedom to practise one's religion, he pointed to the need to resist 'a dictatorship of positivist reason that excludes God from the life of the community and from public organisations'.[31] He saw the dialogue between Christians and Muslims to be especially one of working together to find the right solution to this challenge of the Enlightenment.

He also spoke of his visit to the Ecumenical Patriarch Bartholomew and of a letter he had received from him in which, as he said, 'the words of gratitude welling up from the depths of his heart reminded me very vividly of the experience of communion of those days'. [32]

During the Orthodox Liturgy in Istanbul, Patriarch Bartholomew for the first time exchanged a greeting of peace with Pope Benedict within the liturgy rather than after the liturgy. This was noted as a very significant gesture by many observers. Just as they had been quite amazed by observing the pope meditating or praying in his own way while the Muslims prayed in the Blue Mosque.

I think one can see, as some commentators have observed, a transition from the brilliant Cardinal Ratzinger clarifying theological issues and raising critical questions to a profound teacher in Pope Benedict XVI who continues to use his powerful intellect and vast knowledge, and places them now at the service of the papal ministry of serving the unity of the Church and its relationship in Christ with other Christians and through Christ with other world religions. He may have had to learn rather quickly an extra skill of papal diplomacy as is evident in some of the incidents of the past eighteen months. However, I think he has now established his approach and will, with great serenity, offer intelligent, challenging and wise reflections for all of us to hear. He is clearly continuing the passion of commitment of Pope John Paul II to ecumenical and inter-religious relations, but he is doing the latter somewhat differently though with equal commitment and even passion.

---

31. 'Themes of the Pope's 2006 Travels', 494.
32. 'Themes of the Pope's 2006 Travels', 494.

Tenth Anniversary of the Formal Signing of the Joint Declaration on the Doctrine of Justification, 29 October 2009

On 19 November 2008, when speaking about St Paul in the *Year of St Paul*, Pope Benedict XVI said that 'it is precisely because of [his] personal experience of the relationship with Jesus that Paul places at the centre of his Gospel, an irreducible opposition between two alternative paths to justice: one based on the works of the law, the other founded on the grace of faith in Christ'.

He went on to say towards the end of his address:

> it is Christ who unites us with and in the one God: it is Christ who guarantees our true identity in the diversity of cultures; and it is He who makes us just. To be 'just' means simply to be with Christ and in Christ. And this suffices. Other observances are no longer necessary. That is why Luther's expression 'sola fide' is true if faith is not opposed to charity, to love. Faith is to look at Christ, to entrust oneself to Christ, to be united to Christ, to be conformed to Christ, to his life. And the form, the life of Christ, is love; hence, to believe is to be conformed to Christ and to enter into his love. That is why, in the letter to the Galatians, St Paul develops above all his doctrine on Justification; he speaks of faith that operates through love.[1]

This paper is the text of an address presented during a special Vespers service at St Francis Xavier's Cathedral, Adelaide, on 29 October 2009 to mark the tenth anniversary of the signing of the Joint Declaration on the Doctrine of Justification. It was published in *Lutheran Theological Journal*, 43/3 (December 2009): 148–50.

1. Pope Benedict XVI, General Audience, St Peter's Square, 19 November 2008.

Pope Benedict XVI quoted Luther very easily and spoke very easily of justification by faith without any need to refer to the division that occurred in the Church because of the debates, in Luther's day, about his message of 'sola fide'.

This is illustrative of the new relationship that exists between Lutherans and Catholics because of their involvement together for the past forty years in ecumenical dialogue and collaboration. It is a result also of their shared participation in the journey of spiritual ecumenism, of praying together and for each other, that we might be one. There is no more significant illustration of this new relationship that made Pope Benedict's comments so possible than the signing of the Joint Declaration on the Doctrine of Justification on 31 October 1999.[2]

As we mark its tenth anniversary, the question arises of how this Joint Declaration has shaped us and will shape us in the future. It has already shaped us in many ways. Most fundamentally it has created a new level of communion between Lutherans and Catholics. They can now view each other differently because the Joint Declaration established a new foundation upon which to base all their collaboration and prayer and dialogue. They can now look at each other and recognise faith in the same gospel of Christ in very different expressions of faith about how we are saved and how we are one with Christ.

When the Joint Declaration was signed in Augsburg, the signing was also celebrated in different ways in Australia, certainly here in Adelaide, and in Brisbane. Those public ecclesial acts, very formal actions by leaders of two Christian communions, were the public acknowledgement of a gift that had been received from God. The gift was the discovery of shared faith despite efforts over 400 years to condemn each other's expression of the one faith and to try to express our own version of it in a way that was as opposed as possible to that of the other.

A gift has been given to us which creates in us a responsibility to live in a new way because of that gift. The claim that we now have a new level of communion and therefore a new foundation for all

2. 'The Signing of the Joint Declaration on the Doctrine of Justification, Augsburg, Germany, 31 October 1999', in *Information Service*, 103/1–11 (2000): 3.

aspects of our relationship can be mere words unless it begins to affect the actual lived experience of Lutherans and Catholics.

The most obvious example of how this new relationship has borne fruit, and an example which I think illustrates very powerfully that the signing of the Joint Declaration was a gift, is the association with that Joint Declaration by the World Methodist Council. I was a Catholic observer at a meeting of the Executive of the World Methodist Council in Hong Kong a year or so after the signing of the Joint Declaration. I represented the Pontifical Council for Promoting Christian Unity because of my role as Catholic Co-Chairman of the International Dialogue with the World Methodist Council. At a meeting of their committee concerned with relations with other Christian Churches, I was privileged to observe the decision being made to approach the World Lutheran Federation and the Pontifical Council for Promoting Christian Unity to see if it were possible to expand the accord that had been reached in this Joint Declaration by including another party, the World Methodist Council.

Conversations did take place with Methodists and in fact with the World Alliance of Reform Churches. As it turned out, it was only the World Methodist Council that produced a statement of their faith in the Doctrine of Justification which was found acceptable by Lutherans and by Catholics so that this new level of communion, this new foundation for ecumenical relations, has expanded to include member churches of the World Methodist Council.

Because of the formal inclusion of the World Methodist Council in this new relationship, the Uniting Church in Australia is also involved. They are a member church of the World Methodist Council and took part in the consultations within that communion before the new relationship was established at the World Conference of the World Methodist Council in Seoul, Korea, on 23 July 2006.[3]

I think one of the tasks that lies ahead is to formalise an agreement with other Christian churches, especially the family of Reformed Churches and the Anglican Communion, so that we can state before the world that we have all reached some new level of agreement on

---

3. 'The Affirmation of the Joint Declaration on the Doctrine of Justification by the World Methodist Council, Seoul, South Korea, 23 July 2006', in *Information Service*, 122 (2006/II).

the most divisive issue at the time of the Reformation. This also needs to include newer churches who are often more imprisoned by the polemics of the Reformation than Lutherans and Catholics have been for most of last century.

However, the gift of and the responsibility arising from the Joint Declaration must not be seen only in terms of institutional relationships between world communions. The Declaration also needs to be taken seriously by churches in their ordinary living of the gospel in local contexts. The fact that we have entered in Christ into a deeper level of communion which we formally acknowledged in Augsburg ten years ago and in Seoul three years ago must affect the way we relate to each other. If it does not, we cannot claim to take seriously the gift we have been given by Christ who has achieved this within us.

My sense is that most ordinary Catholics and perhaps even some Lutherans today have forgotten how important the doctrine of justification is in their understanding of their relationship with God in Christ, despite the fact that the Australian Lutheran–Catholic Dialogue, based here in Adelaide, produced a more accessible account of this doctrine in their own Statement on Justification published in November 1998.[4] Somehow we have to find a way to help ordinary Catholics and Lutherans not only to discover for themselves the importance of the doctrine of justification by faith, but also to discover that they share this doctrine to a great extent with other Christians and especially with Lutherans or Catholics and the members of the Uniting Church in Australia. As President of the Pontifical Council, Cardinal Cassidy phrased it this way when he said that the consensus on justification 'must be brought into the heart of our churches, into the very life of our congregations and parishes'.[5]

Of course, any attempts to do this will be hampered by the loss of interest in ecumenism that is prevalent right throughout the Western world. Churches, congregations and communities are more focused now on their own survival. If they look towards other communities

---

4. 'Justification: A Common Statement of the Australian Lutheran–Roman Catholic Dialogue'.
5. Edward Idris Cassidy, 'The Joint Declaration on the Doctrine of Justification: Pastoral Consequences', LWF Ninth Assembly (Hong Kong, 8–16 July 1997), Exhibit 9.1.2.

more than their own, they tend to look at the secular world which challenges them so much, or at the Muslim community which challenges them in another way.

The fruits of the ecumenical movement since the Edinburgh World Missionary Conference in 1910, which marked the beginning of the modern ecumenical movement and the centenary of which we will be celebrating in 2010, have been enormous. But because further gains are more difficult, people have tended to settle for what has been achieved or to turn their interest elsewhere. We can't afford to do this because to do so would be unfaithful to Christ who prayed the night before he died that we might be one. We have no right not to continue to try to build deeper relationships with each other and to deal with those things that inhibit a future truly united church.

To ready ourselves for the tenth anniversary of this signing, the Australian Catholic Bishops Conference, in its May 2009 meeting, devoted a session to a discussion of justification by faith. We were assisted by Pastor Robert Bartholomaeus and Fr Gerard Kelly in our discussions. What was interesting is that bishops were as interested in reflecting on the meaning of the doctrine for themselves as they were in the differences between our two communions in describing this doctrine. Ideally that experience of the Australian Catholic Bishops Conference would be replicated for other Australian Catholics and Lutherans. Their own growth in the life of the Spirit, their own relationship with Christ, their own commitment to living the life of Christ in our secular world and engaging in the mission of preaching the gospel of Christ to our world could not but be enhanced by all rediscovering the power of this doctrine and rediscovering it with the aid of the insights that come by seeing it as well through others' eyes.

We cannot simply celebrate this tenth anniversary with a liturgical service. We were given a gift by Christ that bore great fruit in Augsburg, but that gift involves also a great responsibility for us to do something more as a result of this new level of communion that we have been given, solely by God's grace through faith.

A Response to the Collection

Gerard Kelly

You might well ask what prompted the editors to bring these articles together in a single volume. There could be many reasons. The articles give an insight into the ecumenical engagement of the Catholic Church over a few decades. Their particular origin in Australia also highlights the vibrancy of the ecumenical movement in that country. In this sense, these articles are a testament to the ecumenical advances that have taken place such that a land with deep sectarian roots now lives with a different Christian engagement. Churches in this land have joined in covenanting to work with each other in various areas of church life, to seek unity, and to pray for each other. These articles also give an insight into Bishop Michael Putney's personal ecumenical journey. This is a journey that is truly theological and because of this, deeply spiritual. For this reason the articles are a testament to the leadership that he has exercised in the Catholic Church and in the ecumenical community. The success of all ecumenical leaders is their capacity to find ways to move forward, even in the face of the most intractable problems. A combination of factors makes this possible: a deep knowledge of the Christian tradition; a willingness to listen carefully; the capacity to bring to our imagination a new way of looking at things; an ability to remain patient and to respect the timeline (*kairos*) of the Spirit; and a profound trust in the movement of the Holy Spirit that reinforces hope. The quality and style of Bishop Putney's ecumenical leadership is on display in these articles.

However, the above are not the principal reasons for gathering the articles together in this volume. We are not attempting to give a snapshot of a particular time in the ecumenical movement, worthy and all as that may be. Rather the articles are published here with the conviction that they have an enduring value and can be read with profit even some years after their original publication or presentation. Of course, they have a new audience here, and they will be read in a different context to that which prompted them. They are still able to provide insights that will help us continue on the ecumenical journey, help us address the questions that we now face, and help us develop a spirituality that will sustain us in a patient dialogue. I wish to illustrate this by focusing on three areas that stand out for me in this ensemble of articles. First, they show us the characteristics of the ecumenical methodology of the Catholic Church. In this sense, they help us recognise the gifts that Catholics bring to the ecumenical encounter. Second, they show us why ecumenism is at the heart of the Catholic understanding of the church and its mission and not just an appendix that is for the devotees of ecumenism. Third, these articles give solid foundations for engaging in the tasks that presently face the churches. One of the principal tasks is to reach a common ecclesiological understanding. These articles will continue to contribute to that dialogue.

The Ecumenical Methodology of the Catholic Church

The way Catholics participate in ecumenical dialogue is very much governed by the way they understand the unity of the church. While there is a very clear sense of the direction in which we need to head in order to arrive at the visible unity willed by Christ, there is also a profound consciousness that we cannot pre-determine what such unity will look like. The thing required of us is that we remain open to the shape that unity will take according to God's plan as it continues to be revealed by the Holy Spirit. The framework for the Catholic understanding of unity was clearly presented at the Second Vatican Council. The central idea, that the church is a communion, was developed in the Dogmatic Constitution on the Church, *Lumen gentium*, and its application in the ecumenical context was worked out in the Decree on Ecumenism, *Unitatis redintegratio*. The starting point for the Catholic Church's relationship with other churches and ecclesial communities is that it is already in some sort of communion with these bodies—a real but imperfect communion. The ecumenical task is to deepen this existing communion so that it becomes full communion. This is a very different understanding to what is sometimes called an 'ecumenism of return', where other churches would be expected to 'return' to the Catholic Church. Rather, the Catholic understanding is that ecumenism is based on continual renewal and reform in all churches—including the Catholic Church—in order to purify church life so that the churches manifest that unity given by God. None of this, however, diminishes the claims that the Catholic Church makes for itself in terms of visible continuity in the apostolic faith. Bishop Putney addresses this delicate issue in a very direct way, referring to those occasions that have brought pain to our ecumenical partners. This is still an unresolved ecumenical problem.

Beyond a consideration of those specific references, however, a study of his writing will tell us something about the larger framework within which the Catholic Church understands itself. In short, the Catholic worldview is a sacramental worldview. Such a worldview allows two very important realities to be affirmed simultaneously: that God is sovereign and Christ is the one mediator; and that God's mighty actions are mediated in the world by way of the stuff of the world and the human institutions of the world. The church does not take the place of Christ, but is the vehicle that makes Christ visible in every time and place. In this understanding, the claims of the Catholic Church are claims about the fidelity of God throughout history, and the concrete manifestation of this fidelity. The Catholic Church still struggles to effectively communicate this self-understanding and will no doubt continue to deepen its understanding of the connection between communion and sacrament. This will happen as it further reflects on its starting point for ecumenical engagement, namely an already existing communion, which is concretely manifest in baptism.

The basic self-understanding of the Catholic Church has shaped the way it enters into dialogue. Dialogue is an event of communion and can therefore clarify the apostolic faith in the midst of its various expressions in the different churches and ecclesial communities. This process will expose the diversity and difference that exists among the churches, and be a catalyst for overcoming difference and for appreciating the necessity of genuine diversity; it will help foster the diversity that is necessary to safeguard the apostolicity of the church. For this reason, dialogue will not result in compromise, but in conversion, change and renewal. Bishop Putney emphasises that the ecumenical endeavour is about fidelity to the apostolic faith.

There can be no compromise. Fidelity requires both continuity and change. This is a tension that all churches face as they enter into ecumenical dialogue. Ecumenism is not an exercise in learning merely to tolerate the other, nor does it set out to arrive at a sort of non-denominationalism. Participants in dialogue are at their best when they bring clarity to their church's self-understanding. This means that they are effective servants of the whole *oikoumene* when they know thoroughly the life of their church as expressed in its doctrine, worship, and practice, when they can communicate it clearly, and when they have sufficient confidence in their own church's life and teaching that they can allow it to be questioned by others.

While the Catholic Church's participation in dialogue has placed a strong emphasis on theological dialogue, this is never merely an academic exercise. There are two aspects of this. First, ecumenism is a spiritual movement. This, in fact, is central to appreciating Bishop Putney's ecumenical engagement. To be ecumenical is to have a strong spiritual commitment. Participants in ecumenical dialogue pray together; this is how communion is deepened. A second, but not unrelated aspect is that participants in ecumenical dialogue inevitably develop deep friendships. The ecumenical friendships that Bishop Putney has developed and cherished are an example of one of the fruits of dialogue. While the development of such friendships will be attested by all churches, for Catholics it fits well with their basic ecumenical outlook. These friendships are an instance of communion. While they are personal, they are also ecclesial. In other words, these friendships have a theological, and therefore spiritual, character about them. Ecumenical dialogue is not just a place to talk about communion; it is the place where we live the communion we share.

Ecumenism: An Organic Part of the Church's Life

Bishop Putney writes from a deep conviction that ecumenical engagement is a central activity of the Catholic Church. To use the words of Pope John Paul II in *Ut unum sint*, ecumenism is not just some sort of appendix which is added to the church's traditional activity; rather it is an organic part of the church's life and work and should pervade all that the church is and does (n 22).

The centrality of unity to the church's life and mission was already developed in the Council's Constitution on the Church and its Decree on Ecumenism. There, drawing on the Letters to the Ephesians and Colossians, unity was understood in cosmic terms, as it were. Since the beginning of creation God has had a plan that involves the communion of the whole of creation with God. Such a communion brings human beings into relationship with one another. This plan has been fully revealed in Christ and realised in the shedding of his blood. One may think of the early biblical image of the tower of Babel as pointing to the break in communion, which needs to be restored. A second image, namely that of Pentecost, shows the restoration of unity in Christ: creation is once again living in the Spirit, and human beings communicate with one another—they are in communion. In this grand vision presented by the Vatican Council unity is the name for salvation, or justification; it is the name for the kingdom. Further, the church exists 'from Abel the just one', as the sign that this plan of God is now realised in Christ. In a very real sense, the church puts flesh on this plan and makes it visible. This is why ecumenism is an organic part of the church's life and work.

For the Catholic Church, ecumenism is never just about getting doctrinal agreement with our various ecumenical partners. Doctrinal agreement will be a sign that the churches take seriously the organic relationship between unity and the revelation of God's plan. However, God's plan cannot remain an idea in our minds, but must be demonstrated in the world. In a very real sense, all that we embark on in terms of mission or pastoral care is related to unity, be it helping distressed individuals to experience the mercy of God and thereby to take a step on the road to (personal) unity, or presenting the world and society with a vision that reconciliation and peace are possible in the Spirit. All of this is about the glory of God and fidelity to God. Ecumenism has a strong doxological dimension and this is why it is an organic part of the church's life and work.

Engaging in the Present and Future with Our Ecumenical Partners

The reader of this collection of articles will no doubt be able to trace the ecumenical agenda for the last few decades. If we are satisfied that real progress has been made on this agenda, then we need to ask where this leaves us. It is generally agreed that the most pressing ecumenical issue is ecclesiology. In 2013 the World Council of Churches presented a new convergence document, *The Church: towards a Common Vision* (Faith and Order paper n 214). As the churches now engage in a process of receiving this text and responding to it, they will be faced with fundamental issues of ecclesiology. In 2009 Cardinal Walter Kasper, former President of the Pontifical Council for Promoting Christian Unity, published *Harvesting the Fruits* (Continuum 2009), where he indicated the importance of ecclesiology as one of the questions requiring further study and dialogue. This will be a challenging dialogue for all churches and ecclesial communities because there are fundamental differences.

For the Catholic Church, the question of ecclesiology includes a range of sub-topics, such as sacrament, authority, ministry and papacy. For our ecumenical partners the ecclesiology of the Catholic Church raises questions that go to fundamental Reformation concerns such as the doctrine of justification by grace alone or the priority of the Word of God. These are all topics that have been studied by Bishop Putney in these articles. He is at heart an ecclesiologist, so ecclesiology is always a sub-text in his writing. The articles do not claim to resolve all the challenges of ecclesiology, but they will be useful for the reader who wishes to understand the horizon from which the Catholic Church takes its ecclesiological self-understanding.

Conclusion

The articles in this book are a reason for hope. There is a sober reality about them: they do not pretend that all our differences will be quickly overcome. Yet they also demonstrate that much has been achieved in the years since the Council—in fact more than we often realise. It is not so much that ecumenism has slowed in recent years, but that it has moved to a different phase. We are now at an important juncture. It would be very easy to see the ecumenical question as yesterday's question—and some have done so, believing that other questions have replaced it, especially the questions of interreligious relations. Yes, this new(er) question is very important, and Bishop Putney writes of it. However, this does not mean a lessening of the urgency of the ecumenical agenda. These articles offer hope to those who painstakingly engage in ecumenical dialogue. They help sharpen the focus of today's agenda. The temptation can be to remain locked in yesterday's agenda, and to argue that that agenda has been completed. It has been completed, true, but that in itself paves the way for the new agenda. Bishop Putney's articles will help us see this new agenda with clarity and show us a way forward in taking up the challenge.

Indices

Index of Names

Index of Subjects

A

Aborigines, xiv.

Alleged culpability, 130, 133.

Anglican Church, the xvi, 2, 4, 9, 10, 29, 30, 34, 46, 47, 49f, 51, 54, 55, 57, 58, 59, 61, 62, 73, 82, 88, 96, 99, 102, 103, 107, 141, 156, 170, 223, 239.

Anglicanism, 58.

Anti-Judaism, 130, 131, 132, 135.

Anti-Semitism, 132, 135, 193, 194, 199, 228, 229.

Apostolicae Curae, 58.

Apostolic Faith, xiii, 5, 24, 32, 33, 44, 162, 226.

Apostolic tradition, 32, 36, 76, 94, 98, 101, 124, 141, 181, 186, 227.

Apostolic succession, 23, 29, 36, 43, 44, 53, 54, 55, 58, 101

Apostolicity, 30, 32, 43, 53, 77, 245.

Archdiocese of Brisbane, 3, 4.

ARCIC I and II, 29, 30, 32, 34, 35, 36, 40, 50, 52–59, 61, 112, 164.

Ascension, the, 4, 159, 224.

B

Banyo Institute for the Study of Ecumenism, 5.

Baptism, xvii, 2, 24, 26, 31, 33, 36, 38, 41, 45, 62, 90, 94, 119, 124, 137f, 142, 143, 144, 148, 149, 161, 146, 150, 154, 156, 162, 170, 189, 196, 210.

Baptism, Eucharist and Ministry, 26, 27,

Baptist-Roman Catholic Dialogue, 39.

Baptist World Alliance, 39.

Bishops' Commission for Ecumenical and Inter faith Relations, 7, 193.

Bishop of Rome, the, 17, 40, 60, 61, 67, 68, 96, 97, 99, 102–118, 127, 181, 212, 213, 227.

Body of Christ, the, 29, 36, 38, 39, 40, 93, 170.

C

Canberra, xv, 6, 9, 13, 16, 18, 19, 23, 24, 25, 27, 45, 47, 219.

Catholicism, 70, 87.

CPSIA information can be obtained
at www.ICGtesting.com
Printed in the USA
FFOW05n1749280514